Teacher's Resource Book

MATH*Thematics*
MIDDLE GRADES
Book 1

MODULE 5 Creating Things

MODULE 6 Comparisons and Predictions

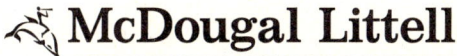

The STEM Project

McDougal Littell
A HOUGHTON MIFFLIN COMPANY

Evanston, Illinois • Boston • Dallas

McDougal Littell: www.mcdougallittell.com
Middle School Mathematics: www.mlmath.com

Acknowledgments

Writers

The authors of *Middle Grades Math Thematics, Books 1-3,* wish to thank the following writers for their contributions to the Teacher's Resource Books for the *Math Thematics* program: **Mary Buck, Roslyn Denny, Jean Howard, Sallie Morse, Patrick Runkel, Thomas Sanders-Garrett, Christine Tuckerman.**

Photography

Front Cover Bob Daemmrich/Stock Boston (t);
Louis Psihoyos/Matrix (b);
5-1 Bob Daemmrich/Stock Boston;
6-1 Louis Psihoyos/Matrix;
Back Cover Robert Frerck/Odyssey.

The STEM Project

Middle Grades Math Thematics is based on the field-test version of the STEM Project curriculum. The STEM Project was supported in part by the

NATIONAL SCIENCE FOUNDATION

under Grant No. ESI-9150114. Opinions expressed in *Middle Grades Math Thematics* are those of the authors and not necessarily those of the National Science Foundation.

Copyright © 2002, 1999 by McDougal Littell Inc.
All rights reserved.

Permission is hereby granted to teachers to reprint or photocopy in classroom quantities the pages or sheets in this work that carry a McDougal Littell copyright notice. These pages are designed to be reproduced by teachers for use in their classes with accompanying McDougal Littell material, provided each copy made shows the copyright notice. Such copies may not be sold and further distribution is expressly prohibited. Except as authorized above, prior written permission must be obtained from McDougal Littell Inc. to reproduce or transmit this work or portions thereof in any other form or by any other electronic or mechanical means, including any information storage or retrieval system, unless expressly permitted by federal copyright laws. Address inquiries to Manager, Rights and Permissions, McDougal Littell Inc., P.O. Box 1667, Evanston, IL 60204.

ISBN: 0-395-89464-6
5 6 7 8 9 10–BMW–06 05 04

About the Teacher's Resource Book

This Resource Book contains all of the teaching support that you need to teach *Math Thematics*, Book 1, Modules 5 and 6. This teaching support includes the following material:

Spanish Glossary

A Spanish translation of the Glossary from the pupil textbook in blackline master form. The Spanish Glossary is located at the beginning of the Teacher's Resource Book for Modules 1 and 2.

Teaching Commentary

Planning the Module Contains a Module Overview and charts showing Module Objectives, Topic Spiraling, Topic Integration, Materials needed, and Teacher Support Materials. Also included are a Guide for Assigning Homework for regular and block schedules, Classroom Ideas, and a Home Involvement Math Gazette. For more information on the Guide for Assigning Homework and pacing, see pages vii-viii.

Teaching Suggestions Complete and comprehensive teaching suggestions for each section of the module. These include a Section Planner, a Section Overview, Materials List, Section Objectives, Assessment Options, Classroom Examples, Closure Questions, a Section Quiz, and notes on Customizing Instruction. Each page features a two-page pupil edition reduced facsimile for easy visual reference to the pupil textbook.

Blackline Masters

Labsheets Blackline masters used in conjunction with various Exploration questions to present data and extend the scope of the Exploration. Answers are provided at point of use in the annotated Teacher's Edition.

Extended Exploration Solution Guide A comprehensive discussion of the Extended Exploration in the pupil textbook, including how to assess student responses and performance.

Alternate Extended Exploration An extended exploration that can be substituted for the one in the pupil textbook, including teaching notes and assessment procedures.

Warm-Up Exercises and Quick Quizzes A page featuring the Warm-Up Exercises from the annotated Teacher's Edition and the Section Quizzes from the Teaching Suggestions of this Resource Book. Each page is printed in large easy-to-read type and can be used to create an overhead visual or used as a hand-out. Answers for the exercises and the quiz are provided at the bottom of each page.

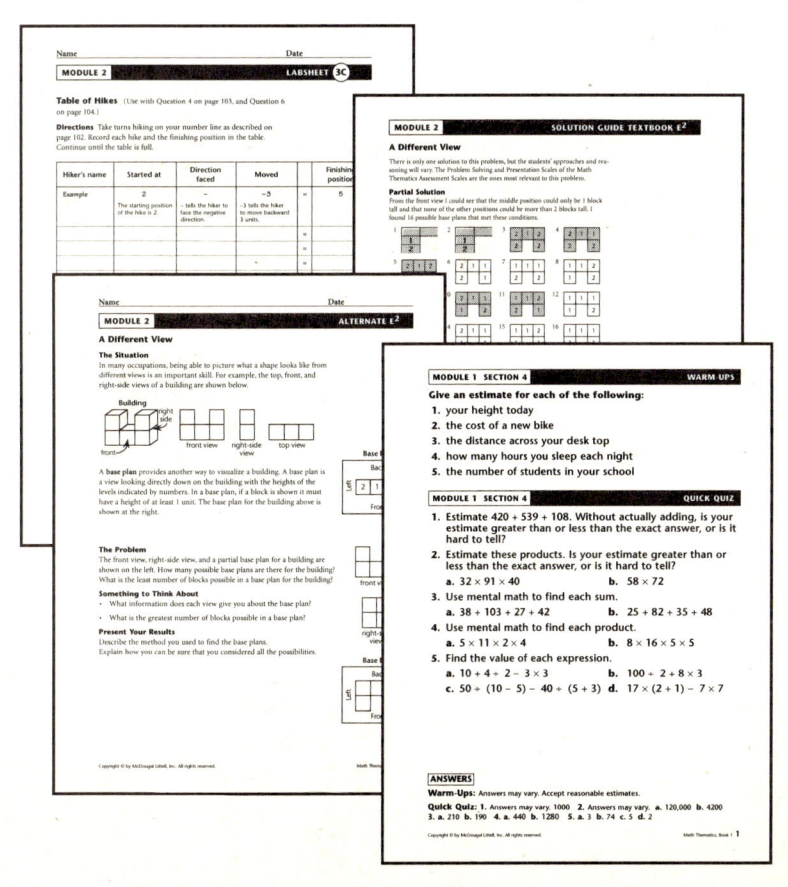

iii

Practice and Applications One to two pages of additional practice for each section of the module. Answers are provided in the Answer section of this Resource Book.

Study Guide Two to three pages of Study Guide for each section of the module. These Study Guide pages feature key concepts, worked-out examples, exercises, and spiral review. They can be used for review and reteaching. Answers are provided in the Answer section of this Resource Book.

Technology Activity A technology activity related to the technology page of each module. Answers are provided in the Answer section of this Resource Book.

Assessment Assessment options include a mid-module quiz and two module tests, Forms A and B. Answers are provided in the Answer section of this Resource Book.

Standardized Assessment A page of standardized multiple-choice questions for each module. Answers are provided in the Answer section of this Resource Book.

Module Performance Assessment A Performance Assessment task for each module. Answers are provided in the Answer section of this Resource Book.

Answers Complete answers to all blackline masters.

Cumulative Test with Answers A cumulative test on both the modules of this Resource Book. Answers to the test follow immediately.

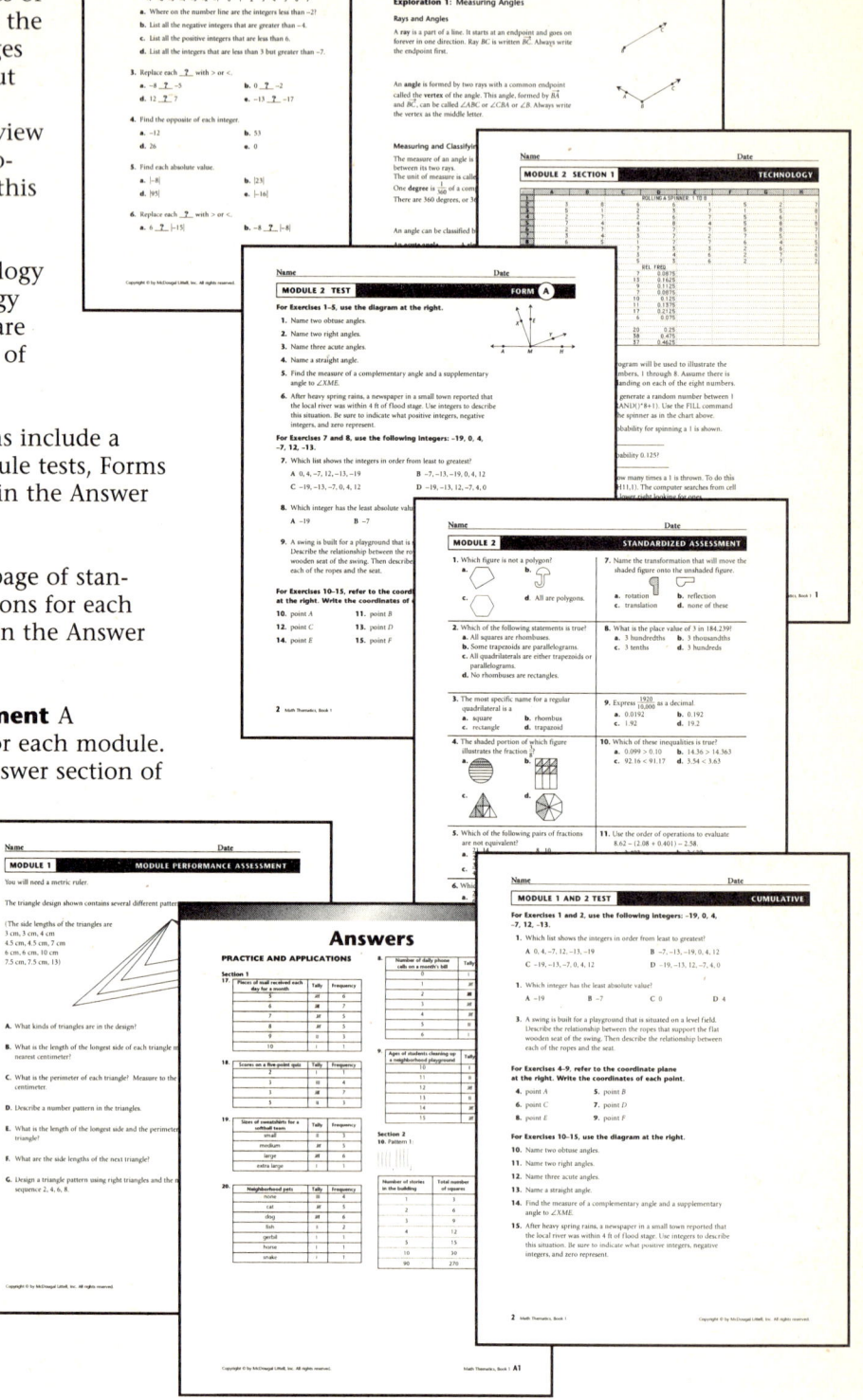

Table of Contents

Pacing and Making Assignments vii

Module 5 5-1

    Module Overview 5-2

    Home Involvement 5-6

    Teaching Suggestions 5-8

    Labsheets 5-47

    Extended Exploration Guide 5-54

    Alternate Extended Exploration 5-55

    Warm-Up Exercises and Quick Quizzes 5-57

    Practice and Applications 5-63

    Study Guide 5-74

    Technology Activity 5-87

    Assessment 5-89

    Standardized Assessment 5-94

    Module Performance Assessment 5-95

    Answers 5-96

Module 6 6-1
    Module Overview 6-2
    Home Involvement 6-6
    Teaching Suggestions 6-8
    Labsheets 6-49
    Extended Exploration Guide 6-59
    Alternate Extended Exploration 6-60
    Warm-Up Exercises and Quick Quizzes 6-62
    Practice and Applications 6-68
    Study Guide 6-79
    Technology Activity 6-96
    Assessment 6-98
    Standardized Assessment 6-103
    Module Performance Assessment 6-104
    Answers 6-106

Cumulative Test on Modules 5 and 6 .... CT1
Answers to Cumulative Test CT3

Pacing and Assigning Homework

Pacing Chart

The Pacing Chart below shows the number of days allotted for each of the three courses: a Core Course, an Extended Course, and a Block Scheduling Course. The Core and Extended Courses require 140 days, and the Block Scheduling Course, 70 days. The time frames include the Module Projects, the Extended Explorations (E^2), and time for review and assessment.

Module	1	2	3	4	5	6	7	8
Core Course	19	18	18	18	16	18	17	16
Extended Course	19	18	18	18	16	18	17	16
Block Scheduling	9	9	9	9	8	9	8	9

Core Course

The Core Course is intended for students who enter with typical, or about average, mathematical skills. The daily assignment provides students with about 20–30 minutes of homework a night taken from appropriate Practice and Application (P&A) exercises. Exercises range from straightforward skill practice, to applications that require reasoning, problem solving, and making connections across mathematical strands. The assignments include all the exercises suggested for use as embedded assessment. Each section's Spiral Review (SR) is included, as are all Reflecting on the Section (ROS) problems. Because of all the elements to be covered, assignments for the one-day sections may take more time. Also, sometimes a lengthy Reflecting on the Section problem (or other essential exercise) may cause an assignment to run longer. These problems have been denoted with a star (*). In such cases, teachers may want to spread the assignment out over more than one day, or may wish to provide class time for students to complete the work.

Extended Course

The Extended Course is designed for students who enter with strong or above average mathematical skills. Daily assignments cover all the essential material in the Core Course, including the embedded assessment exercises, the Spiral Review (SR), and the Reflecting on the Section (ROS) problems. Assignments also contain more difficult problems, including all the Challenge (Chal) and Extension (Ext) exercises. As in the Core Course, each assignment is designed to be completed in about 20–30 minutes. Some Extension or Reflecting on the Section problems may cause assignments to run long. These longer problems are denoted by a star (*).

Block Scheduling Course

The Block Scheduling course is intended for schools that use longer periods, typically 90-minute classes, for instruction. The course covers all eight modules. The assignments range from straightforward application of the material to exercises involving higher-order thinking skills. Daily assignments are designed to provide about 40–50 minutes of homework, and to cover all the essential material in the Core Course, including the embedded assessment exercises, the Spiral Review (SR), and Reflecting on the Section (ROS).

Guide for Assigning Homework

The Guide for Assigning Homework appears on each module's opening pages. The first chart suggests Core and Extended Assignments. The second chart offers assignments and pacing for Block Scheduling.

Regular Scheduling (45 min class period)

			exercises to note		
Section/ P&A Pages	Core Assignment	Extended Assignment	Additional Practice/Review	Open-ended Problems	Special Problems
1 pp. 88–93	Day 1: 1–8, SR 19–28	1–8, SR 19–28	Sec 1 Ex Prac, p. 92; TB, p. 589	E^2, p. 93	E^2, p. 93
	Day 2: 9, 11–13, 15–16, *ROS 18	9, 11–13, 15–16, Chal 17, *ROS 18		ROS 18; Mod Proj 2	P&A 10, 14; Mod Proj 1–2
2 pp. 102–106	Day 1: 1–11, SR 20–29	3–6, 8–11, Chal 12, SR 20–29	Sec 2 Ex Prac, p. 106		
	Day 2: 13–17, ROS 19, Career 30	13–17, Chal 18, ROS 19, Career 30, Ext 32–34		Career 31	Career 31

Additional Practice/Review
Each section contains additional support and practice for the objectives:
- **Extra Skill Practice (Ex Prac)** A page for each section, including exercises for each day and a set of Standardized Testing or Study Skills exercises.
- **Practice and Application (P&A)** Exercises beyond the 20–30 minute homework period, covering the same skills and concepts as the Core Assignment.
- **Toolbox (TB)** Teaching and practice for pre-book skills applied in this section or in upcoming sections.

Open-ended Problems
Included in this category are exercises where students generate examples, create designs, or use original ideas. The Extended Exploration (E^2) from each module appears here. It is designed to provide a rich problem solving experience, with multiple approaches or solutions. The listing may include Reflecting on the Section (ROS), Career Connection (Career), Module Project (Mod Proj), Study Skills (St Sk), or Standardized Testing (Std Test) exercises, as well as other Practice and Application (P&A) exercises where appropriate.

Special Problems Exercises in this category require extra time or additional materials, such as a calculator or a newspaper. All Extended Exploration (E^2) and Module Project (Mod Proj) activities are listed, as well as many Practice and Application (P&A) exercises labeled Research, Create Your Own, or Home Involvement. (The E^2 and the final Module Project questions are listed with the sections they follow.) Although Special Problems are not included in the Core Assignment, they are accessible to all students. Teachers may allot class time or extra days for students to complete them.

Block Scheduling (90 min class period)

	Day 1	Day 2	Day 3	Day 4	Day 5	Day 6	Day 7	
Teach	Sec 1	Sec 2 Expl 1–2	Sec 2 Expl 3; Sec 3 Expl 1	Sec 3 Expl 2–3	Sec 4 Expl 1–2	Sec 4 Expl 3; Sec 5	Sec 6	Allow 2 days review/assess/projects
Apply/ Assess (P&A)	Sec 1: 3–12, ROS 15, SR 16–27	Sec 2: 2–11, 14–15 SR 33–38	Sec 2: 16–19, 22–25, 31, ROS 32; Sec 3: 2–4	Sec 3: 6, 8–10, 12, ROS 15, SR 16–33	Sec 4: 1–2, 4–5, 8, 10, 12, 15–16, 17–20, SR 43–46	Sec 4: 27, 30, 32, 34, 40 ROS 42; Sec 5: 1, 4, 6, ROS 9, SR 10–15	Sec 6: 1, 2, 5 ROS 7, SR 8–12	
Yearly Pacing	**Mod 1:** 9 days				**Remaining:** 61 days		**Total:** 70 days	

viii

BOOK 1

TEACHER'S RESOURCES FOR MODULE 5

MATHThematics

MODULE 5 — Creating Things

- Planning and Teaching Suggestions, p. 5-8
- Labsheets, p. 5-47
- Extended Explorations, p. 5-54
- Blackline Masters, p. 5-57

MODULE 5: CREATING THINGS

Module Overview

Themes such as mask design, origami, cooking, weaving, and geometric puzzle design are the settings for developing fraction operations using models, measurement, mental math, estimation, calculators, and algorithms. Students also explore benchmarks and conversions for customary units of capacity.

Module Objectives

Section	Objectives	NCTM Standards
1	◆ Use number sense to compare fractions. ◆ Use common multiples to find common denominators. ◆ Compare fractions by writing equivalent fractions with a common denominator. ◆ Compare fractions by rewriting as decimals. ◆ Choose mental math, paper/pencil, or a calculator to compare fractions.	**1, 2, 3, 4, 5, 6**
2	◆ Use benchmarks to estimate customary length. ◆ Use a ruler to measure in fractions of an inch. ◆ Choose a customary unit or combination of units to measure a length. ◆ Convert between customary units of length. ◆ Add and subtract lengths measured in customary units.	**1, 2, 3, 4, 7, 13**
3	◆ Add and subtract fractions with the same or different denominators.	**1, 2, 3, 4, 7**
4	◆ Add mixed numbers. ◆ Estimate mixed number sums. ◆ Subtract mixed numbers. ◆ Use mental math to subtract a mixed number from a whole number.	**1, 2, 3, 4, 7**
5	◆ Use benchmarks to estimate capacity in customary units. ◆ Convert between customary units of capacity. ◆ Use the distributive property to multiply a mixed number by a whole number. ◆ Multiply with fractions and mixed numbers. ◆ Find reciprocals.	**1, 2, 3, 4, 5, 6, 7, 13**
6	◆ Use a reciprocal to divide a whole number by a fraction. ◆ Interpret the quotient in division by a fraction. ◆ Use number sense to estimate when dividing with fractions. ◆ Use reciprocals to divide any combination of whole numbers, fractions, or mixed numbers.	**1, 2, 3, 4, 5, 6, 7**

Topic Spiraling

Section	Connections to Prior and Future Concepts
1	In Section 1 students apply and extend skills from Modules 2–4 as they develop and choose between different methods of comparing fractions. They use number sense, common denominators, and decimal form. Fractions are also compared in the Module 6 work on ratios.
2	Section 2 presents the customary units of length. Students develop benchmarks and use them to estimate lengths, measure to the nearest fraction of an inch, and convert between units.
3	Section 3 explores fraction addition and subtraction, both with the same denominator and with different denominators. Students apply common denominators, introduced in Section 1.
4	Section 4 extends addition and subtraction to mixed numbers. Estimation and mental math are used as well as paper and pencil methods.
5	Section 5 extends fraction multiplication, taught in Module 4, to mixed numbers. Reciprocals are introduced. The distributive property is used to mentally multiply a mixed number by a whole number. This property is revisited in Book 2 Module 4. The customary units of capacity are also presented in this section. The customary units of weight are covered in Module 7.
6	Section 6 uses a ruler model to introduce division by fractions or mixed numbers. Students build their number sense and interpret the quotient in problem situations. Fractions and mixed numbers continue to be used in Book 1 and are reviewed in Book 2 Toolbox and Modules 3–4.

Integration

Mathematical Connections	1	2	3	4	5	6
algebra (including patterns and functions)	317			346–349, 351	355–363	373
geometry	318, 319	**321–331***	332–335, 337, 338	341–346, 348–351	**353–363**	**364–374**
data analysis, probability, discrete math	318, 319	330	337, 338	350	361	371
Interdisciplinary Connections and Applications						
social studies and geography		321–326	332, 338	341	353	
reading and language arts	320	321			360	
science		329			361	372
home economics		327			353–357, 360, 363	
arts	310	326, 330	332–333, 337	341–349, 354	359, 362	375
construction, cuisine, finance, sports	318	329	337	349, 350	362	371

* **Bold page numbers** indicate that a topic is used throughout the section.

Guide for Assigning Homework

Regular Scheduling (45 min class period)

Section/ P&A Pages	Core Assignment	Extended Assignment	Additional Practice/Review	Open-ended Problems	Special Problems
1 pp. 317–320	**Day 1:** 1–10, 14–15, SR 39–45	1–2, 4, 6, 10–15, SR 39–45, Ext 46–49	Sec 1 Ex Prac, p. 320		
	Day 2: 16–20, 22–24, 26, 31–33, 35–36, ROS 38	16–27, 31–36, Chal 37, ROS 38	P&A 28–30	P&A 34, ROS 38	P&A 28–30
2 pp. 328–331	**Day 1:** 1–13, SR 34–36	1–13, SR 34–36	Sec 2 Ex Prac, p. 331		
	Day 2: 14–16, 20, 22, 24–28, ROS 33, SR 37	14–16, 20, 22, 24–28, Chal 32, ROS 33, SR 37	P&A 17–19, 21, 23, 29–31	Std Test, p. 331	Mod Proj 1–2
3 pp. 337–340	**Day 1:** 4–6, 10–12, 14, 15, ROS 17, SR 18–24	4–6, 10–12, 14, 15, Chal 16, ROS 17, SR 18–24	Sec 3 Ex Prac, p. 339; P&A 1–3, 7–9	E^2, p. 340; Std Test, p. 339; ROS 17	P&A 13 E^2, p. 340
4 pp. 348–352	**Day 1:** 1, 2, 4–6, 10, 12, 13, SR 32–40	1–14, SR 32–40	Sec 4 Ex Prac, p. 352; P&A 14		
	Day 2: 15–18, 20–24, 27, 28, ROS 31	16, 18, 20–25, 27–28, ROS 31, Ext 41–43	P&A 19, 29–30	ROS 31; Ext 42–43	P&A 26; Mod Proj 3–4
5 pp. 359–363	**Day 1:** 1–12, SR 41–49	1–12, SR 41–49	Sec 5 Ex Prac, p. 263		
	Day 2: 13–16, 19–22, 25, 29–32, 34, 36, ROS 40	14, 16–22, 25–26, 29–32, 34, 36, 39, ROS 40, Career 50	P&A 23, 24, 27, 28, 33, 35, 37, 38		Career 50; Mod Proj 5
6 pp. 371–375	**Day 1:** 1–4, 8–11, SR 25–33	1–11, SR 25–33	Sec 6 Ex Prac, p. 374		
	Day 2: 12–14, 18, 19, 21, ROS 24	12–14, 18–21, Chal 23, ROS 24	P&A 15–17		P&A 22; Mod Proj 6–10
Review/ Assess	Review and Assess (PE), Quick Quizzes (TRB), Mid-Module Quiz (TRB), Module Tests— Forms A and B (TRB), Standardized Assessment (TRB)				Allow 5 days
Enrich/ Assess	E^2 (PE) and Alternate E^2 (TRB), Module Project (PE), Module Performance Assessment (TRB)				
Yearly Pacing	**Mod 5:** 16 days	**Mods 1–5:** 89 days	**Remaining:** 51 days	**Total:** 140 days	

Key: P&A = Practice & Application; ROS = Reflecting on the Section; SR = Spiral Rev; TB = Toolbox; Ex Prac= Extra Skill Practice; Ext = Extension; * more time

Block Scheduling (90 min class period)

	Day 1	Day 2	Day 3	Day 4	Day 5	Day 6	
Teach	Sec 1	Sec 2	Sec 3	Sec 4	Sec 5	Sec 6	Allow 2 days review/assess/projects
Apply/ Assess (P&A)	Sec 1: 1–2, 4, 6, 10, 14–15, 16–26 (even) 31–33, 35–36, ROS 38, SR 39–45	Sec 2: 2–8 (even), 9–13, 20–28 (even), 25, ROS 33, SR 34–37	Sec 3: 4–6, 10–12, 14–15, ROS 17, SR 18–24	Sec 4: 4, 6, 12, 13, 16, 18, 20, 21, 23, 24, 27, 28, ROS 31, SR 32–40	Sec 5: 2–3, 4–16 (even), 19–22, 25, 30–32, 34, 36, ROS 40, SR 41–49	Sec 6: 2–8 (even), 9–12, 14, 18, 21, ROS 24, SR 25–33	
Yearly Pacing	**Mod 5:** 8 days		**Mods 1–5:** 44 days		**Remaining:** 26 days	**Total:** 70 days	

Materials List

Section	Materials
1	Labsheets 1A and 1B, scissors, fraction calculator (optional), paper folding, hole punch, scissors
2	ruler, yardstick, tape measure (optional)
3	fraction strips from Section 1, scissors, tape, colored paper, ruler
4	Labsheet 4A, ruler, fraction calculator (optional)
5	milk containers ($\frac{1}{2}$ pint, pint, quart, and gallon), other containers of various sizes, pattern blocks
6	Labsheets 6A and 6B, scissors, ruler, tape, trapezoid-shaped puzzle pieces; for R and A: ruler and nickel

Support Materials in this Resource Book

Section	Practice	Study Guide	Assessment	Enrichment
1	Section 1	Section 1	Quick Quiz	
2	Section 2	Section 2	Quick Quiz	Technology Activity
3	Section 3	Section 3	Quick Quiz, Mid-Module Quiz	Alternate Extended Exploration
4	Section 4	Section 4	Quick Quiz	
5	Section 5	Section 5	Quick Quiz	
6	Section 6	Section 6	Quick Quiz	
Review/Assess	Sections 1–6		Module Tests Forms A and B, Standardized Assessment, Module Performance Assessment	

Classroom Ideas

Bulletin Boards:
- customary units for length and capacity with students' benchmarks
- pictures of traditional masks with world map
- display of favorite recipes

Student Work Displays:
- exhibits from the Module Project
- penguins and other origami
- student solutions to the E²

Interest Centers:
- origami books and paper
- tangrams or geometric puzzles
- materials for relief masks and pins

Visitors/Field Trips:
- artist, carpenter, chef
- restaurant kitchen

Technology:
- *Interactions: Real Math—Real Careers*, McDougal Littell, 1994, videodisc
- *An Odyssey of Discovery: Fractions*, Pierian Spring Software, 1997, CD, Mac/Win

Home Involvement

The Math Gazette
Creating Things

Sneak Preview!

Over the next four weeks in our mathematics class, we will be comparing fractions, determining lengths and capacities of objects, and adding, subtracting, multiplying, and dividing fractions and mixed numbers, while completing a thematic unit on Creating Things. Some of the topics we will be discussing are:

- ✗ origami
- ✗ the Great Wall of China
- ✗ weaving
- ✗ ceremonial masks
- ✗ geometric puzzles

Ask Your Student

How can you use the least common denominator to help you compare two fractions? (Sec. 1)

How can you use a ruler to add $1\frac{1}{2}$ and $2\frac{1}{4}$? (Sec. 4)

How do you use the distributive property when you multiply $1\frac{1}{2}$ by 5? (Sec. 5)

Connections

Literature:
Students will read an excerpt from *Sadako and the Thousand Paper Cranes*, by Eleanor Coerr, in which the tradition of folding origami cranes is described.

Students will read about the construction of the Great Wall of China in *The Great Wall*, by Leonard Everett Fisher. They may be interested in tracing the route of the Great Wall on a modern map and finding cities that are on or near it.

In an excerpt from *Justin and the Best Biscuits in the World*, by Mildred Pitts Walter, students read about a young boy who learns of his grandfather's experiences as a cowhand on the American western frontier. Your students may be interested in reading the rest of this book to find out more about African-Americans and the American West.

Art and Social Studies:
Students will learn that weaving fabrics and other materials has been a part of many cultures throughout history.

Students will also learn about the mask used in celebrating *Día de Muertos*. They may be interested in designing and creating their own masks for this holiday.

E² Project

Following Section 3, students will have about one week to complete the E² project, *A Weighty Question*. Students will investigate how to measure any mass between 1 kg and 40 kg using only four different weights.

A Weighty Question

MODULE 5

5-6

Creating Things

Section Title	Mathematics Your Student Will Be Learning	Activities
1: Paper Folding	◆ comparing fractions ◆ finding equivalent fractions and decimals	◆ model fractions with fraction strips
2: Building the Great Wall	◆ developing benchmarks for units of length ◆ reading fractional measures on a ruler ◆ converting between customary units of length ◆ adding and subtracting measurements	◆ measure the lengths of different objects ◆ begin work on the Module Project, *Create an Exhibit of Everyday Objects*
3: Over and Under	◆ adding and subtracting fractions	◆ use fraction strips to add and subtract fractions ◆ weigh objects on a balance scale
4: Masks	◆ adding and subtracting mixed numbers	◆ use string and a ruler to measure lengths ◆ continue work on the Module Project
5: Recipe for Success	◆ developing benchmarks for units of capacity ◆ converting between customary units of capacity ◆ multiplying mixed numbers ◆ using the distributive property	◆ estimate the capacities of different containers ◆ model multiplication of mixed numbers with pattern blocks ◆ continue work on the Module Project
6: Dividing the Puzzle	◆ dividing a whole number by a fraction ◆ dividing fractions and mixed numbers	◆ solve a geometric puzzle ◆ model division of fractions on a ruler ◆ complete the Module Project

MODULE 5

Activities to do at Home

◆ Collect newspapers, magazines, and mail-order catalogs. Notice how fractions are used to describe sale prices, dimensions, or other information. If possible, use information in the advertisements or articles to find amounts described by fractions. (After Sec. 3)

◆ Choose several containers of different sizes. Use sketches or photographs to make a visual display of the relationships between the capacities of the containers, such as "five cereal bowls are approximately equal to one juice can." (After Sec. 5)

Related Topics

You may want to discuss these related topics with your student:

- Crafts
- Fund-raising
- Cooking
- Stock market

Section 1: Comparing Fractions

Section Planner

DAYS FOR MODULE 5

| 1 | 2 | 3 | 4 | 5 | 6 | 7 | 8 | 9 | 10 | 11 |

SECTION 1

First Day
Setting the Stage, p. 310
Exploration 1, pp. 311–313

Second Day
Exploration 2, pp. 314–315
Key Concepts, p. 316

Block Schedule

Day 1
Setting the Stage, Exploration 1, Exploration 2, Key Concepts

RESOURCE ORGANIZER

Teaching Resources
- Practice and Applications, Sec. 1
- Study Guide, Sec. 1
- Warm-Up, Sec. 1
- Quick Quiz, Sec. 1

Section Overview

In Module 5, students will study how mathematics is used to create things. The explorations in Section 1 use the art of Japanese paper folding to show students how they can use paper folding to make fraction strips to model and compare fractions. Students will also use mental math to compare fractions to $\frac{1}{2}$. The inequality symbols for "greater than" and "less than" are introduced. Where denominators are different, students will learn how to compare fractions using equivalent fractions with a least common denominator. Since the least common denominator of two fractions is defined as the least common multiple (LCM) of their denominators, students who need to review finding the LCM can do so by looking back at page 300 in Module 4. Students may also need a review of writing fractions as decimals, which is another technique they will use in this section to compare fractions. Reviews of writing fractions as decimals can be found in Module 3 on pages 176 and 202. Exploration 2 shows the calculator keystrokes for writing a fraction as a decimal.

SECTION OBJECTIVES

Exploration 1
- use number sense to compare fractions

Exploration 2
- use common multiples to find common denominators
- compare fractions by writing equivalent fractions with a common denominator
- compare fractions by rewriting as decimals
- choose mental math, paper and pencil, or a calculator for comparing fractions

ASSESSMENT OPTIONS

Checkpoint Questions
- Question 9 on p. 313
- Question 12 on p. 313
- Question 17 on p. 315

Embedded Assessment
- For a list of embedded assessment exercises see p. 5-12.

Performance Task/Portfolio
- Exercise 30 on p. 318 (create your own)
- Exercise 38 on p. 319 (journal)

SECTION 1 MATERIALS

Setting the Stage
- Labsheet 1A
- scissors

Exploration 1
- Labsheet 1B
- scissors

Exploration 2
- fraction calculator (optional)

Teacher Support for Pupil Pages 310–311

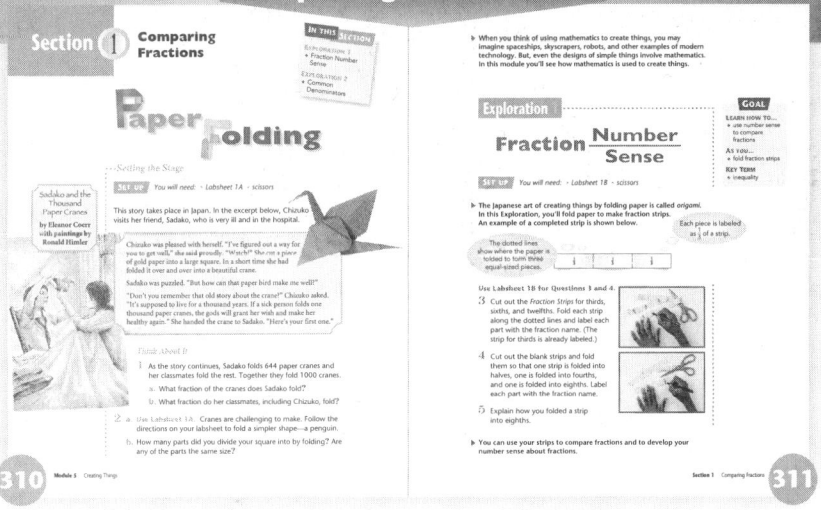

Setting the Stage

MOTIVATE

The reading on page 310 should be done in class, either in groups or individually. You may wish to spend an extra day to explore geometric relationships using origami. Some students may be interested in trying to fold a paper crane like the one in the story. The book, *Joy of Origami*, contains a simple pattern for a paper crane.

Question 1 provides an opportunity to connect fractions, decimals, and percents. Students can write $\frac{644}{1000}$ as 0.644. Help them see that 0.644 is between 64% (0.64) and 65% (0.65).

Exploration 1

PLAN

Classroom Management
Students should work through Exploration 1 individually with teacher guidance or in groups of two to four. In *Questions 3* and *4*, students will be cutting and folding their own fraction strips. You may want to cut some extra strips (Labsheet 1B) ahead of time to use as replacements. Students should keep the fraction strips they make in this exploration for further work with fractions. *Question 7* is designated as appropriate for class or group discussion so students will all have the same understanding of comparing with $\frac{1}{2}$.

GUIDE

Using Manipulatives After folding to make fraction strips for fourths and eighths (*Question 4*), it is helpful to re-fold them so each fold faces under. This will help the strips lay flat. If students have trouble seeing the fold lines, have them use a ruler and a pencil to mark the fold lines. After completing the exploration, you may want to have each student paper clip their strips together and then collect them so the strips can be used again later in the section and throughout this module.

Customizing Instruction

Multicultural Note Paper folding is the craft of folding paper into objects without cutting or pasting. The origins of paper folding are unknown, but it may have developed from the older custom of cloth folding. In Japan, paper folding is called *origami*. Japanese origami has evolved into an art form using hundreds of intricate folds. Origami is valued in Japan for its ceremonial and decorative functions, often taking the form of birds, fish, insects, flowers, and animals.

Alternative Approach Exploration 1 can also be completed using commercially produced fraction bars available for use in the classroom. The fractional parts on these bars are shaded so that instead of folding the bars, students would simply be comparing the shaded sections.

Second Language Learners The word *inequality* may be a new vocabulary word for some students. Explain that the prefix *in-* means *not* or *without*. Equality comes from the root word *equal*. So, the word inequality means *without equality*, or *the state of being not equal*.

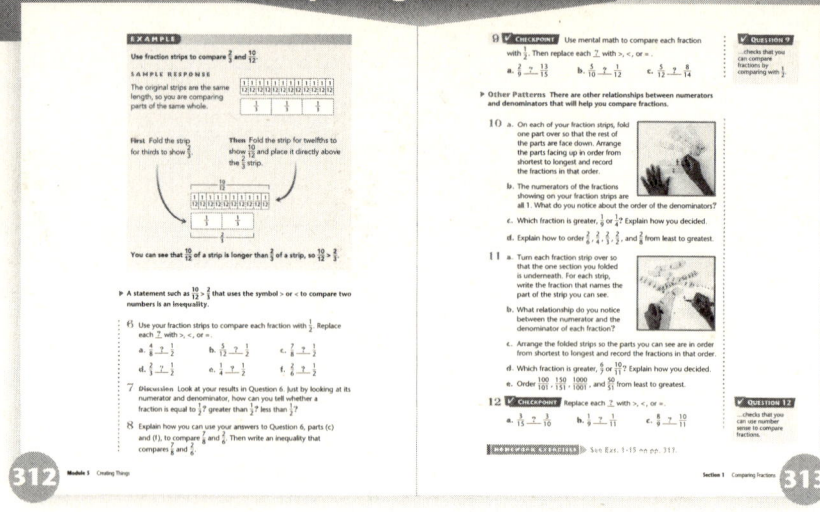

Exploration 1 continued

Classroom Examples
Use fraction strips to compare $\frac{3}{4}$ and $\frac{7}{10}$.

Answer: The original strips are the same length, so you are comparing parts of the same whole.

| $\frac{1}{10}$ | $\frac{1}{10}$ | $\frac{1}{10}$ | $\frac{1}{10}$ | $\frac{1}{10}$ | $\frac{1}{10}$ | $\frac{1}{10}$ | $\frac{1}{10}$ | $\frac{1}{10}$ | $\frac{1}{10}$ |

| $\frac{1}{4}$ | $\frac{1}{4}$ | $\frac{1}{4}$ | $\frac{1}{4}$ |

First Fold the strip for fourths to show $\frac{3}{4}$.

Then Fold the strip for tenths to show $\frac{7}{10}$ and place it directly above the $\frac{3}{4}$ strip.

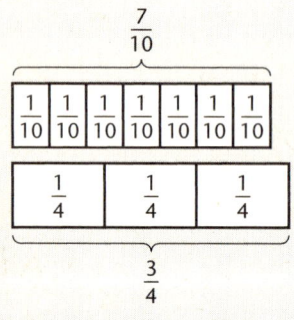

$\frac{7}{10}$

| $\frac{1}{10}$ | $\frac{1}{10}$ | $\frac{1}{10}$ | $\frac{1}{10}$ | $\frac{1}{10}$ | $\frac{1}{10}$ | $\frac{1}{10}$ |

| $\frac{1}{4}$ | $\frac{1}{4}$ | $\frac{1}{4}$ |

$\frac{3}{4}$

You can see that $\frac{3}{4}$ of a strip is longer than $\frac{7}{10}$ of a strip, so $\frac{3}{4} > \frac{7}{10}$.

Discussion *Question 7* helps to develop fraction number sense by looking at the relationship between the numerator and denominator of a fraction in order to compare it with $\frac{1}{2}$. This discussion sets the stage for looking at two other numerator and denominator relationships explored in *Questions 10* and *11*.

Developing Math Concepts
Students will use number sense to compare fractions when the numerators or denominators are the same, when both fractions are one part less than a whole, and by comparing each fraction to $\frac{1}{2}$. As students are developing this number sense, it may be helpful to present real-life situations where sizes of fractional parts are considered. In *Question 8*, students should use number sense and logical reasoning to compare the two fractions. In *Question 10(d)*, students use their fraction number sense to put the fractions in order, but if they are unsure, they can check their answer using fraction strips.

Checkpoint In *Question 9*, remind students to mentally compare the two fractions in each problem to $\frac{1}{2}$ first and then to compare them to each other. Students should refer back to *Question 8* if they have difficulty. In *Question 12*, you may want to call on students to explain their thinking and the method they used to compare each pair of fractions.

HOMEWORK EXERCISES

See the Suggested Assignment for Day 1 on page 5-12. For Exercise Notes, see page 5-12.

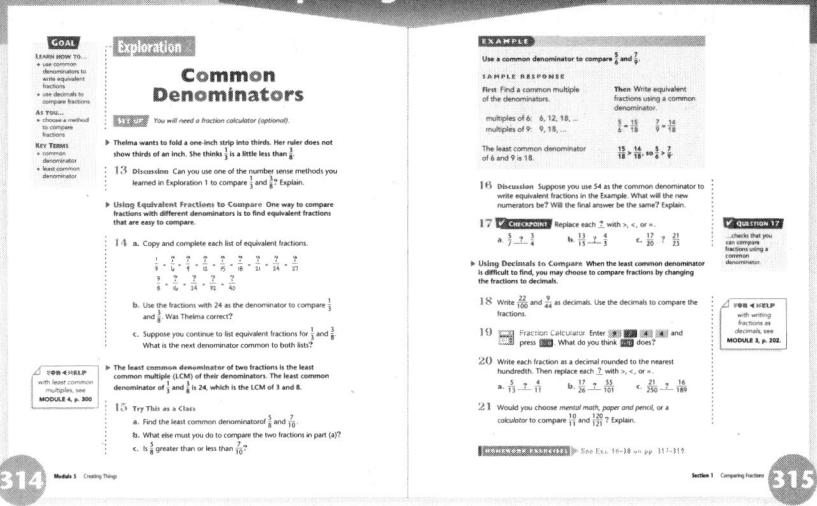

Exploration 2

PLAN

Classroom Management
Students may work through Exploration 2 individually with teacher guidance or in groups of two to four. This exploration builds upon previous learning in several concept areas: finding the least common multiple of two numbers, writing equivalent fractions, and writing fractions as decimals. A brief review of these topics may be helpful. *Questions 13* and *16* are designated as whole class discussion so all students will have the same understandings of the underlying concepts. For *Question 19*, any calculator can be used to change $\frac{9}{44}$ to a decimal. Instead of the F/D key, students can simply use the division key. For *Question 20*, you may want to discuss rounding decimals since students may need to round their decimal answers before comparing them.

GUIDE

Common Error Students may incorrectly think the least common denominator can always be found by multiplying the two denominators together. Point out that this is only sometimes true, but often results in a common denominator that is not the *least* common denominator.

Classroom Examples
Use a common denominator to compare $\frac{5}{9}$ and $\frac{8}{15}$.

Answer:
First Find a common multiple of the denominators.
multiples of 9: 9, 18, 27, 36, 45, …
multiples of 15: 15, 30, 45, …
The least common denominator of 9 and 15 is 45.

Then Write equivalent fractions using a common denominator.
$\frac{5}{9} = \frac{25}{45}$ $\frac{8}{15} = \frac{24}{45}$
$\frac{25}{45} > \frac{24}{45}$, so $\frac{5}{9} > \frac{8}{15}$.

Discussion For *Question 16*, students should understand that using any common denominator to compare fractions will yield the same results as using the least common denominator.

HOMEWORK EXERCISES

See the Suggested Assignment for Day 2 on page 5-12. For Exercise Notes, see page 5-12.

CLOSE

Closure Question Describe how to compare fractions by using a common denominator and by using decimals.

Sample Response: When using common denominators to compare fractions, write equivalent fractions with the same denominators and compare numerators. The fraction with the larger numerator is the larger fraction. When using decimals to compare fractions, divide the numerator by the denominator to get a decimal value. The fraction with the larger decimal value is the larger fraction.

Teacher Support for Pupil Pages 316–317

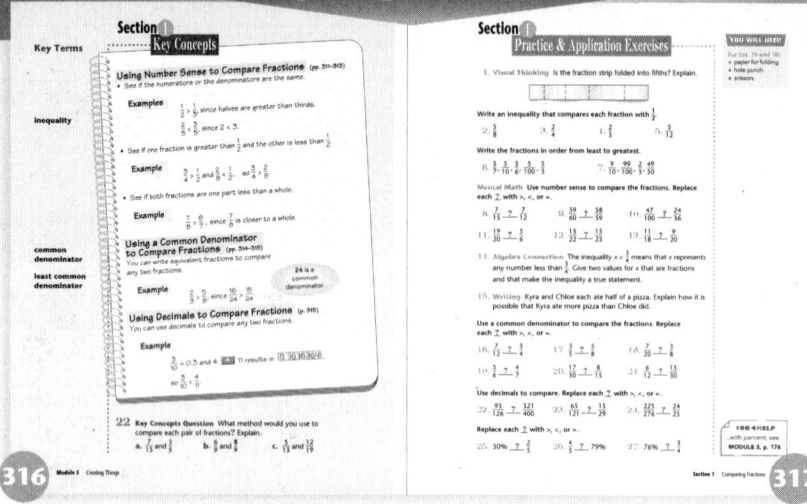

SUGGESTED ASSIGNMENT

Core Course
Day 1: Exs. 1–10, 14, 15, 39–45
Day 2: Exs. 16–20, 22–24, 26, 31–33, 35, 36, 38

Extended Course
Day 1: Exs. 1, 2, 4, 6, 10–15, 39–49
Day 2: Exs. 16–27, 31–38

Block Schedule
Day 1: Exs. 1, 2, 4, 6, 10, 14, 15, 16–26 even, 31–33, 35, 36, 38–45

EMBEDDED ASSESSMENT

These section objectives are tested by the exercises listed.

Use number sense to compare fractions.
Exercises 2, 4, 6, 10, 15

Use common multiples to find common denominators.
Exercises 16, 18, 20, 35

Compare fractions by writing equivalent fractions with a common denominator.
Exercises 16, 18, 20, 36

Compare fractions by rewriting as decimals.
Exercises 22, 24, 26

Choose mental math, paper and pencil, or a calculator for comparing fractions.
Exercises 31–33

Practice & Application
EXERCISE NOTES

Writing For *Ex. 15* suggest that students think about comparing parts of the same whole. Remind students that the fraction strips they made were all the same length, so in comparing them they were comparing parts of the same whole. This may help students come up with the idea that the pizzas are different sizes.

Developing Math Concepts In *Exs. 25–27*, students must compare a fraction to a percent. Students may choose to change the fraction to a percent and compare, or change the percent to a fraction and compare. Students may need to refer to page 176 of Module 3 if they need to review how to write a fraction as a percent, and vice versa.

Customizing Instruction

Home Involvement Those helping students at home will find the Key Concepts on page 316 a handy reference to the key ideas, terms, and skills of Section 1.

Absent Students For students who were absent for all or part of this section, the blackline Study Guide for Section 1 may be used to present the ideas, concepts, and skills of Section 1.

Extra Help For students who need additional practice, the blackline Practice and Applications for Section 1 provides additional exercises that may be used to confirm the skills of Section 1. The Extra Skill Practice on page 320 also provides additional exercises.

Teacher Support for Pupil Pages 318–319

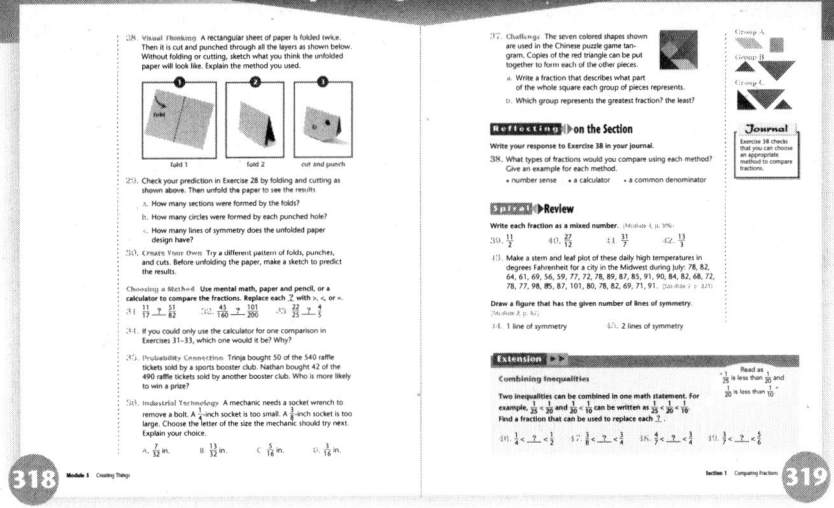

Practice & Application

Real World Connection For *Ex. 36* you may want to point out that socket wrenches come in a range of sizes and that being able to use number sense to estimate which size you will need is a valuable and time-saving advantage. Many industrial mechanics have a highly developed number sense that they use frequently in their work.

Closing the Section

While creating and using fraction strips in Exploration 1, students learned to use number sense to compare fractions. In Exploration 2, they learned when to use number sense and when to use a common denominator or a calculator to compare fractions. Students will be able to reflect on these understandings while answering the Reflecting on the Section exercise on page 319. You may wish to have students share their answers to this exercise with the class.

QUICK QUIZ ON THIS SECTION

1. Write from least to greatest.
   $\dfrac{1}{2}, \dfrac{5}{4}, \dfrac{5}{7}, \dfrac{3}{9}, \dfrac{4}{11}, \dfrac{4}{3}$

2. Use number sense to compare.
   a. $\dfrac{46}{47} \underline{\ ?\ } \dfrac{211}{212}$
   b. $\dfrac{3}{11} \underline{\ ?\ } \dfrac{3}{13}$

3. Use a common denominator to compare.
   a. $\dfrac{8}{11} \underline{\ ?\ } \dfrac{2}{3}$
   b. $\dfrac{14}{24} \underline{\ ?\ } \dfrac{21}{36}$

4. Use decimals to compare.
   a. $\dfrac{4}{38} \underline{\ ?\ } \dfrac{11}{94}$
   b. $\dfrac{10}{53} \underline{\ ?\ } \dfrac{42}{200}$

5. Eight out of 23 students in Ms. Silver's class got an A on their midterm exam. Ten out of 27 students in Mr. Gold's class got an A on the exam. Which class had the greater fraction of A's on the midterm exam?

For answers, see Quick Quiz blackline on p. 5-57.

Section 2: Customary Units of Length

Section Planner

DAYS FOR MODULE 5
1 2 3 4 5 6 7 8 9 10 11

SECTION 2

First Day
Setting the Stage, p. 321
Exploration 1, pp. 322–323

Second Day
Exploration 2, pp. 324–326
Key Concepts, p. 327

Block Schedule

Day 2
Setting the Stage, Exploration 1, Exploration 2, Key Concepts

RESOURCE ORGANIZER

Teaching Resources
- Practice and Applications, Sec. 2
- Study Guide, Sec. 2
- Technology Activity, Sec. 2
- Warm-Up, Sec. 2
- Quick Quiz, Sec. 2

Section Overview

In Section 2, the design of the Great Wall of China introduces students to customary units of length. As they did for metric units of measure in Module 3 on page 161, students will develop their own benchmarks for inch, foot, yard, and mile, which they will then use to estimate the lengths of objects. Refer to page 161 for a review of benchmarks, if necessary. In order to get more accurate measurements than their benchmarks allow, students will measure with a ruler. They will learn to read the markings for inches, half-inches, quarter-inches, and eighth-inches. Students will also discuss the merits of writing a measurement using a combination of units, such as feet and inches.

In a number of exercises involving the measures of well-known structures, students will practice converting customary units of measure. Conversions are necessary where students will add and subtract customary units of measure.

SECTION OBJECTIVES

Exploration 1
- use benchmarks to estimate customary length
- use a ruler to measure in fractions of an inch
- choose an appropriate customary unit or combination of units to measure a length

Exploration 2
- convert between customary units of length
- add and subtract lengths measured in customary units

ASSESSMENT OPTIONS

Checkpoint Questions
- Question 9 on p. 323
- Question 17 on p. 325
- Question 20 on p. 326

Embedded Assessment
- For a list of embedded assessment exercises see p. 5-19.

Performance Task/Portfolio
- Exercise 33 on p. 329 (research)
- Module Project on p. 330
- Standardized Testing on p. 331

SECTION 2 MATERIALS

Exploration 1
- ruler
- yardstick

Practice & Application Exercises
- tape measure

Module Project on page 330
- customary ruler

Teacher Support for Pupil Pages 320-321

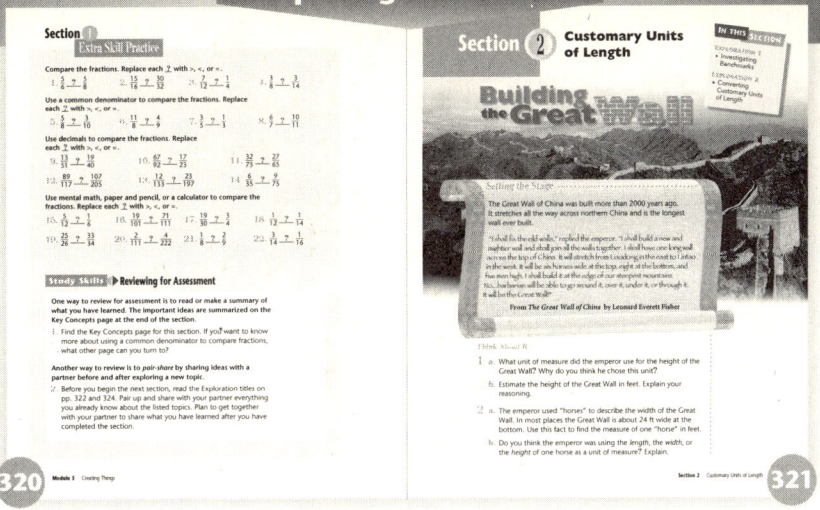

Setting the Stage

MOTIVATE

Before discussing *Questions 1* and *2*, students should do the reading on page 321 in class, either individually or in groups. You may wish to begin this section by presenting the background information on the Great Wall of China provided in the Customizing Instruction section below. Students may also enjoy doing further reading or research on the Great Wall or on China.

Exploration 1

PLAN

Classroom Management
Exploration 1 is best performed in groups of two to four. In *Question 4(a)*, students will be finding everyday objects that can be used as benchmarks for an inch, a foot, and a yard. You may tell students ahead of time to bring in a box of their own items to use, or plan to have available a box of items from which they may choose. Suggested items include pencils, markers, crayons, notebook paper, chalk, erasers, milk or juice containers, coins, paper clips, a baseball or softball bat, and a towel.

In *Question 4(b)*, students are not being asked to measure, but to use their benchmarks to estimate. Be sure students write down each estimate, since in *Question 9* they will be comparing their estimates to the actual measures. You will want to measure and record each object named in *Question 4(b)* before students begin the exploration. Knowing each measure ahead of time will help you identify any students who measure incorrectly.

Customizing Instruction

Background Note The Great Wall of China extends some 1500 mi across the northern part of China. First built for protection and to mark a northern boundary, the Great Wall as we know it today is not a single wall, but a series of walls that have been rebuilt over the years. The height of the wall ranges from 20 ft to 50 ft and the width ranges from 12 ft to 40 ft. Although it was only partially successful in preventing invasions, troops could race quickly across the top of the Great Wall to ward off intruders.

Teacher Support for Pupil Pages 322–323

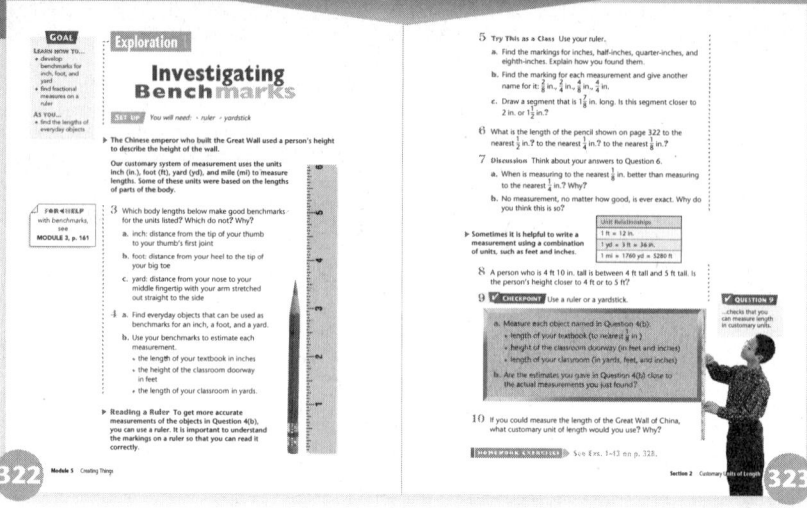

Exploration 1 continued

GUIDE

Try This as a Class *Question 5* is designed to be done with teacher guidance so you can be sure all students can read a ruler correctly. This is an important prerequisite for *Question 9* so students will be able to measure and record accurately.

Developing Math Concepts As students determine their own benchmarks and become familiar with them, you may want to encourage students to consider which real-life situations would be appropriate for using benchmarks and which situations would require an exact measure.

Discussion While discussing *Question 7*, you may want to ask students to share the occupations or hobbies of any of their family members or friends, and then discuss what types of measurements these people might make or use in their work.

Common Error When recording their measurements in *Question 9(a)*, students may incorrectly write the measures using only one unit instead of a combination of units (80 in. instead of 6 ft 8 in.). Remind students to refer to the unit relationships table on page 323 to be sure they have written their measures correctly.

Managing Time If students are working in groups, they may be able to find and record the measures in *Question 9* more efficiently if group members are assigned various roles for the activity. The roles might be: 2 members to measure, 1 member to double check the measure for accuracy, and 1 member to record the measure. Group members should switch roles as they measure each object so that each member has a chance to practice reading a ruler or yardstick.

HOMEWORK EXERCISES

See the Suggested Assignment for Day 1 on page 5-19. For Exercise Notes, see page 5-19.

Customizing Instruction

Alternative Approach Students who finish the exploration early may enjoy estimating and then measuring other objects in the classroom. Suggestions include measuring the height of their desk, the length and width of a bulletin board, the width of the doorway, or the dimensions of a classroom window.

Visual Learners Visual learners will benefit from a classroom display of the benchmarks they find in Exploration 1. You could display the benchmarks on a table with the objects divided into three groups for 1-inch, 1-foot, and 1-yard benchmarks. Challenge students to add objects to each group of benchmarks as they work through this section.

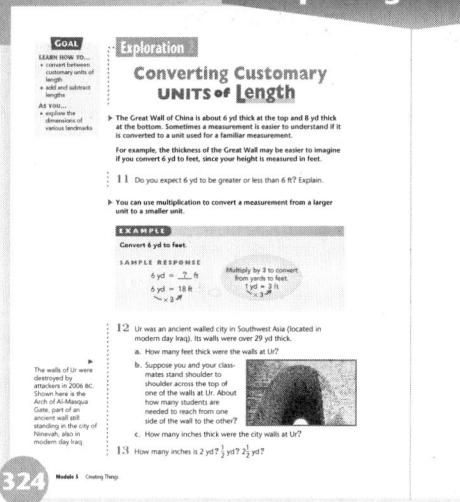

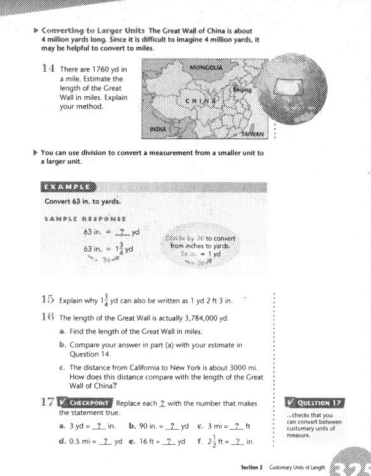

Exploration 2

PLAN

Classroom Management
Students may work through Exploration 2 individually or in groups of two to four. This exploration develops students' number sense and estimation skills as they learn to convert units. The unit relationships table on page 323 is an important reference for students as they practice these conversions. It may be helpful to post a copy of this table somewhere in the room for students to use as a quick reference as they work through the exploration. *Question 18* is designated as class discussion so students can discuss their thinking as they add and convert units.

GUIDE

Classroom Examples
Convert 4 ft to inches.

Answer: Multiply by 12 to convert from feet to inches.

1 ft = 12 in.
$\searrow \times 12 \nearrow$

So, 4 ft = 48 in.
$\searrow \times 12 \nearrow$

Convert 44 in. to feet.

Answer: Divide by 12 to convert from inches to feet.

12 in. = 1 ft
$\searrow \div 12 \nearrow$

So, 44 in. = $3\frac{2}{3}$ ft
$\searrow \div 12 \nearrow$

Developing Math Concepts
Encourage students to think about the benchmarks they found in Exploration 1 when answering *Question 12(b)*. *Question 13* provides an incremental, number sense approach to converting fractional amounts, a skill that is revisited throughout the exploration. If students have difficulty understanding the mixed number result in the Example on page 325, remind them of how the remainder of a division problem can be written as a fraction in lowest terms.

Checkpoint In *Question 17*, make sure students understand how to convert measures as this is a prerequisite for adding and subtracting measures in *Questions 18–21*.

Customizing Instruction

Second Language Learners Second language learners may be familiar with the word *change* which is often listed as a synonym for *convert*. Be sure students understand that when you convert a measure you are not changing its value, but merely writing it in a different form. You may also need to explain the two forms of the word *convert* as used in the exploration: *converting* (verb) and *conversion* (noun).

Multicultural Note The ruins of Ur were discovered in 1852. The walls of the city surround an oval area of about 82 acres. Excavations carried out on the site have contributed much of the present day knowledge of early Mesopotamian culture.

Background Information The Great Wall of China branches out at various points on its route. If these branches are included in the total length, the Great Wall approaches 4000 mi. in length.

Teacher Support for Pupil Pages 326–327

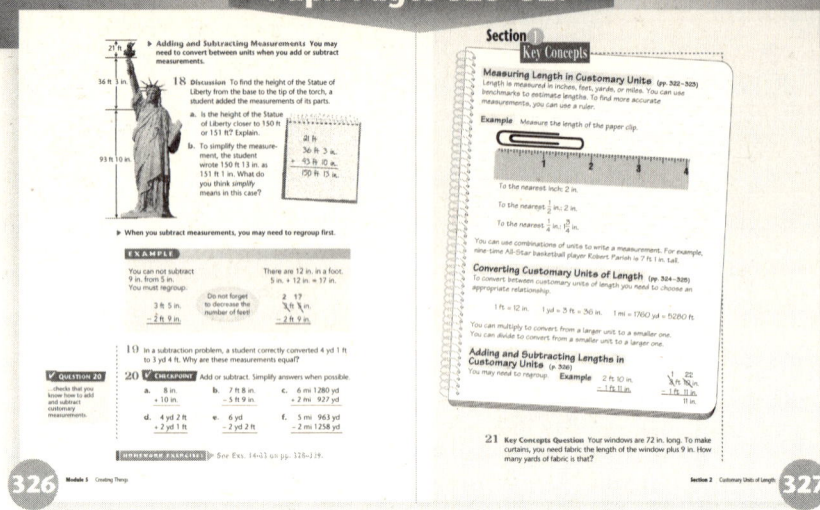

MODULE 5 ◆ SECTION 2

Exploration 2 continued

Discussion As you discuss *Question 18*, point out to students how their previous learning about conversions applies to adding measures. Be sure all students understand the use of the term *simplify* since it is used in several places after *Question 18*.

Classroom Examples
Subtract:

    5 yd 1 ft
– 3 yd 2 ft

Answer: You cannot subtract 2 ft from 1 ft. You must regroup first.

  4   4   ← Regroup 1 yd
  5̸ yd 1̸ ft   as 3 ft.
– 3 yd 2 ft
—————
  1 yd 2 ft

HOMEWORK EXERCISES

See the Suggested Assignment for Day 2 on page 5-19. For Exercise Notes, see page 5-19.

CLOSE

Closure Question How are the conversion of customary units of length and benchmarks used in adding and subtracting lengths that are measured in different units?

Sample Response: When adding and subtracting lengths measured in one or more customary units, you may need to regroup, or convert from one measurement to another. Then you can use benchmarks as an estimate to check that the final values make sense.

Customizing Instruction

Home Involvement Those helping students at home will find the Key Concepts on page 327 a handy reference to the key ideas, terms, and skills of Section 2.

Absent Students For students who were absent for all or part of this section, the blackline Study Guide for Section 2 may be used to present the ideas, concepts, and skills of Section 2.

Extra Help For students who need additional practice, the blackline Practice and Applications for Section 2 provides additional exercises that may be used to confirm the skills of Section 2. The Extra Skill Practice on page 331 also provides additional exercises.

5-18

Teacher Support for Pupil Pages 328–329

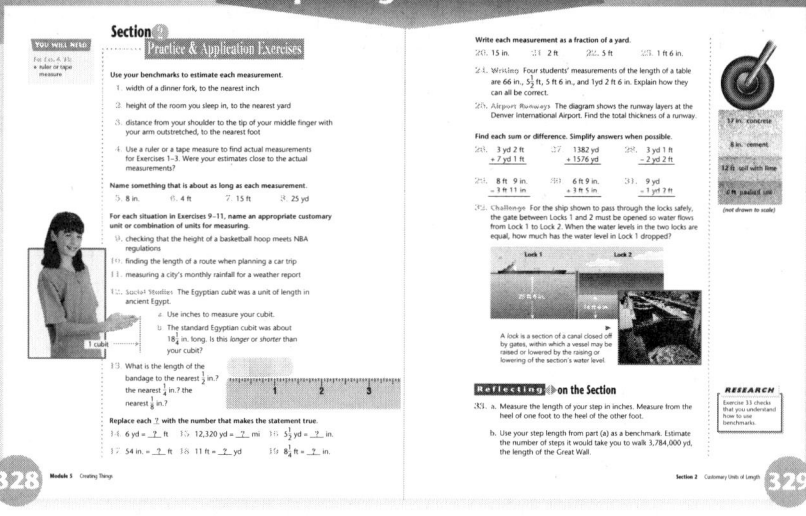

SUGGESTED ASSIGNMENT

Core Course
Day 1: Exs. 1–13, 34–36
Day 2: Exs. 14–16, 20, 22, 24–28, 33, 37

Extended Course
Day 1: Exs. 1–13, 34–36
Day 2: Exs. 14–16, 20, 22, 24–28, 32, 33, 37

Block Schedule
Day 2: Exs. 2–8 even, 9–13, 20–28 even, 25, 33–37

EMBEDDED ASSESSMENT

These section objectives are tested by the exercises listed.

Use benchmarks to estimate customary length.
Exercises 2, 4, 6, 8

Use a ruler to measure in fractions of an inch.
Exercises 12, 13

Choose an appropriate customary unit or combination of units to measure a length.
Exercises 9, 10, 11

Convert between customary units of length.
Exercises 20, 22, 24

Add and subtract lengths measured in customary units.
Exercises 25, 26, 28

Practice & Application
EXERCISE NOTES

Writing For *Ex. 24*, you may wish to have students look back at *Question 15* if they have difficulty explaining their answer. Students may also find it helpful to organize their explanation using a pre-writing web such as the one below.

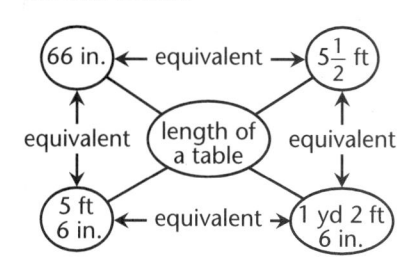

Measurement In *Ex. 33(a)*, guide students to make accurate measurements. Students should take several steps in order to establish a natural stride.

Customizing Instruction

Background Information Units of measure in early systems were based on natural objects. It was easy to use dimensions of the human body for standards of measure. The ancient Egyptians who devised the unit of length called the *cubit* may have been the first people to use standard measurements for length and weight. The Egyptian cubit was defined as the distance between the elbow and the tip of the longest finger.

The cubit was further divided into smaller units, called *digits*, that were the width of one finger. Four digits made a larger unit called a *palm*, and thus there were twenty-eight digits (or seven palms) in the Egyptian cubit.

Beginning the Module Project

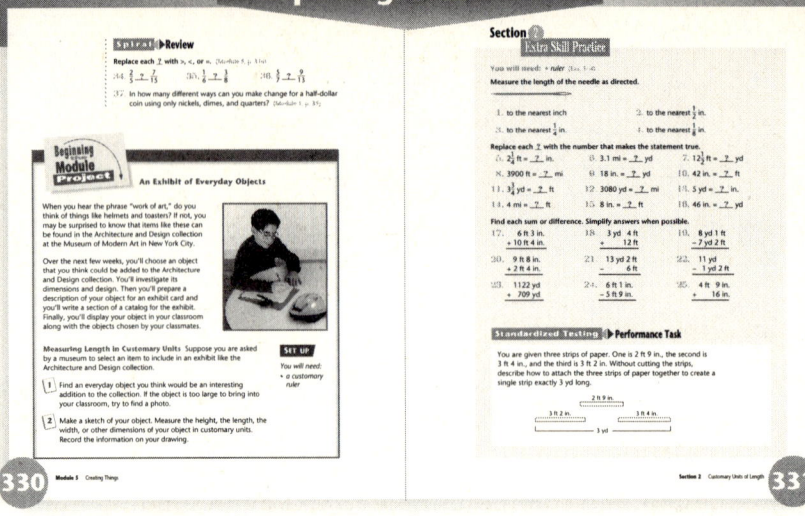

Choosing an object to be added to the Architecture and Design collection is an important first step in the Module Project. You may wish to have the class choose a theme for their exhibit. The theme could define some common aspect for the objects: color (things that are green), use (kitchen tools), age (things your grandparents used), or design (objects with symmetry).

Encourage students to be creative in their choice of objects, but to choose their object carefully and thoughtfully since they will use the object for several different activities. To help students choose an appropriate object, you may want to tell them what some of these activities will be: adding and subtracting measures from the dimensions of the object, determining the dimensions of a crate to pack the object in, and analyzing how the design of the object relates to its function. Since students will be working with measurements for the height, length, and width of the object, you may wish to point out that spherical or irregularly-shaped objects may present a particular challenge. One strategy for choosing an object is to have students brainstorm a list of possible objects, then briefly discuss the various choices on the list. This brainstorming could be done in small groups or as a class.

Closing the Section

After working through this section, students should be able to understand and apply the relationships between customary units of length. They also learned to find fractional measures on a ruler as they measured the lengths of everyday objects. The benchmarks students found for inch, foot, and yard will empower them to estimate lengths confidently and accurately in their everyday lives. Converting between units of length and adding and subtracting lengths are skills that students will use frequently in real-life situations. To bring closure to the section, you may wish to ask students to respond to the question "How will what you have learned in this section be useful to you, either now or in the future?"

QUICK QUIZ ON THIS SECTION

1. If you could measure the wingspan of an airplane, what customary unit of length would you use?

2. Replace each ___?___ with the number that makes the statement true.
   a. 18 yd = ___?___ ft
   b. 114 in. = ___?___ ft
   c. 3960 ft = ___?___ mi

3. Write each measurement as a fraction of a foot.
   a. 4 in.   b. $2\frac{1}{2}$ in.
   c. 69 in.

4. Jose jogged 2160 yd, then after resting jogged 1800 yd more. How many miles did he jog in all?

5. Monica had 12 ft 8 in. of a decorative edging. She used $2\frac{1}{2}$ yd to make a craft project. How many feet of edging does she have left?

For answers, see Quick Quiz blackline on p. 5-58.

Section 3: Addition and Subtraction of Fractions

Section Planner

DAYS FOR MODULE 5

1 2 3 4 **5** 6 7 8 9 10 11

SECTION 3

First Day
Setting the Stage, *p. 332*
Exploration 1, *pp. 333–335*
Key Concepts, *p. 336*

Block Schedule

Day 3
Setting the Stage, Exploration 1, Key Concepts

RESOURCE ORGANIZER

Teaching Resources
- Practice and Applications, Sec. 3
- Study Guide, Sec. 3
- Mid-Module Quiz
- Warm-Up, Sec. 3
- Quick Quiz, Sec. 3

Section Overview

Continuing the theme of mathematics in design, Section 3 on fraction addition and subtraction begins with a discussion of weaving. Students will use their fraction strips from Section 1 to find the width of two rows of ribbon that have been woven together to create a design. Using their fraction strips to model the addition and subtraction of fractions, students will formulate methods for adding and subtracting fractions with either like or unlike denominators. Students investigated methods for comparing fractions in Section 2 of this module. They will use the same methods to rename pairs or larger sets of fractions with unlike denominators before they add or subtract those fractions.

In Practice & Application Exercise 13, students will have the opportunity to create their own woven design using fractional dimensions.

SECTION OBJECTIVES

Exploration 1
- add and subtract fractions with the same or different denominators

ASSESSMENT OPTIONS

Checkpoint Questions
- Question 9 on p. 334
- Question 13 on p. 335

Embedded Assessment
- For a list of embedded assessment exercises see p. 5-24.

Performance Task/Portfolio
- Exercise 17 on p. 338 (oral report)
- Standardized Testing on p. 339
- ★ Extended Exploration on p. 340
- ★ = a problem solving task that can be assessed using the Assessment Scales

SECTION 3 MATERIALS

Exploration 1
◆ fraction strips from Section 1

Teacher Support for Pupil Pages 332–333

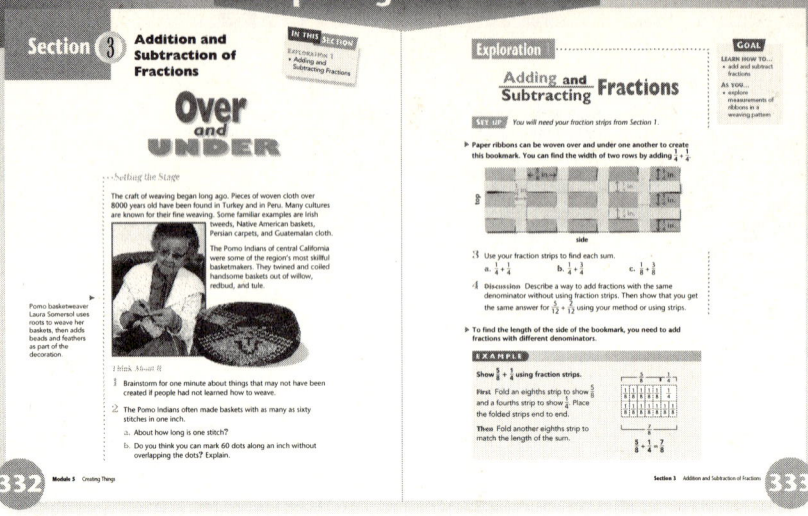

Setting the Stage

MOTIVATE

Before discussing *Questions 1* and *2*, students should do the reading on page 332 in class, either individually or in groups. You might consider having students do additional reading on how mathematics is used to create woven items such as baskets and blankets. Students could also bring in woven items from home such as baskets, placemats, wall hangings, blankets, small rugs, or fabric to display in the classroom. Classmates could look for patterns in the weave, and discuss how the weaver may have used mathematics to create the item.

Exploration 1

PLAN

Classroom Management You may also wish to have students work through Exploration 1 in pairs. Working together, they will have more fraction strips available for modeling the problems. Students will be using their fraction strips from Section 1 to find common denominators and to add and subtract fractions. *Questions 4* and *11* are designated as class discussion so students can discuss the procedure for adding and subtracting fractions with the same denominator before moving on to problems where the denominators are different.

GUIDE

Discussion While discussing *Question 4*, you will want to emphasize why the denominators remain the same when adding or subtracting fractions. The remainder of the exploration builds on this understanding.

Classroom Examples
Show $\frac{2}{3} + \frac{1}{9}$ using fraction strips.

Answer: **First** Fold a thirds strip to show $\frac{2}{3}$ and a ninths strip to show $\frac{1}{9}$. Place the folded strips end to end.

Then Fold another ninths strip to match the length of the sum.

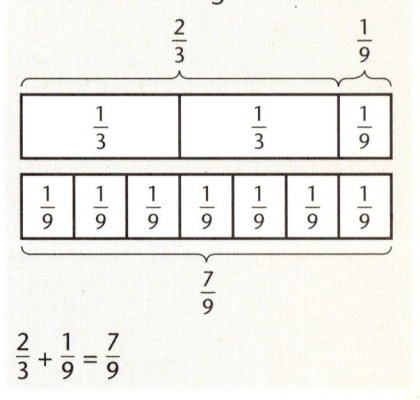

$\frac{2}{3}$		$\frac{1}{9}$
$\frac{1}{3}$	$\frac{1}{3}$	$\frac{1}{9}$
$\frac{1}{9}$ $\frac{1}{9}$ $\frac{1}{9}$	$\frac{1}{9}$ $\frac{1}{9}$ $\frac{1}{9}$	$\frac{1}{9}$

$$\frac{7}{9}$$

$$\frac{2}{3} + \frac{1}{9} = \frac{7}{9}$$

5-22

Teacher Support for Pupil Pages 334–335

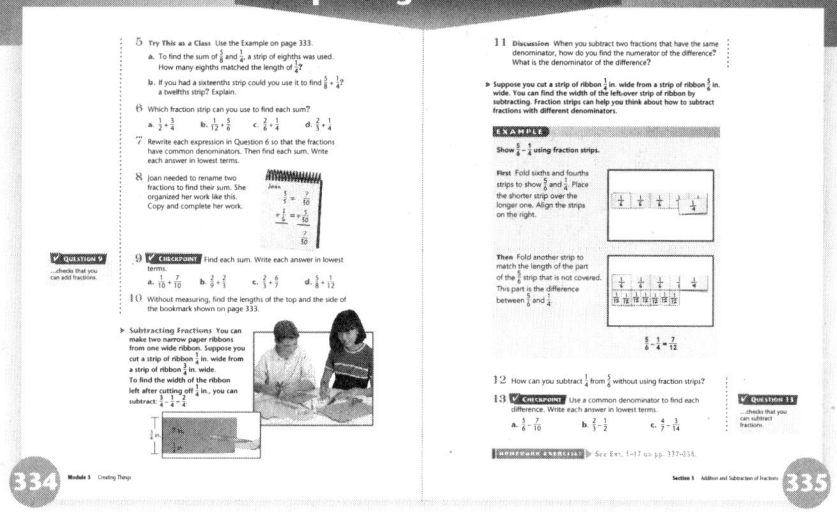

Exploration 1 continued

Try This as a Class To stimulate students' thinking in *Question 5(b)*, encourage them to think back to their work with equivalent fractions. Since 12 is a multiple of 4, some students may incorrectly think the twelfths strip will work. It may be helpful to use the fraction strips to demonstrate why it will not work.

Developing Math Concepts Some students may need to use their fraction strips to find the denominators in *Question 7*. Students should be comfortable with this method before moving on to paper and pencil methods. It is important that students have a thorough understanding of adding and subtracting fractions since these are prerequisite skills for Section 4.

Discussion When discussing the Example on page 335, you may wish to have students explore with their fraction strips in order to determine why a twelfths strip was used.

Classroom Examples
Show $\frac{3}{5} - \frac{1}{2}$ using fraction strips.

Answer: **First** Fold a fifths strip to show $\frac{3}{5}$ and a halves strip to show $\frac{1}{2}$. Place the shorter strip over the longer one. Align the strips on the left.

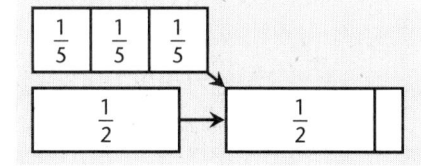

Then The part of the strip modeling $\frac{3}{5}$ that is not covered represents the difference between $\frac{3}{5}$ and $\frac{1}{2}$. Since the least common denominator of the fractions is 10, fold a tenths strip to match the length of this uncovered portion.

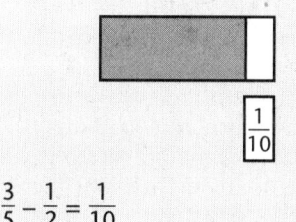

$$\frac{3}{5} - \frac{1}{2} = \frac{1}{10}$$

HOMEWORK EXERCISES

See the Suggested Assignment for Day 1 on page 5-24. For Exercise Notes, see page 5-24.

Customizing Instruction

Background Information Weaving is a very popular craft today. Modern looms produce woven products rapidly and efficiently, but the weaving of heavy pieces, such as rugs and tapestries, is often still done by hand by skilled artisans. Many people also weave by hand as a hobby or art form.

Second Language Learners Some students may be familiar with the word *common* when used to mean "usual" or "widespread." You may want to explain that *common* as used in the phrase *common denominator* means "belonging equally to all" or "belonging to two or more quantities."

Multicultural Note The Pomo Indians of California are widely regarded as spectacular basketmakers. Unlike most Native American tribes, Pomo men as well as women wove baskets. Pomo Indians liked to weave bird feathers, shells, and many other ornaments into their designs, with striking results. Their highly developed weaving skills allowed them to make beautiful baskets as large as four feet wide or as small as a human thumbnail.

Teacher Support for Pupil Pages 336-337

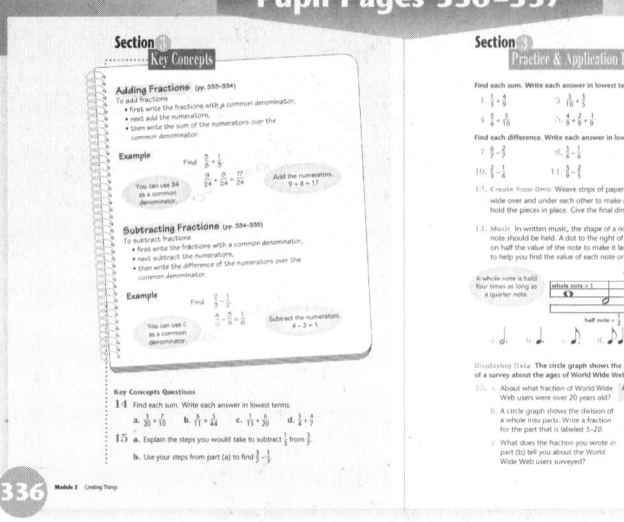

CLOSE

Closure Question Describe the steps involved in adding and subtracting fractions.

Sample Response: To add fractions, first write them with a common denominator, then add the numerators, and then write the sum of the numerators over the common denominator. Rewrite the fraction in the lowest terms if necessary. To subtract fractions, follow the same steps you use for adding fractions except subtract the numerators and write the difference over the common denominator.

SUGGESTED ASSIGNMENT

Core Course
Day 1: Exs. 4–6, 10–12, 14, 15, 17–24

Extended Course
Day 1: Exs. 4–6, 10–12, 14–24

Block Schedule
Day 3: Exs. 4–6, 10–12, 14, 15, 17–24

EMBEDDED ASSESSMENT

This section objective is tested by the exercises listed.

Add and subtract fractions with the same or different denominators.

Exercises 4, 6, 10, 12, 14, 15

Practice & Application

EXERCISE NOTES

Developing Math Concepts
For *Exs. 5* and *6*, you may want to point out that the rules for adding more than two fractions are the same as the rules for adding exactly two fractions.

Create Your Own For *Ex. 13*, students may want to bring in their completed mats to show their classmates. Students could estimate the dimensions of their classmates' mats and then measure to check their estimates.

Customizing Instruction

Home Involvement Those helping students at home will find the Key Concepts on page 336 a handy reference to the key ideas, terms, and skills of Section 3.

Absent Students For students who were absent for all or part of this section, the blackline Study Guide for Section 3 may be used to present the ideas, concepts, and skills of Section 3.

Extra Help For students who need additional practice, the blackline Practice and Applications for Section 3 provides additional exercises that may be used to confirm the skills of Section 3. The Extra Skill Practice on page 339 also provides additional exercises.

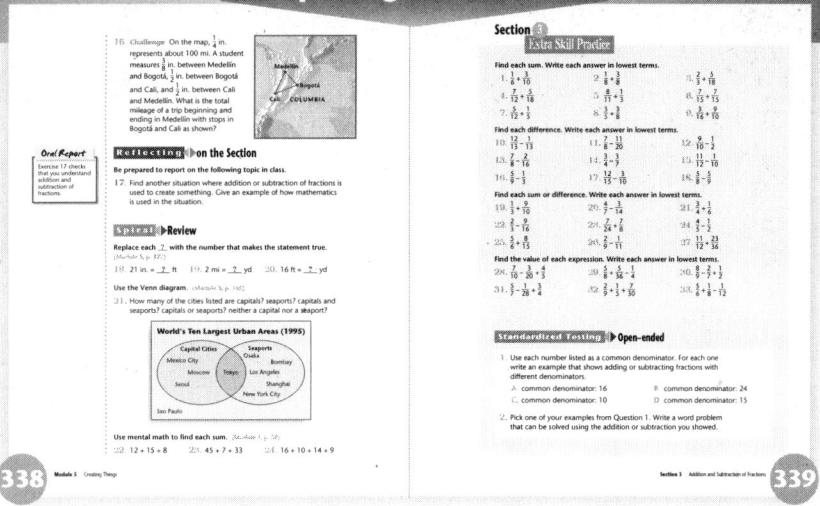

Practice & Application

Ongoing Assessment You might wish to have students save their responses to **Ex. 17** for their portfolio, to show their understanding of the real life applications of adding and subtracting fractions.

Closing the Section

In Section 3, students used fraction strips to learn how to add and subtract fractions. Students will be able to reflect on what they have learned as they answer the Reflecting on the Section exercise on page 338.

QUICK QUIZ ON THIS SECTION

1. Find each sum. Write each answer in lowest terms.

   a. $\dfrac{3}{14} + \dfrac{4}{7}$ b. $\dfrac{5}{10} + \dfrac{1}{10} + \dfrac{1}{5}$

   c. $\dfrac{1}{8} + \dfrac{3}{16} + \dfrac{10}{32}$

2. Find each difference. Write each answer in lowest terms.

   a. $\dfrac{5}{9} - \dfrac{2}{5}$ b. $\dfrac{3}{4} - \dfrac{2}{3}$

   c. $\dfrac{6}{7} - \dfrac{1}{3}$

3. It rained $\dfrac{1}{4}$ in. on Tuesday, $\dfrac{5}{16}$ in. on Wednesday, and $\dfrac{3}{8}$ in. on Thursday. How much rain fell during the three days?

4. In a survey $\dfrac{5}{9}$ of the people said they preferred orange juice. Only $\dfrac{1}{6}$ of the people preferred tomato juice. What fraction of the people surveyed preferred neither?

For answers, see Quick Quiz blackline on p. 5-59.

Section 4: Addition and Subtraction of Mixed Numbers

Section Planner

DAYS FOR MODULE 5
1 2 3 4 5 **6 7** 8 9 10 11

SECTION 4

First Day
Setting the Stage, p. 341
Exploration 1, pp. 342–343

Second Day
Exploration 2, pp. 344–346
Key Concepts, p. 347

Block Schedule

Day 4
Setting the Stage, Exploration 1, Exploration 2, Key Concepts

RESOURCE ORGANIZER

Teaching Resources
- Practice and Applications, Sec. 4
- Study Guide, Sec. 4
- Warm-Up, Sec. 4
- Quick Quiz, Sec. 4

Section Overview

In Section 4, a discussion of relief masks introduces students to the procedures for adding and subtracting mixed numbers. Students will first estimate the sum of mixed number measurements. Then they will use a ruler to find the actual sum. In a third activity, students will see that when adding mixed numbers, it is easier to find the sum if the whole numbers are added first. Next, the students will use paper and pencil to find the sum of the mixed numbers. Two paper and pencil techniques are introduced. In Exploration 2, students will be introduced to subtraction of mixed numbers using mental math, a ruler, estimation, and paper and pencil. When students use paper and pencil to subtract, they can either rename fractions where necessary, or they can rewrite the mixed numbers as fractions and then subtract.

Refer students to page 50 of Module 1 to review compatible numbers and to the Toolbox, page 601, to review elapsed time. Both skills are necessary to complete the exercises in this section.

SECTION OBJECTIVES

Exploration 1
- add mixed numbers
- estimate mixed number sums

Exploration 2
- subtract mixed numbers
- use mental math to subtract a mixed number from a whole number

ASSESSMENT OPTIONS

Checkpoint Questions
- Question 10 on p. 343
- Question 25 on p. 346

Embedded Assessment
- For a list of embedded assessment exercises see p. 5-31.

Performance Task/Portfolio
- Exercise 31 on p. 350 (journal)
- ★ Exercises 41–43 on p. 351 (extension)
- Module Project on p. 351

★ = a problem solving task that can be assessed using the Assessment Scales

---

SECTION 4 MATERIALS

Setting the Stage
◆ Labsheet 4A

Exploration 1
◆ Labsheet 4A
◆ ruler

Exploration 2
◆ ruler

Teacher Support for Pupil Pages 340-341

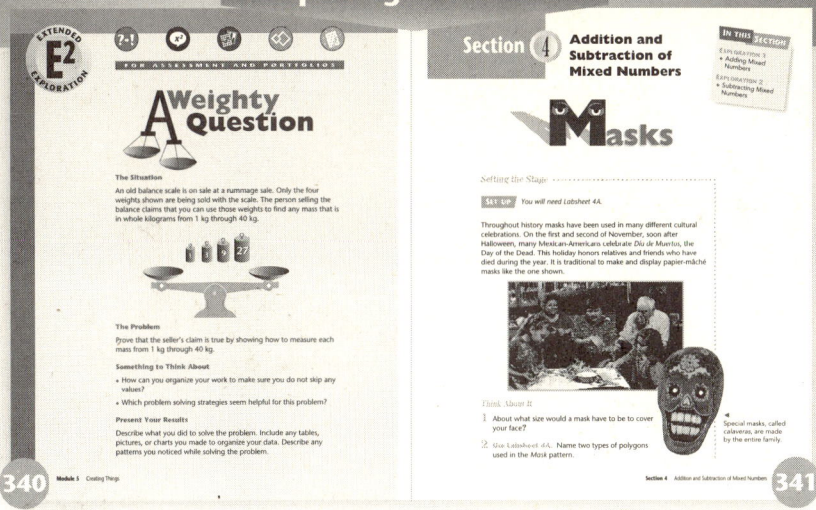

Setting the Stage

MOTIVATE

Before discussing *Questions 1* and *2*, students should do the reading on page 341 in class either individually or in groups. Students may want to do further reading or research on masks, or they may be interested in creating their own relief masks using inexpensive materials they find around the house. Students could bring their masks to class and discuss how they used mathematics to create them. Some students may want to try to make a papier-mâché mask like the one pictured on page 341.

Exploration 1

PLAN

Classroom Management

Students should work with a partner to complete Exploration 1. Since this exploration builds on students' previous skills of using a ruler, finding a common denominator to add and subtract fractions, and simplifying improper fractions, a brief review of these topics may be helpful. *Question 6* is designated as whole class discussion to be sure students can apply the skills of finding a common denominator and simplifying improper fractions to the new skill of adding mixed numbers. After discussing *Question 8*, students could use either method they prefer to add mixed numbers.

For *Question 11*, students may fail to consider *both* lengths and widths of the rectangles that make the mouth and eyes since only one length and width is recorded on the labsheet.

Customizing Instruction

Background Information *Papier-mâché* is a French term meaning "chewed paper." *Papier-mâché* was developed in Paris in the 18th century and used to make boxes, trays, decorative items, and statuettes. Today it is used for such purposes as store window displays, masks, puppets, jewelry, and even furniture. *Papier-mâché* is a popular craft medium because it is lightweight, easy to handle, and the completed objects last a long time.

Multicultural Note The *Dia de Muertos* (Day of the Dead) is not a sad affair, but rather a day to celebrate the lives of friends and relatives who have died. On this holiday, also called *All Souls' Day*, families visit the graves of loved ones to leave flowers, pray, sing, and eat the favorite foods of the people they are honoring.

MODULE 5 ◆ SECTION 4

5-27

Teacher Support for Pupil Pages 342–343

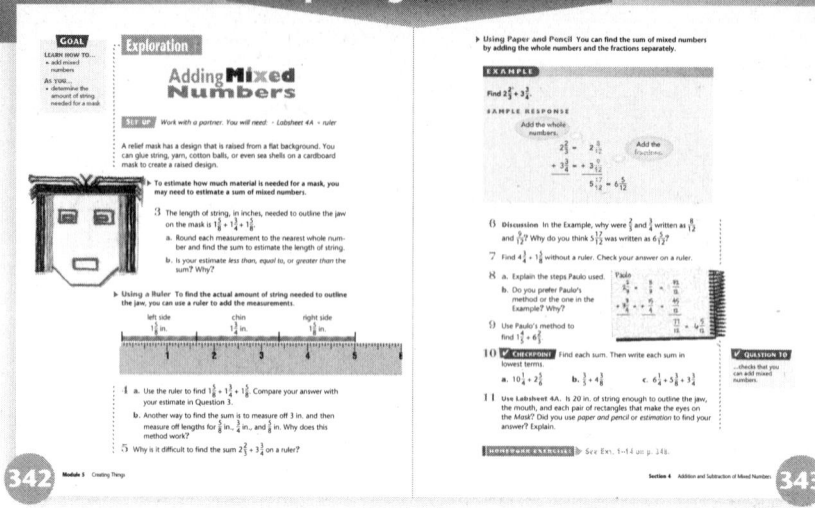

Exploration 1 continued

GUIDE

Developing Math Concepts In *Question 4(a)*, some students may intuitively want to add whole numbers and fractions separately before being shown this method in *Question 4(b)*. If so, use their intuition as a basis for discussing *Question 4(b)*. For *Question 5*, ask students to name other fractions whose sums would be difficult to find on a ruler. It is important that students have a thorough grasp of how to simplify mixed number sums, as this will help them understand the regrouping required for subtracting mixed numbers in Exploration 2.

Classroom Examples
Find $1\frac{4}{5} + 2\frac{5}{6}$.

Answer:
$$1\frac{4}{5} = 1\frac{24}{30}$$
$$+ 2\frac{5}{6} = + 2\frac{25}{30}$$
$$\overline{\phantom{+ 2\frac{5}{6} =}} \quad 3\frac{49}{30} = 4\frac{19}{30}$$

Common Error When finding a common denominator, students may fail to write the whole number beside the equivalent fraction, causing them to forget to add the whole number part when finding the sum. Remind students that to write equivalent mixed numbers, the whole number part must be written.

Discussion In *Question 6*, you may want to ask students to explain how adding mixed numbers is similar to adding fractions. Students should be able to make the connection between the two skills.

Checkpoint In *Question 10(c)*, you may want to point out that the steps for finding the sum of more than two mixed numbers are the same as the steps for finding the sum of two mixed numbers.

HOMEWORK EXERCISES

See the Suggested Assignment for Day 1 on page 5-31. For Exercise Notes, see page 5-31.

Customizing Instruction

Alternative Approach 1 Students can complete Exploration 1 individually with teacher guidance. For some students, the pictured ruler may be adequate for understanding the *Using a Ruler* example on page 342 and answering *Question 4*. Some students may need to use an actual ruler as they work through the questions.

Alternative Approach 2 Students who finish the exploration with extra time may enjoy sketching a mask of their own similar to the one on Labsheet 4A. They could then challenge another student to estimate how much string is needed to outline the mask and then have them measure to check their estimate. Encourage students to use a variety of polygons to create the features on their masks.

Teacher Support for Pupil Pages 344–345

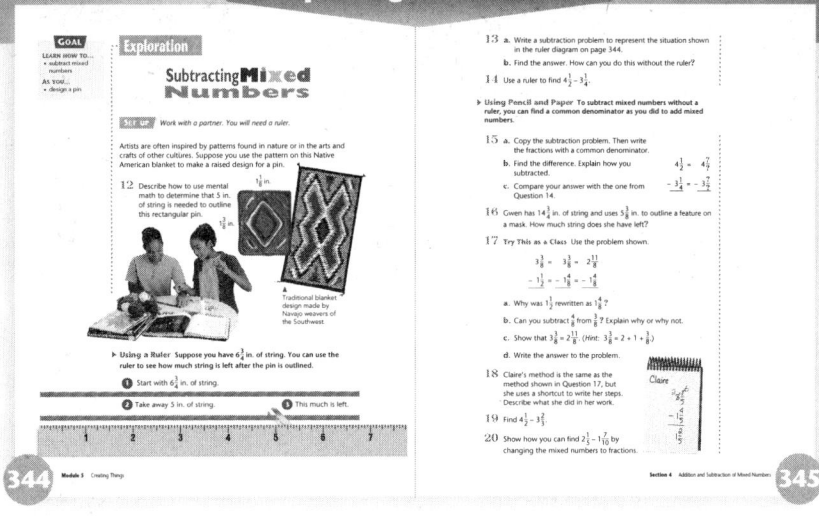

Exploration 2

PLAN

Classroom Management
Students should work in pairs to complete Exploration 2. This exploration builds on students' previous knowledge of adding mixed numbers. It may be helpful to review equivalencies such as $4\frac{2}{2} = 5$, as this is the conceptual knowledge students will need to understand the regrouping process for mixed number subtraction. Teacher guidance is recommended for the Try This as a Class problems (*Questions 17* and *21*) to be sure students understand the regrouping process.

GUIDE

Developing Math Concepts
Students should be comfortable subtracting mixed numbers where regrouping is not necessary before moving on to the questions where regrouping is required. Some students may prefer the shortcut method presented in *Question 18* as a way to subtract mixed numbers.

Classroom Examples
Find $5\frac{1}{6} - 2\frac{3}{4}$.

Answer:
$$5\frac{1}{6} = 5\frac{2}{12} = 4\frac{14}{12}$$
$$-2\frac{3}{4} = -2\frac{9}{12} = -2\frac{9}{12}$$
$$\overline{2\frac{5}{12}}$$

Try This as a Class If students have trouble understanding how to regroup $3\frac{3}{8}$ as $2\frac{11}{8}$ in *Question 17(c)*, it may be helpful to have them think back to their work on simplifying their mixed number sums from Exploration 1. Present $2\frac{11}{8}$ as if it were a mixed number sum and ask students how they would simplify it. This strategy of *working backward* may help them better understand the relationship between the two values.

Customizing Instruction

Alternative Approach Exploration 2 can be completed individually with teacher guidance. Students who finish the exploration early may enjoy trying the Extension problems (Exs. 41–43) on page 351.

Visual Learners Some students may need to use a sketch, a diagram, or a manipulative to help them understand the regrouping step in subtracting mixed numbers. Pattern blocks or fraction strips work well for demonstrating this concept.

5-29

Teacher Support for Pupil Pages 346–347

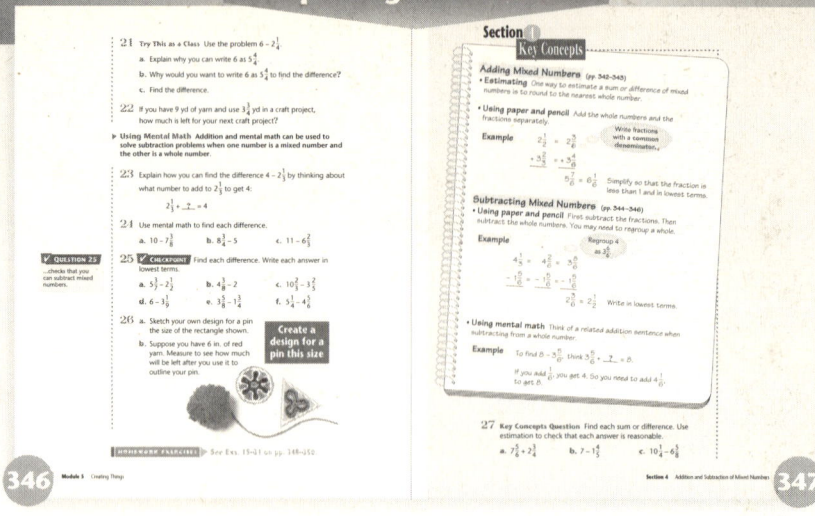

Exploration 2 continued

Checkpoint As students complete *Question 25*, ask them to think about the methods they have learned in this exploration, and to decide which methods are appropriate for each problem.

HOMEWORK EXERCISES

See the Suggested Assignment for Day 2 on page 5-31. For Exercise Notes, see page 5-31.

CLOSE

Closure Question How is adding and subtracting mixed numbers like adding and subtracting fractions? How is it different?

Sample Response: When adding or subtracting both types of numbers, you need to find a common denominator for the fractions, add or subtract the fractions, and write your answer in lowest terms. When adding or subtracting mixed numbers, you may also need to regroup to solve, and the whole number part of the mixed number must also be added or subtracted.

Customizing Instruction

Home Involvement Those helping students at home will find the Key Concepts on page 347 a handy reference to the key ideas, terms, and skills of Section 4.

Absent Students For students who were absent for all or part of this section, the blackline Study Guide for Section 4 may be used to present the ideas, concepts, and skills of Section 4.

Extra Help For students who need additional practice, the blackline Practice and Applications for Section 4 provides additional exercises that may be used to confirm the skills of Section 4. The Extra Skill Practice on page 352 also provides additional exercises.

Teacher Support for Pupil Pages 348–349

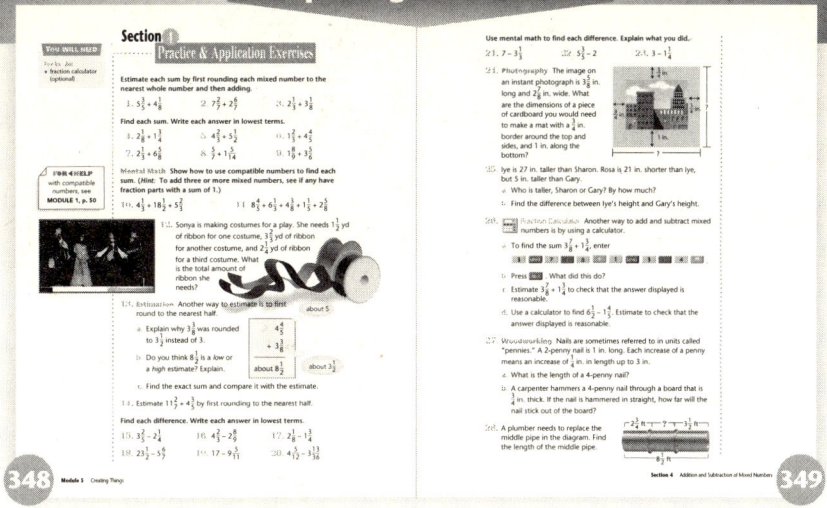

SUGGESTED ASSIGNMENT

Core Course
Day 1: Exs. 1, 2, 4–6, 10, 12, 13, 32–40
Day 2: Exs. 15–18, 20–24, 27, 28, 31

Extended Course
Day 1: Exs. 1–14, 32–40
Day 2: Exs. 16, 18, 20–25, 27, 28, 31, 41–43

Block Schedule
Day 4: Exs. 4, 6, 12, 13, 16, 18, 20, 21, 23, 24, 27, 28, 31–40

EMBEDDED ASSESSMENT

These section objectives are tested by the exercises listed.

Add mixed numbers.
Exercises 4, 6, 12

Estimate mixed number sums.
Exercises 1, 2, 13

Subtract mixed numbers.
Exercises 16, 18, 20, 27, 28

Use mental math to subtract a mixed number from a whole number.
Exercises 21, 23

Practice & Application
EXERCISE NOTES

Real World Connection For *Ex. 12*, students may be interested to know that cloth and ribbon are often sold by the yard. People who make clothing, or people who sell materials to make clothing, frequently need to add or subtract mixed numbers.

Developing Math Concepts
Ex. 13 presents another way of estimating mixed number sums by rounding to the nearest $\frac{1}{2}$. You could use fraction strips to show why $3\frac{3}{8}$ rounds to $3\frac{1}{2}$ instead of 3 or 4. You may also want to discuss real life situations where rounding to the nearest half would be better than rounding to the nearest whole number.

5-31

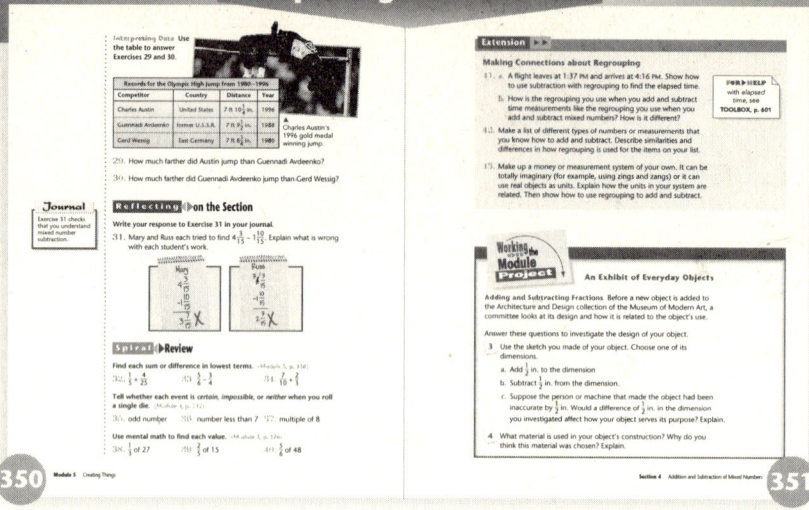

Practice & Application

Ongoing Assessment You may want to have students save their answers to the Reflecting on the Section exercise on page 350 for their portfolio to show their progress in understanding mixed number subtraction. After explaining what is wrong with each student's work, your students could solve the problem to show the correct steps of the subtraction.

Working on the Module Project

To complete *Question 3*, students could create two other sketches which show the new dimensions, then compare the new sketches to the original one. Or they could simply record the new dimensions on another sheet of paper and then answer part *(c)*.

For *Question 4*, if the object is made of several different materials, students could identify the main ones and include just these in their discussion rather than discussing all of them. To stimulate students' thinking for this part of the project, you may want to hold a class discussion of the properties and characteristics of various materials.

Closing the Section

In Section 4, students have built upon their previous knowledge of adding and subtracting fractions as they learned how to add and subtract mixed numbers. You may want to summarize the section by asking students to answer questions which help connect the two sets of skills. How is adding and subtracting mixed numbers like adding and subtracting fractions? How is it different? What new skills did you learn in this section? What previously learned skills did you use?

QUICK QUIZ ON THIS SECTION

1. Find each sum. Write each answer in lowest terms.

   a. $2\frac{3}{7} + 3\frac{6}{7}$ **b.** $1\frac{3}{5} + 3\frac{7}{10}$

2. Find each difference. Write each answer in lowest terms.

   a. $4\frac{2}{9} - 1\frac{2}{3}$ **b.** $10\frac{7}{10} - 4\frac{3}{5}$

3. Carmen needs $18\frac{1}{2}$ yd of material to make costumes for a play. She has $5\frac{2}{3}$ yd. How much more does she need?

4. Seth ran $6\frac{1}{2}$ mi on Monday, $4\frac{2}{5}$ mi on Wednesday, and $8\frac{7}{10}$ mi on Friday. How far did he run during these three days?

5. Estimate $1\frac{23}{42} + 3\frac{61}{78}$ by rounding to the nearest half.

For answers, see Quick Quiz blackline on p. 5-60.

Section 5: Capacity and Mixed Number Multiplication

Section Planner

DAYS FOR MODULE 5
1 2 3 4 5 6 7 **8 9 10 11**

SECTION 5

First Day
Setting the Stage, p. 353
Exploration 1, pp. 354–355

Second Day
Exploration 2, pp. 355–357
Key Concepts, p. 358

Block Schedule

Day 5
Setting the Stage, Exploration 1, Exploration 2, Key Concepts

RESOURCE ORGANIZER

Teaching Resources
- Practice and Applications, Sec. 5
- Study Guide, Sec. 5
- Warm-Up, Sec. 5
- Quick Quiz, Sec. 5

Section Overview

In Section 5, students will work with customary units of capacity, using milk containers as benchmarks for estimating capacity. Key terms in this section are *capacity, fluid ounce, cup, pint, quart,* and *gallon*. Students will use benchmarks to determine the reasonableness of statements involving capacity. They will also convert between customary units of measure. For help in converting, students should recall from Section 2 that division is used to convert from a smaller unit to a larger one, and multiplication is used to convert from a larger unit to a smaller one. Some of the conversions will involve mixed numbers.

The distributive property will be introduced for those exercises in Exploration 2 that require multiplying a whole number by a mixed number. Students will also multiply two mixed numbers in this exploration by first expressing the mixed numbers as fractions. For a review of the multiplication of fractions, refer students to page 268 in Module 4. Students will also explore the relationship between *reciprocals*, another key term in Section 5.

SECTION OBJECTIVES

Exploration 1
- use benchmarks to estimate capacity in customary units
- convert between customary units of capacity

Exploration 2
- use the distributive property to multiply a mixed number by a whole number
- use fraction form to multiply any combination of fractions, whole numbers, or mixed numbers
- find reciprocals

ASSESSMENT OPTIONS

Checkpoint Questions
- Question 7 on p. 354
- Question 9 on p. 355
- Question 14 on p. 356
- Question 18 on p. 357
- Question 24 on p. 357

Embedded Assessment
- For a list of embedded assessment exercises see p. 5-37.

Performance Task/Portfolio
- Exercise 12 on p. 359 (writing)
- Exercise 40 on p. 361 (discussion)
- Module Project on p. 362

SECTION 5 MATERIALS

Setting the Stage
- $\frac{1}{2}$ pint, pint, quart, and gallon milk containers

Exploration 1
- containers of various sizes

Exploration 2
- pattern blocks

Teacher Support for Pupil Pages 352–353

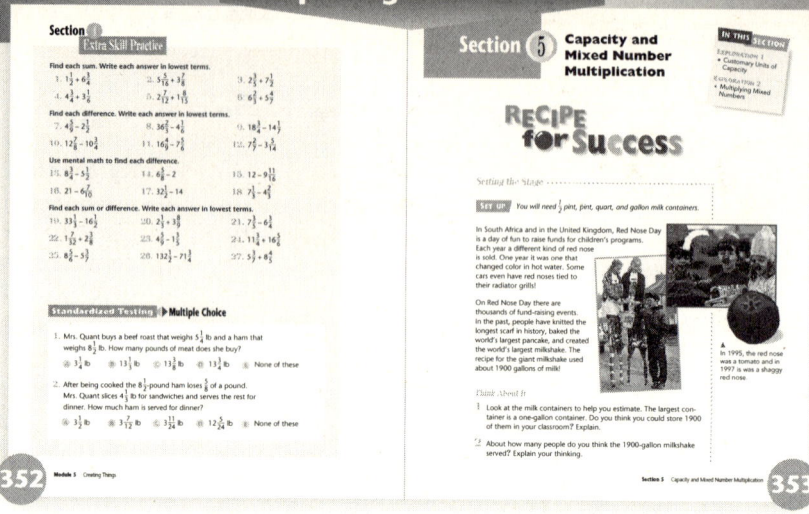

Setting the Stage

MOTIVATE

Before discussing *Questions 1* and *2*, students should do the reading on page 353 in class, either individually or in groups. The milk containers should be set up so that students can refer to them as they complete *Questions 1* and *2*. It may be helpful to bring in enough milk containers so that each group has their own set of containers to use as a reference. You could ask several students to save their milk cartons from lunch and to bring containers from home. Students may also be interested in reading about other record breaking events from sources such as the *Guinness Book of World Records*.

Exploration 1

PLAN

Classroom Management
Exploration 1 can be completed individually or in groups of 2 to 4. For *Question 4* on page 354, students will be estimating the capacity of various containers, but it is not necessary that each group have a sample of each one. As you tell students the capacities in *Question 4*, you may want to use masking tape to label each container with the amount it holds. Students would then have a visual reference for a variety of capacities to use as they complete the exploration.

If time permits, you may want to fill the containers with water and pour the amounts from one container to another so students can better see the relationships between the various units. Teacher guidance is recommended for *Question 5* on page 354 to insure that students interpret the diagram correctly. *Question 8* on page 355 is appropriate for whole class discussion so students can learn from each others' thinking about converting units.

Customizing Instruction

Visual Learners Some students may benefit from a pictorial visual to help them understand the relationships among customary units of capacity. Students could create their own visual or use the one at the right.

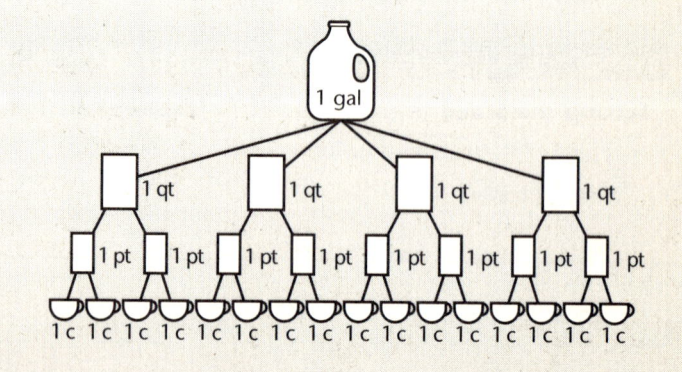

Teacher Support for Pupil Pages 354-355

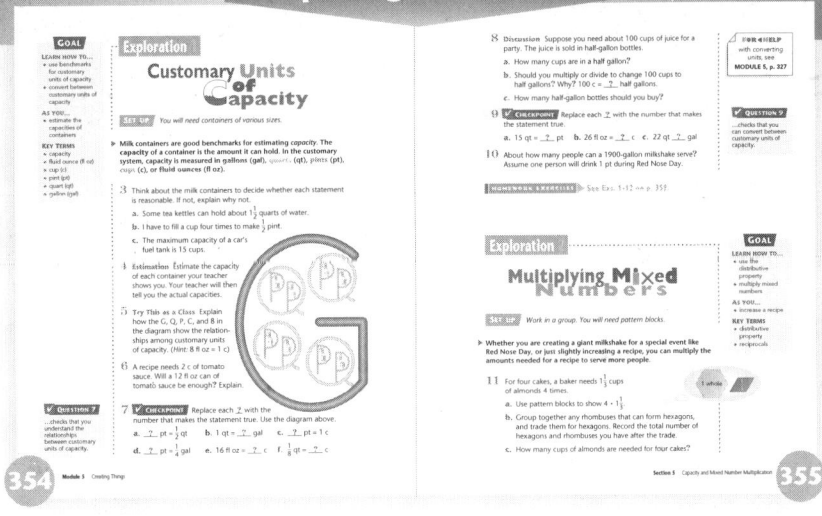

Exploration 1 continued

GUIDE

Developing Math Concepts
This exploration develops students' intuitive number sense regarding conversions between customary units of capacity. As students work through the exploration, you may want to review the rules for converting units of length presented in Section 2. It may be helpful to discuss how these same rules apply to converting units of capacity.

Estimation In *Question 4*, if the capacity of a container is shown on its label, be sure that students cannot see it as you display the container.

Common Error Students may choose the wrong operation when converting between customary units of capacity. Encourage students to refer to the relationships presented in the diagram in *Question 5* or to the capacity table on page 358. Students should always use number sense to check that their answer is reasonable.

Try This as a Class Before beginning *Question 5*, be sure students understand what each letter in the diagram stands for. Students can keep track of the capacity relationships they discover by writing down the equivalencies, or by creating their own charts, diagrams, or tables to display the relationships.

Checkpoint In *Questions 7* and *9*, be sure students can use the relationships they discovered in *Question 5* to convert between units.

Discussion *Question 8* provides an intuitive, number sense approach to converting units. Although some students may remember the rules for converting between units from Section 2, the discussion here will encourage students to use their number sense as they think about conversions.

HOMEWORK EXERCISES

See the Suggested Assignment for Day 1 on page 5-37. For Exercise Notes, see page 5-38.

Customizing Instruction

Second Language Learners You may want to help students distinguish between the meaning of *capacity* as presented in this exploration and other meanings of the word, such as its usage in these phrases: *a capacity crowd, the capacity to learn new things, the factory is operating below full capacity,* and *in his capacity as president*.

Alternative Approach Students can complete Exploration 2 individually with teacher guidance. If overhead pattern blocks are not available, a blackline master can be copied onto a transparency and then the blocks can be cut out. If available, you could use colored transparencies that correspond with the different-colored blocks, or you can use permanent markers to color in the shapes.

Visual Learners Some students may find it helpful to use pattern blocks to understand the distributive property as shown in the Example on page 356. These students may also need more practice with pattern blocks before moving on to paper-and-pencil computation.

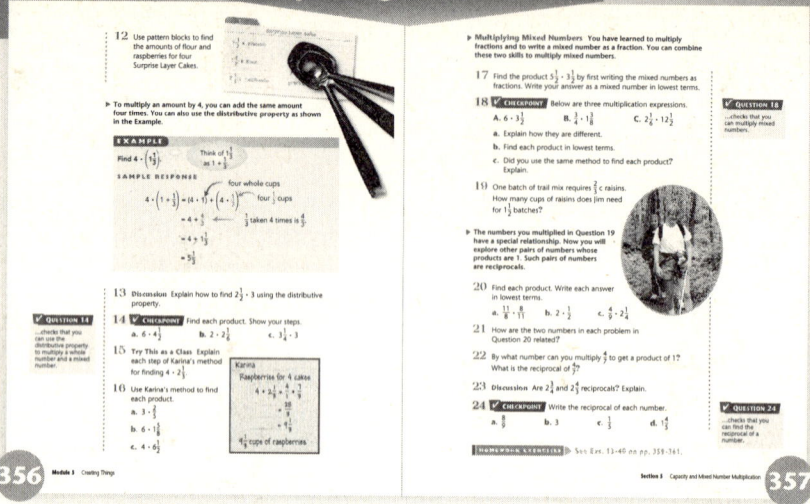

Exploration 2

PLAN

Classroom Management
Students should complete Exploration 2 in groups of 2 to 4. Each group will need a set of pattern blocks that contains at least 9 hexagons, 4 trapezoids, and 4 rhombuses. *Question 13* is highlighted as appropriate for class discussion so that all students have an understanding of how to use the distributive property. The discussion in *Question 23* insures that students understand how to find the reciprocal of a mixed number.

GUIDE

Classroom Examples
Find $3 \cdot \left(2\frac{5}{6}\right)$.

Answer:
$$3 \cdot \left(2 + \frac{5}{6}\right) = (3 \cdot 2) + \left(3 \cdot \frac{5}{6}\right)$$
$$= 6 + \frac{15}{6}$$
$$= 6 + 2\frac{3}{6}$$
$$= 6 + 2\frac{1}{2}$$
$$= 8\frac{1}{2}$$

Developing Math Concepts
Students may need to use pattern blocks to understand the Example on page 356. Using a hexagon to represent 1 and a rhombus to represent $\frac{1}{3}$, the product $4 \cdot \left(1 + \frac{1}{3}\right)$ can be modeled as 4 hexagons $(4 \cdot 1)$ plus 4 rhombuses $\left(4 \cdot \frac{1}{3}\right)$.

Common Error When multiplying a mixed number and a whole number, some students may simply multiply the whole numbers and write the fraction beside the result. To correct this error, encourage students to think about their work in *Questions 11* and *12*.

Discussion Some students may need to use pattern blocks to help them explain *Question 13*. A discussion of the word *distribute* as meaning "to spread out or over" may be helpful.

Try This as a Class As you work through *Question 15*, you may want to point out how Karina's method, insures that *both* parts of the mixed number are multiplied by the whole number.

Checkpoint It is important for students to develop the habit of using estimation to check the reasonableness of their answers. Encourage them to do this for the products in *Question 18(b)*. It may be helpful for students to share their responses to *Question 18(c)* verbally so that all students have a clear understanding of the various methods and of the types of problems for which they are used.

Discussion In *Question 23*, students should be able to explain why the numbers are not reciprocals. You may want to ask students to give the reciprocal of each mixed number as part of their explanation.

HOMEWORK EXERCISES

See the Suggested Assignment for Day 2 on page 5-37. For Exercise Notes, see page 5-38.

Teacher Support for Pupil Pages 358–359

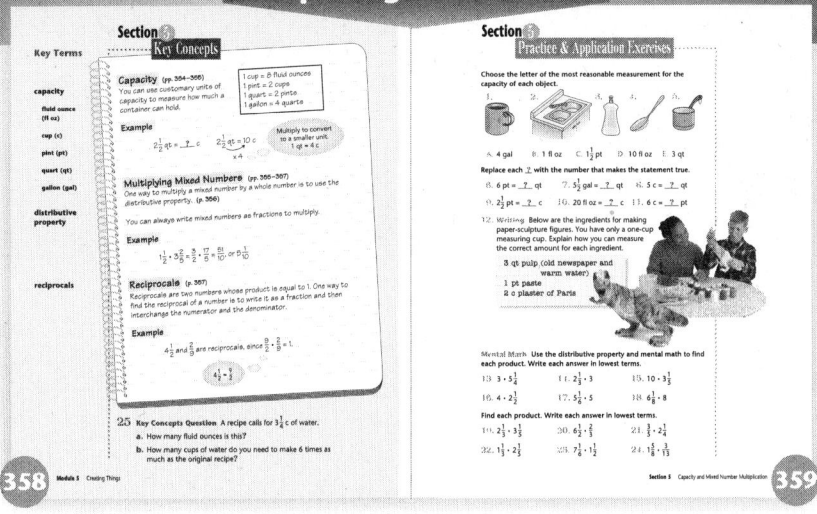

Exploration 2 continued

CLOSE

Closure Question State the two ways of multiplying mixed numbers described in this section. How is multiplication of mixed numbers used when converting customary units of capacity? How are a fraction and its reciprocal related?

Answer: Use the distributive property and write the mixed numbers as fractions; *Sample Response:* When a measurement of capacity is given as a mixed number and you are converting to a smaller unit, you multiply the two values to convert. The product of a number and its reciprocal is 1.

SUGGESTED ASSIGNMENT

Core Course
Day 1: Exs. 1–12, 41–49
Day 2: Exs. 13–16, 19–22, 25, 29–32, 34, 36, 40

Extended Course
Day 1: Exs. 1–12, 41–49
Day 2: Exs. 14, 16–22, 25, 26, 29–32, 34, 36, 39, 40, 50

Block Schedule
Day 5: Exs. 2, 3, 4–16 even, 19–22, 25, 30–32, 34, 36, 40–49

EMBEDDED ASSESSMENT

These section objectives are tested by the exercises listed.

Use benchmarks to estimate capacity in customary units.
Exercises 2, 3, 4

Convert between customary units of capacity.
Exercises 6, 8, 10, 12

Use the distributive property to multiply a mixed number by a whole number.
Exercises 14, 16, 25

Use fraction form to multiply fractions, whole numbers, and/or mixed numbers.
Exercises 20, 21, 25

Find reciprocals.
Exercises 30, 31, 32

Customizing Instruction

Home Involvement Those helping students at home will find the Key Concepts on page 358 a handy reference to the key ideas, terms, and skills of Section 5.

Absent Students For students who were absent for all or part of this section, the blackline Study Guide for Section 5 may be used to present the ideas, concepts, and skills of Section 5.

Extra Help For students who need additional practice, the blackline Practice and Applications for Section 5 provides additional exercises that may be used to confirm the skills of Section 5. The Extra Skill Practice on page 363 also provides additional exercises.

MODULE 5 ◆ SECTION 5

5-37

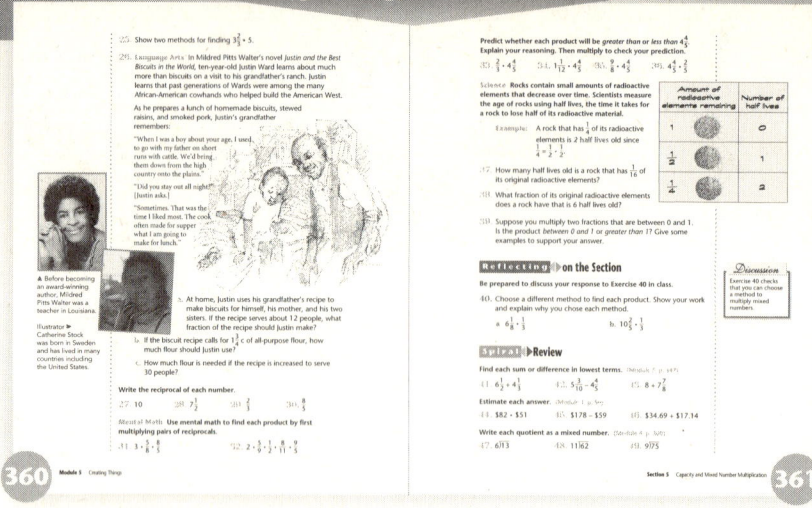

Practice & Application

Developing Math Concepts
For *Ex. 26(b)*, discuss how Justin might handle the recipe if it called for $\frac{7}{12}$ c flour. You may need to explain to students that there are no measuring cups that show twelfths, so Justin would need to come up with an alternative way to measure the correct amount. He could combine $\frac{1}{3}$ c $\left(\frac{4}{12}\right)$ and $\frac{1}{4}$ c $\left(\frac{3}{12}\right)$ to get the correct amount. *Exs. 33–36* help develop students' number sense about multiplying fractions and mixed numbers. When predicting each product, it may be helpful if students think back to their work on finding a fraction of a number where the multiplication symbol is replaced with the word *of*. For *Ex. 33*, they might think: "Is $\frac{2}{3}$ of $4\frac{4}{5}$ more than or less than $4\frac{4}{5}$?"

Ongoing Assessment You may want to have students save their answers to the Reflecting on the Section exercise *(Ex. 40)* for their portfolio to show their understanding of the different methods used to multiply mixed numbers.

Working on the Module Project

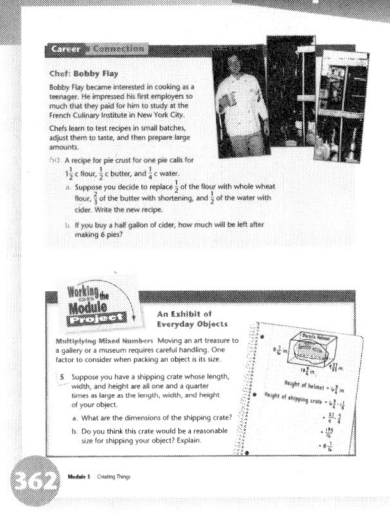

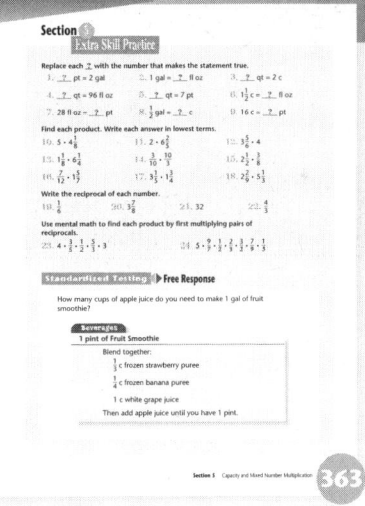

Students should calculate the dimensions of the shipping crate by multiplying each dimension of their object (length, width, and height) by $1\frac{1}{4}$. You will want to be sure their calculations are correct before they move on to part (b). As students answer part (b), you may want to have them explore the sizes of boxes that objects are shipped in by asking them to examine any boxes they have at home. You could ask students to bring in examples of these boxes and, if possible, to record the dimensions of the object that was shipped in the box. Students could then determine the relationship between the dimensions of the object and the dimensions of the box. A large box used to ship an appliance such as a refrigerator, washing machine, or dryer may be interesting to display in the classroom. It may be possible to obtain one of these boxes from a local appliance store.

Closing the Section

In this section, students discovered the relationships between customary units of capacity, and learned to convert between these units. Students learned to multiply mixed numbers by using the distributive property and by writing the mixed numbers as improper fractions. Students also learned to write reciprocals of fractions and mixed numbers. Students will be able to reflect on these understandings when answering the following questions: Suppose you are a chef in a large restaurant. You prepare a wide variety of dishes by creating your own recipes, and by increasing or decreasing ingredients in the recipes used by other chefs. Why is a knowledge of customary units of capacity important for the work you do? How might you use what you know about customary units of capacity in your work? How might you use your knowledge of multiplying mixed numbers? What other tasks or occupations might require you to use the skills you learned in this section?

QUICK QUIZ ON THIS SECTION

1. Replace each ___?___ with the number that makes the statement true.
   a. 18 pt = ___?___ qt
   b. 40 c = ___?___ gal
   c. 50 fl oz = ___?___ c

2. Find each product. Write each answer in lowest terms.
   a. $4\frac{1}{2} \cdot 1\frac{2}{3}$
   b. $3\frac{1}{4} \cdot \frac{7}{13}$
   c. $2\frac{3}{4} \cdot 1\frac{5}{8}$

3. Theo needs $2\frac{3}{4}$ c of flour to make 1 batch of cookies. How many cups of flour does he need to make 5 batches?

4. Write the reciprocal of each number.
   a. $2\frac{3}{11}$
   b. $\frac{7}{9}$
   c. $3\frac{1}{3}$

For answers, see Quick Quiz blackline on p. 5-61.

5-39

Section 6 — Division with Fractions

Section Planner

DAYS FOR MODULE 5
1 2 3 4 5 6 7 8 9 **10** 11

SECTION 6

First Day
Setting the Stage, p. 364
Exploration 1, pp. 365–367

Second Day
Exploration 2, pp. 368–369
Key Concepts, p. 370

Block Schedule

Day 6
Setting the Stage, Exploration 1,
Exploration 2, Key Concepts

RESOURCE ORGANIZER

Teaching Resources
- Practice and Applications, Sec. 6
- Study Guide, Sec. 6
- Module Tests Forms A and B
- Standardized Assessment
- Module Performance Assessment
- Warm-Up, Sec. 6
- Quick Quiz, Sec. 6

Section Overview

The designs formed by geometric puzzle pieces in Section 6 are used to introduce students to procedures for dividing by fractions and mixed numbers. Students will use a ruler to solve a puzzle problem that involves dividing a whole number by a decimal. In the activity, students will be reintroduced to reciprocals, a topic presented in the previous section. They will discover how they can use a reciprocal and multiplication to divide any number by a fraction. As students investigate how to divide a fraction by another fraction or by a mixed number in Exploration 2, they will formulate a general rule for estimating a quotient in relation to 1 given the relative values of the numbers being divided. This rule will also allow them to determine the reasonableness of the quotient when two mixed numbers are divided. All exercises in Section 6 require students to write their quotients in lowest terms.

SECTION OBJECTIVES

Exploration 1
- use a reciprocal to divide a whole number by a fraction
- interpret the quotient in division by a fraction

Exploration 2
- use number sense to estimate when dividing with fractions or mixed numbers
- use reciprocals to divide any combination of whole numbers, fractions, or mixed numbers

ASSESSMENT OPTIONS

Checkpoint Questions
- Question 7 on p. 366
- Question 11 on p. 367
- Question 16 on p. 369
- Question 20 on p. 369

Embedded Assessment
- For a list of embedded assessment exercises see p. 5-44.

Performance Task/Portfolio
- ★Exercise 22 on p. 372 (create your own)
- Exercise 24 on p. 374 (visual thinking)
- Module Project on p. 375

★ = a problem solving exercise that can be assessed using the Assessment Scales

SECTION 6 MATERIALS

Setting the Stage
- ◆ Labsheet 6A
- ◆ scissors

Exploration 1
- ◆ Labsheet 6B
- ◆ ruler
- ◆ tape
- ◆ trapezoid-shaped puzzle pieces

Teacher Support for Pupil Pages 364–365

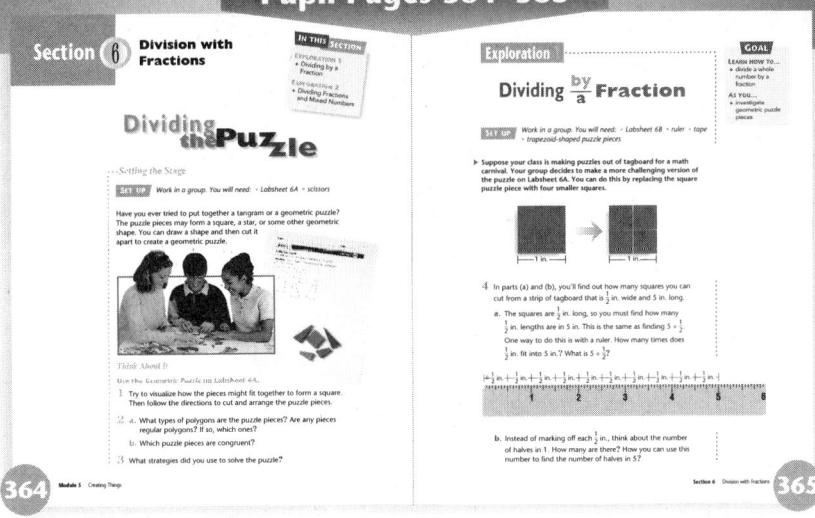

Setting the Stage

MOTIVATE

Students will enjoy discussing other geometric puzzles they have solved. Some students may have worked tangram puzzles before and could share their strategies for solving them. The puzzle pieces are easier to work with if Labsheet 6A is pasted onto construction paper before cutting out the shapes. Students might wish to make a sketch of the answer to the puzzle, then take the puzzle pieces home for family members or friends to try to solve. If time permits, students can also create their own geometric puzzles by drawing a shape and then cutting it apart.

Students could solve each other's puzzles or they could challenge each other to make a more difficult version of their puzzle by cutting one of their pieces into two or more smaller pieces.

Exploration 1

PLAN

Classroom Management
Exploration 1 should be completed in groups of 2 to 4. Before beginning the exploration, you may want to briefly review reciprocals from Section 5 since this exploration builds on that knowledge. When using Labsheet 6B for **Questions 5** and **6** on page 366, be sure students know to draw and label the fraction sections above the ruler as shown in Problem 1.

Customizing Instruction

Alternative Approach Division of a whole number by a fraction can also be shown with pattern blocks. For *Question 4*, students would count out 5 yellow hexagons and then see how many red trapezoids would cover the 5 hexagons. Problems that can be shown easily with pattern blocks include any whole number divided by $\frac{1}{2}$, $\frac{1}{3}$, or $\frac{1}{6}$. Quotients that are not whole numbers can also be shown using pattern blocks.

When modeling these problems, be sure students understand that the "leftover" pattern block piece is written not as the piece itself, but as *what fraction that piece is of the divisor*. For instance, when students divide 1 by $\frac{2}{3}$ the leftover piece is a blue thirds block. The thirds block is "$\frac{1}{2}$ of the divisor $\frac{2}{3}$," so the answer is written as $1\frac{1}{2}$ (not $1\frac{2}{3}$).

5-41

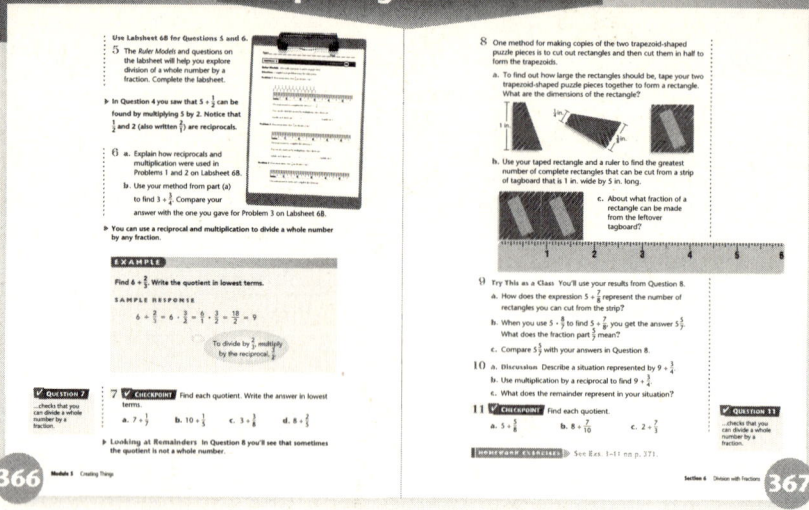

Exploration 1 continued

GUIDE

Developing Math Concepts
Guide students to understand the division algorithm as it stems from their manipulative work, first with the ruler and then with the taped rectangle. Some students may need more manipulative work before moving on to paper and pencil computation for dividing fractions. Although the rule for division by a fraction as multiplication by the reciprocal is not presented until after *Question 6*, students should be able to discover this connection on their own as they work through Labsheet 6B and answer *Questions 5* and *6*. Be sure students have a thorough grasp of division with whole number quotients before moving on to *Questions 8–10* where the quotients are not whole numbers. After students use the taped rectangle to explore quotients that are not whole numbers in *Questions 8–10*, you may wish to provide additional practice with a manipulative to further reinforce this understanding.

Common Error Students may forget to write the reciprocal of the fraction before they multiply. Use the Example and students' work from Problems 1 and 2 on Labsheet 6B as a reminder of the correct procedure.

Classroom Examples
Find $8 \div \frac{4}{5}$. Write the quotient in lowest terms.

Answer: To divide by $\frac{4}{5}$, multiply by its reciprocal $\frac{5}{4}$.

$$8 \div \frac{4}{5} = 8 \cdot \frac{5}{4}$$
$$= \frac{8}{1} \cdot \frac{5}{4}$$
$$= \frac{40}{4} = 10$$

Try This as a Class *Question 9* is to be done as a class so students can more easily make the connection between using a manipulative and using an algorithm. Students who have difficulty relating the use of their taped rectangle to the actual paper and pencil computation may need to look back at *Question 8(b–c)*.

Discussion The discussion in *Question 10* insures that students are able to use the division algorithm, and further ties together their work from *Questions 8* and *9*. By this time in the exploration, look to see that students are able to make the transition from manipulative to paper and pencil.

Checkpoint For *Question 11*, you may want to have students explain the meaning of each division before they complete the problems. (5 divided by $\frac{5}{8}$ means how times does $\frac{5}{8}$ fit into 5?) This will reinforce their work from the beginning of the exploration and help strengthen their conceptual understanding of division.

HOMEWORK EXERCISES

See the Suggested Assignment for Day 1 on page 5-44. For Exercise Notes, see page 5-45.

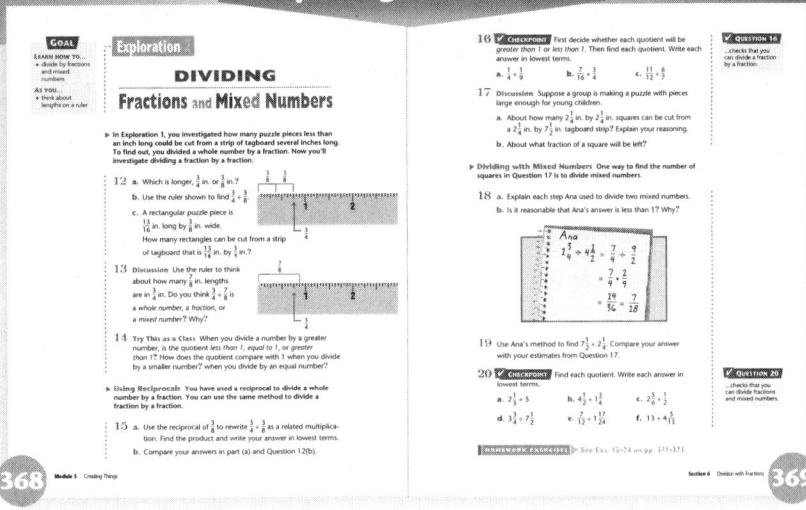

Exploration 2

PLAN

Classroom Management
Students can work through Exploration 2 individually or in groups of 2 to 4. Comparing fractions is an important prerequisite skill for this exploration, so you may want to do a quick review before beginning. *Questions 13* and *17* are designated as whole class discussion to develop students' number sense about dividing fractions and mixed numbers. *Question 14* is a Try This as a Class problem so that students can hear and benefit from their classmates' understanding of division quotients.

GUIDE

Developing Math Concepts
Although students may want to apply the rules they learned in Exploration 1 to divide the fractions in *Questions 12* and *13*, encourage them to use the ruler and their number sense. When dividing fractions and mixed numbers, students are often confused when the division problem yields a result that is less than one. The development in *Questions 12–14* is designed to help students understand why (and when) this happens.

Common Error Students often confuse the dividend and the divisor when division problems are written out in words. Students may have been told in the past that the larger number is always the dividend. Point out that this is not always true and that any two numbers can divide each other. You may also want to review the definitions of *dividend* and *divisor*. You will want to pay close attention to this potential error as students complete *Questions 14* and *17*.

Try This as a Class Students should refer to their answers from *Questions 12* and *13* if they have difficulty answering *Question 14*. You may also want to use some simple whole number examples to help students first grasp the concept. Ask: "Is the result of 2 divided by 4 a whole number amount or a fractional amount? How do you know? (Think: How many 4's will *fit into* one 2?) Is 4 divided by 2 greater than or less than 1?"

Checkpoint In *Question 16*, remind students to identify which fraction is greater before deciding whether the quotient will be greater than 1 or less than 1.

Discussion One way of thinking about *Question 17(a)* is to add $2\frac{1}{4}$ three times to get $6\frac{3}{4}$. If another $2\frac{1}{4}$ is added, the answer is greater than $7\frac{1}{2}$, so the answer must be between 3 and 4. Students might also use estimation to determine that 3 times $2\frac{1}{2}$ equals $7\frac{1}{2}$, so the answer will be more than 3. For *Question 17(b)*, students could reason that the fraction will be about $\frac{1}{3}$ or that it will be less than $\frac{1}{2}$.

Checkpoint For *Question 20*, you may want to have students predict whether each answer will be greater than or less than 1. Students could then check their predictions as they work the problems.

HOMEWORK EXERCISES

See the Suggested Assignment for Day 2 on page 5-44. For Exercise Notes, see page 5-45.

Teacher Support for Pupil Pages 370–371

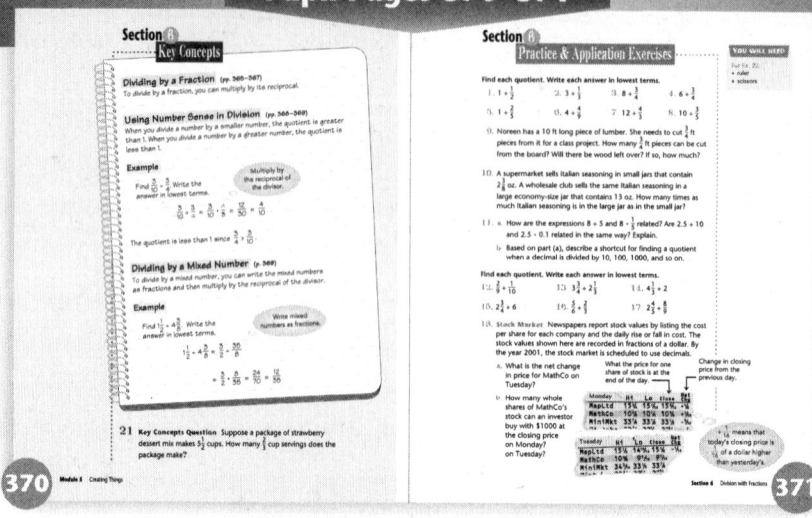

Exploration 2 continued

CLOSE

Closure Question Describe the steps involved in the division of fractions and mixed numbers.

Sample Response: To divide fractions, multiply the first fraction by the reciprocal of the second fraction. Then write the final answer in lowest terms if it is not already written that way. If the division involves mixed numbers, first write each mixed number as an improper fraction and then proceed with the above steps to divide the fractions.

SUGGESTED ASSIGNMENT

Core Course
Day 1: Exs. 1–4, 8–11, 25–33
Day 2: Exs. 12–14, 18, 19, 21, 24

Extended Course
Day 1: Exs. 1–11, 25–33
Day 2: Exs. 12–14, 18–21, 23, 24

Block Schedule
Day 6: Exs. 2–8 even, 9–12, 14, 18, 21, 24–33

EMBEDDED ASSESSMENT

These section objectives are tested by the exercises listed.

Use a reciprocal to divide a whole number by a fraction.
Exercises 2, 4, 8, 10, 11

Interpret the quotient in division by a fraction.
Exercise 9

Use number sense to estimate when dividing with fractions or mixed numbers.
Exercise 21

Use reciprocals to divide any combination of whole numbers, fractions, or mixed numbers.
Exercises 12, 14, 18

Customizing Instruction

Home Involvement Those helping students at home will find the Key Concepts on page 370 a handy reference to the key ideas, terms, and skills of Section 6.

Absent Students For students who were absent for all or part of this section, the blackline Study Guide for Section 6 may be used to present the ideas, concepts, and skills of Section 6.

Extra Help For students who need additional practice, the blackline Practice and Applications for Section 6 provides additional exercises that may be used to confirm the skills of Section 6. The Extra Skill Practice on page 374 also provides additional exercises.

MODULE 5 ♦ SECTION 6

5-44

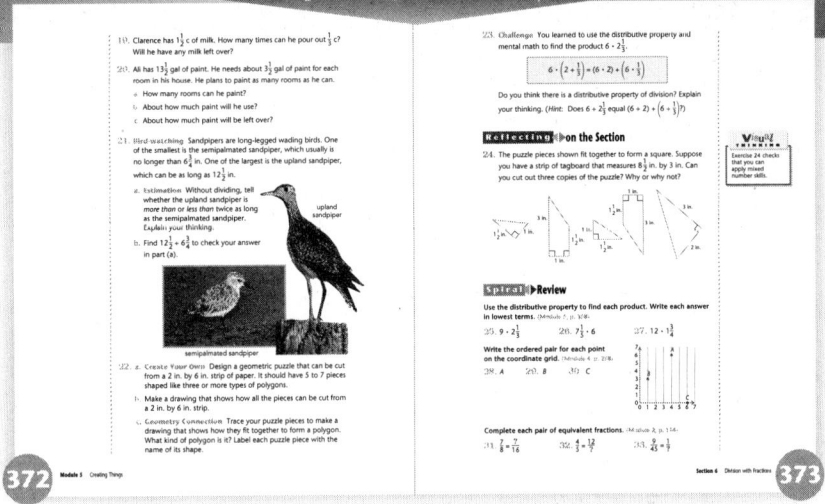

Practice & Application

EXERCISE NOTES

Research For *Ex. 21*, students may be interested in finding out more about birdwatching. If you or a student knows someone who is a birdwatcher, you may wish to invite that person to speak to the class.

Create Your Own For *Ex. 22*, you might wish to ask students to bring their completed polygons to class to use as a class display.

Common Error Some students may think that since there is a distributive property for multiplication, there must be one for division as well. Doing *Ex. 23* should clear up this erroneous reasoning.

Ongoing Assessment You might suggest that students save their answers to *Ex. 24* for their portfolio to show their understanding of dividing fractions and mixed numbers.

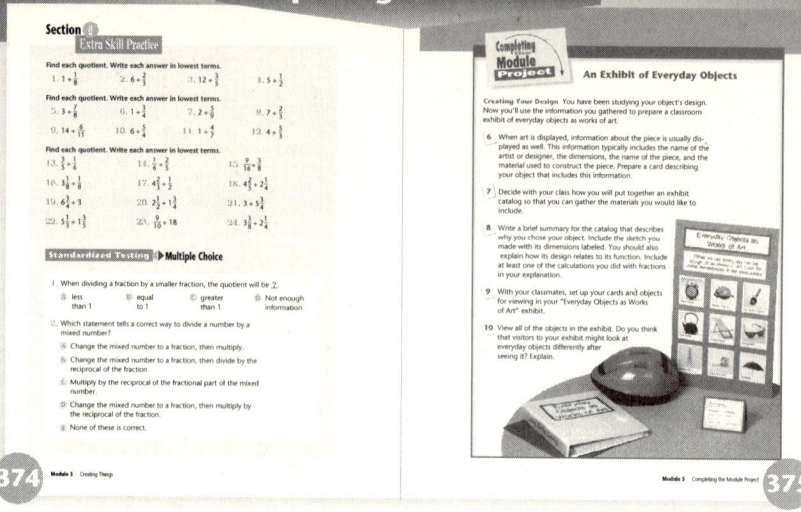

Closing the Section

In Section 6, students have used models to broaden their conceptual understanding of division. They have also developed their number sense about dividing fractions and mixed numbers. To bring closure to the section you may want to ask these questions: What does it mean to divide 6 by $\frac{3}{4}$? When dividing fractions and mixed numbers, how can you use number sense to check the reasonableness of your answer?

Quick Quiz on this Section

1. How many $\frac{3}{4}$ in. strips can you cut from a piece of paper that is 15 in. wide?

2. First decide whether each quotient will be greater than 1 or less than 1. Then find each quotient. Write each answer in lowest terms.
   a. $\frac{1}{4} \div \frac{3}{5}$ b. $\frac{2}{3} \div \frac{1}{10}$

3. How many $\frac{3}{4}$ c servings can you get from a 64 fl oz container?

4. Find each quotient. Write each answer in lowest terms.
   a. $2\frac{3}{4} \div \frac{8}{9}$ b. $4\frac{2}{5} \div \frac{11}{15}$

5. A relay race is $6\frac{1}{2}$ times around a track. Each of the 4 runners ran an equal distance. How many laps did each runner run?

For answers, see Quick Quiz blackline on p. 5-62.

Completing the Module Project

As students prepare the information about their objects, encourage them to create neat and attractive cards. You may want to specify a minimum size for the cards to be sure they are handy and easy to read. If time allows, you will want to provide an opportunity for students to discuss how the class will compile the exhibit catalog. You may want to let class members form committees to help with the task of preparing the classroom exhibit. Committees could have various responsibilities such as gathering the information and putting it in a certain order, checking to be sure all the information is complete (including the summaries, sketches, and explanations from *Question 8*), editing the information to make sure there are no errors, and arranging the objects and the cards so that the display is pleasing and attractive. Once the display is complete, you may want to invite other classes to tour the exhibit and to share their reactions with your class.

Name _____ Date _____

MODULE 5　　　　　　　　　　　　　　　　　　　　　　**LABSHEET 1A**

Penguin Paper Fold   (Use with Question 2 on page 310.)

Directions

Step 1 Cut out the square.

Step 2 Crease all the lines. Unfold your square. Lay the square flat on your desk, with Flap 1 at the bottom. Then turn it over so the blank side faces up.

Step 3 Fold Flap 1 upward. Then fold Flaps 2 and 3 inward so that they overlap Flap 1. This will form a triangle shape.

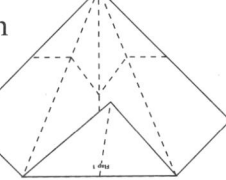

Step 4 Stand the triangle up on your desk. Fold the triangle in half so that Flaps 2 and 3 touch.

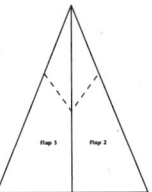

Step 5 Push down on Flaps 4 and 5. Then press Flaps 4 and 5 in toward one another so that they touch. Your completed penguin will look like this:

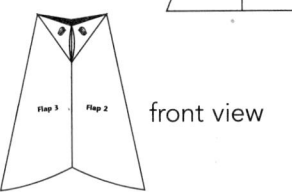

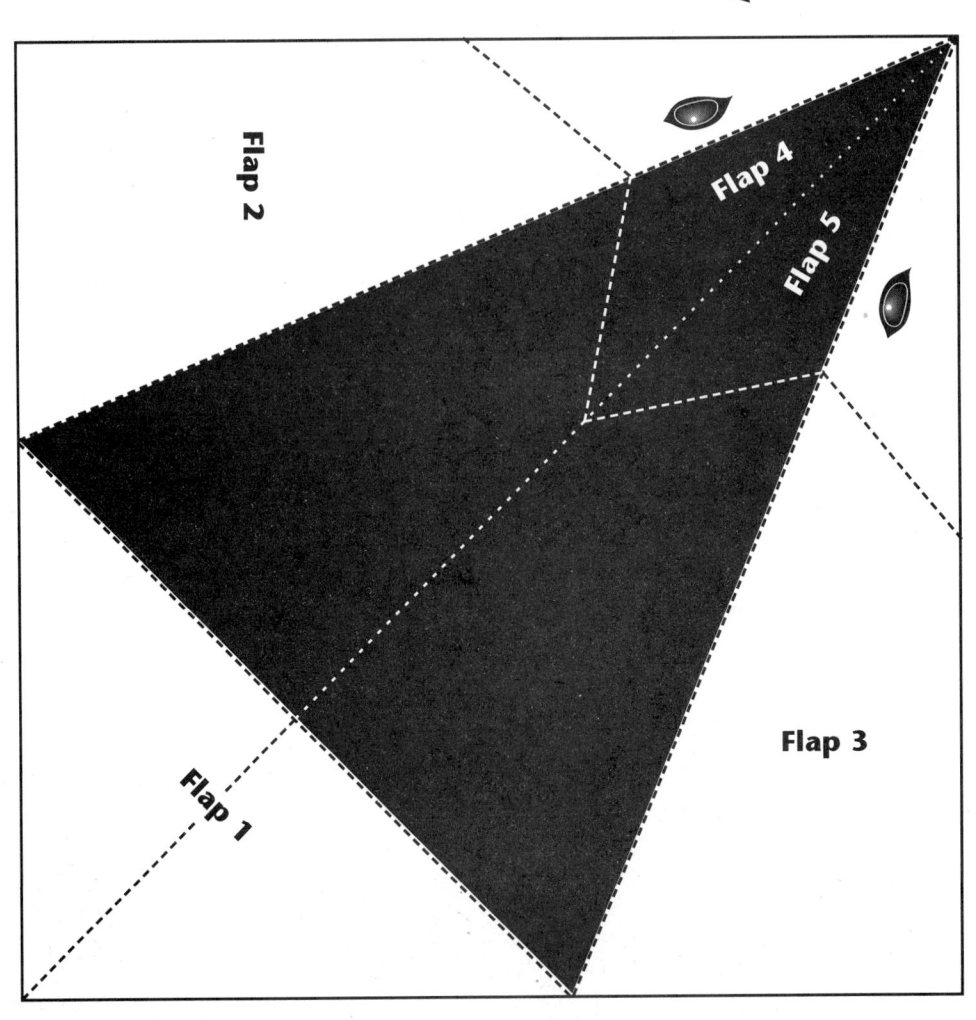

side view　　　　front view

Flap 2

Flap 4

Flap 5

Flap 1

Flap 3

Copyright © by McDougal Littell Inc. All rights reserved.　　　Math Thematics, Book 1 **5-47**

MODULE 5 LABSHEET **1B**

Fraction Strips (Use with Questions 3 and 4 on page 311.)

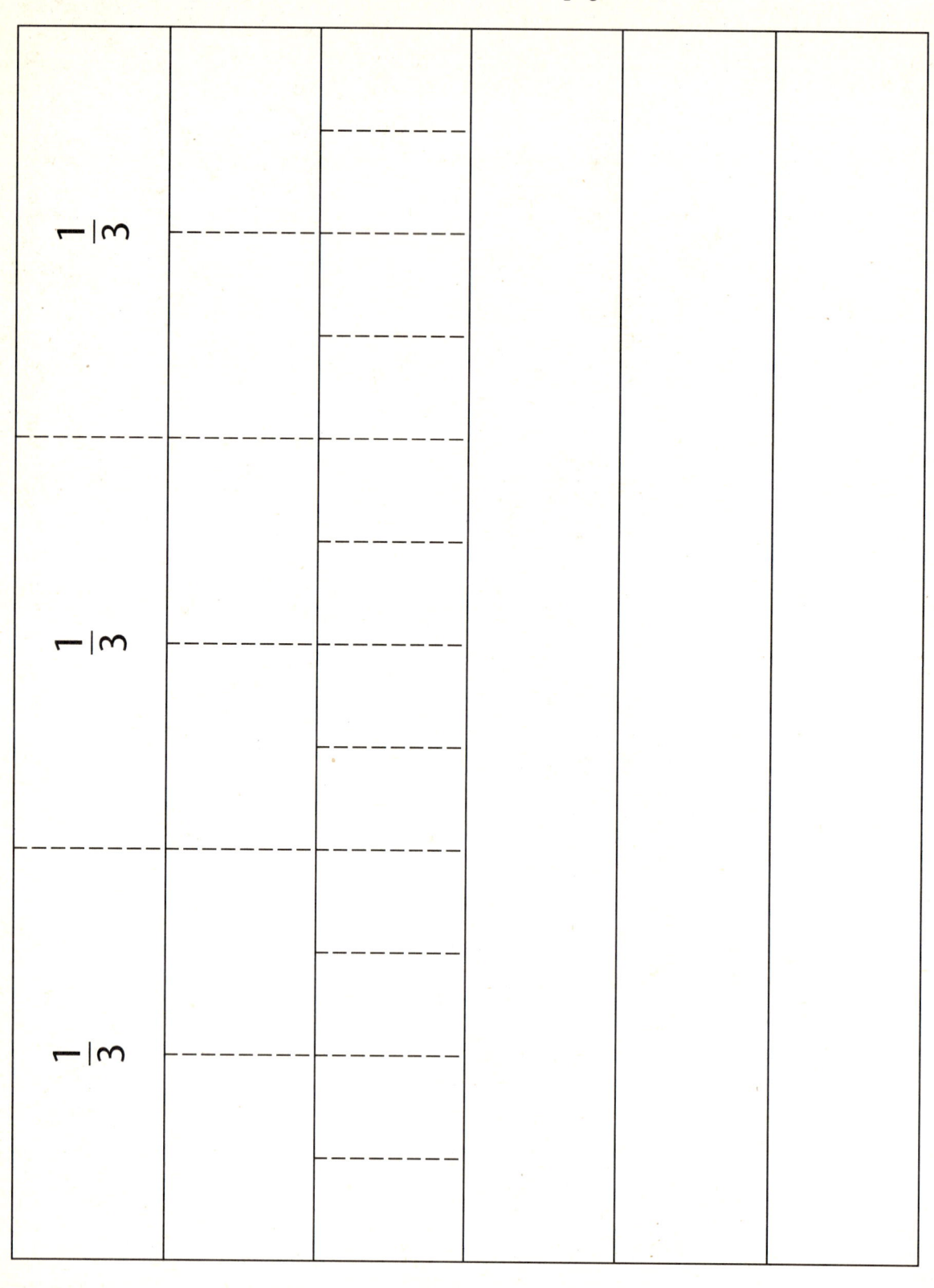

$\frac{1}{3}$

$\frac{1}{3}$

$\frac{1}{3}$

Name   Date

MODULE 5   **LABSHEET 4A**

Mask (Use with Question 2 on page 341 and Question 11 on page 343.)

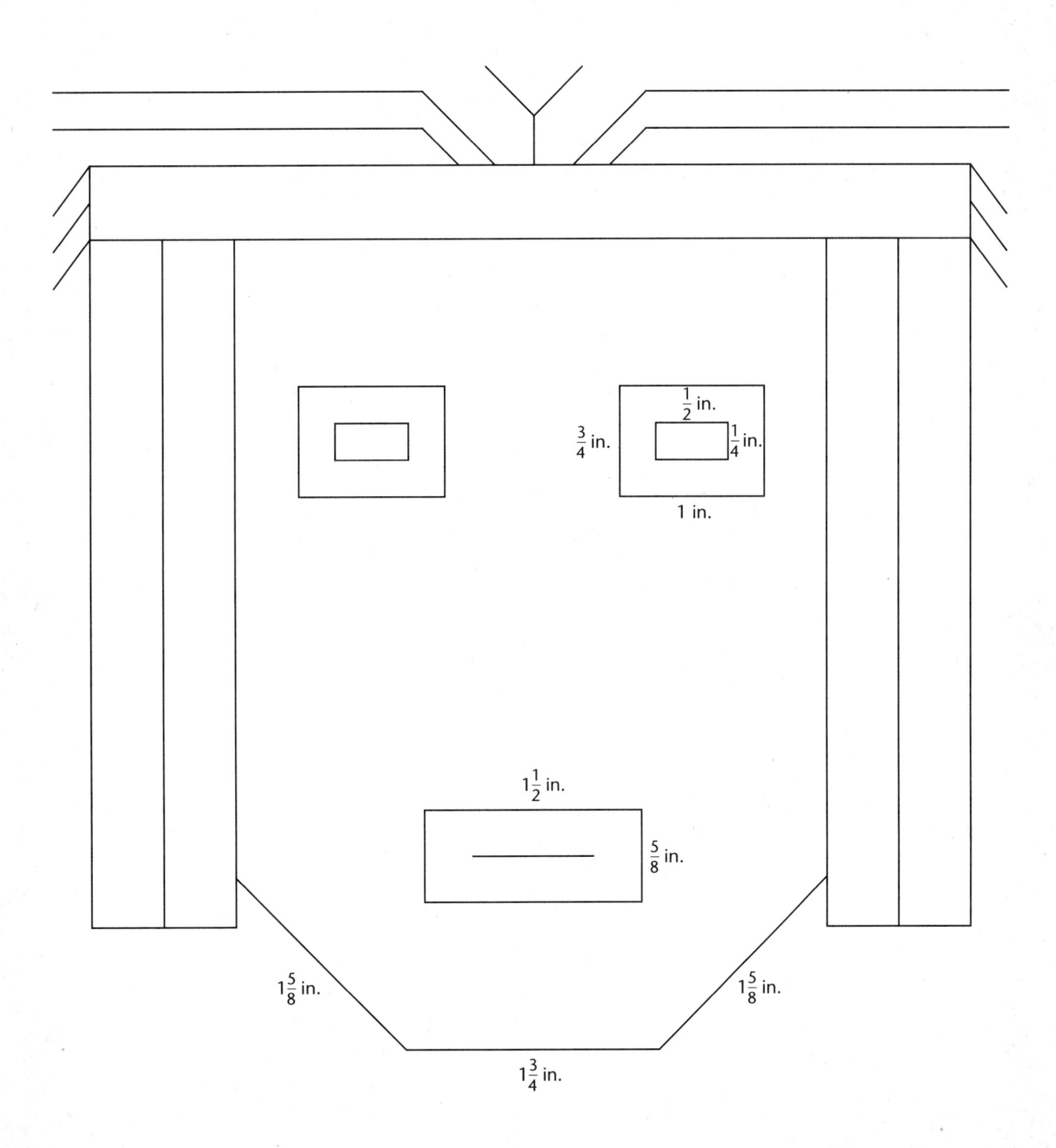

Math Thematics, Book 1 **5-49**

Name _____ Date _____

MODULE 5 LABSHEET **6A**

Geometric Puzzle

(Use with Questions 1–3 on page 364 and Question 8 on page 367.)

Directions Cut out the puzzle pieces and arrange them so that all five pieces form a square.

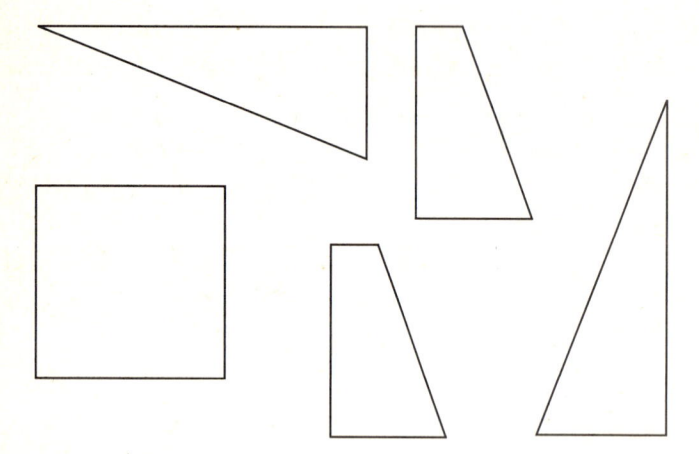

5-50 Math Thematics, Book 1   Copyright © by McDougal Littell Inc. All rights reserved.

Name _____   Date _____

MODULE 5   **LABSHEET 6B**

Ruler Models (Use with Questions 5 and 6 on page 366.)

Directions Complete each problem using the ruler given.

Problem 1 How many times does $\frac{1}{4}$ in. fit into 3 in.?

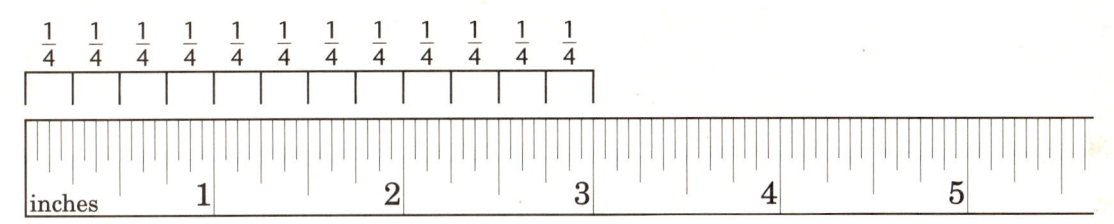

$\frac{1}{4}$ $\frac{1}{4}$ $\frac{1}{4}$ $\frac{1}{4}$ $\frac{1}{4}$ $\frac{1}{4}$ $\frac{1}{4}$ $\frac{1}{4}$ $\frac{1}{4}$ $\frac{1}{4}$ $\frac{1}{4}$ $\frac{1}{4}$

inches 1 2 3 4 5

Use your answer to complete the division: $3 \div \frac{1}{4} =$ _____ .

You can also find the answer by multiplying. Since there are _____

fourths in 1, there are _____ • _____ = _____ fourths in 3.

Problem 2 How many times does $\frac{1}{8}$ in. fit into 2 in.?

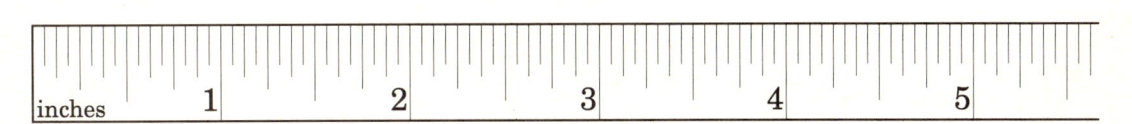

inches 1 2 3 4 5

Use your answer to complete the division: $2 \div$ ____ = ____ .

You can also find out by multiplying. Since there are _____

eighths in 1, there are _____ • _____ = _____ eighths in 2.

Problem 3 How many times does $\frac{3}{4}$ in. fit into 3 in.?

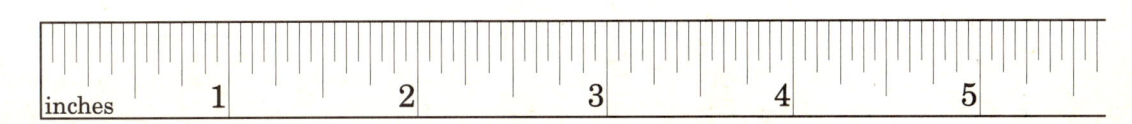

inches 1 2 3 4 5

Use your answer to write and complete the division:

_____ ÷ _____ = _____

Copyright © by McDougal Littell Inc. All rights reserved.   Math Thematics, Book 1 **5-51**

Name _____ Problem _____

TEACHER ASSESSMENT SCALES

☆ *The star indicates that you excelled in some way.*

Problem Solving

① ② ③ ④ ⑤ ☆→

① You did not understand the problem well enough to get started or you did not show any work.

③ You understood the problem well enough to make a plan and to work toward a solution.

⑤ You made a plan, you used it to solve the problem, and you verified your solution.

Mathematical Language

① ② ③ ④ ⑤ ☆→

① You did not use any mathematical vocabulary or symbols, or you did not use them correctly, or your use was not appropriate.

③ You used appropriate mathematical language, but the way it was used was not always correct or other terms and symbols were needed.

⑤ You used mathematical language that was correct and appropriate to make your meaning clear.

Representations

① ② ③ ④ ⑤ ☆→

① You did not use any representations such as equations, tables, graphs, or diagrams to help solve the problem or explain your solution.

③ You made appropriate representations to help solve the problem or help you explain your solution, but they were not always correct or other representations were needed.

⑤ You used appropriate and correct representations to solve the problem or explain your solution.

Connections

① ② ③ ④ ⑤ ☆→

① You attempted or solved the problem and then stopped.

③ You found patterns and used them to extend the solution to other cases, or you recognized that this problem relates to other problems, mathematical ideas, or applications.

⑤ You extended the ideas in the solution to the general case, or you showed how this problem relates to other problems, mathematical ideas, or applications.

Presentation

① ② ③ ④ ⑤ ☆→

① The presentation of your solution and reasoning is unclear to others.

③ The presentation of your solution and reasoning is clear in most places, but others may have trouble understanding parts of it.

⑤ The presentation of your solution and reasoning is clear and can be understood by others.

Content Used: _____ Computational Errors: Yes ☐ No ☐

Notes on Errors: _____

5-52 Math Thematics, Book 1   Copyright © by McDougal Littell Inc. All rights reserved.

Name _____ Problem _____

STUDENT SELF-ASSESSMENT SCALES

▨ If your score is in the shaded area, explain why on the back of this sheet and stop.

☆ The star indicates that you excelled in some way.

Problem Solving

① I did not understand the problem well enough to get started or I did not show any work.

②

③ I understood the problem well enough to make a plan and to work toward a solution.

④

⑤ I made a plan, I used it to solve the problem, and I verified my solution.

Mathematical Language

① I did not use any mathematical vocabulary or symbols, or I did not use them correctly, or my use was not appropriate.

②

③ I used appropriate mathematical language, but the way it was used was not always correct or other terms and symbols were needed.

④

⑤ I used mathematical language that was correct and appropriate to make my meaning clear.

Representations

① I did not use any representations such as equations, tables, graphs, or diagrams to help solve the problem or explain my solution.

②

③ I made appropriate representations to help solve the problem or help me explain my solution, but they were not always correct or other representations were needed.

④

⑤ I used appropriate and correct representations to solve the problem or explain my solution.

Connections

① I attempted or solved the problem and then stopped.

②

③ I found patterns and used them to extend the solution to other cases, or I recognized that this problem relates to other problems, mathematical ideas, or applications.

④

⑤ I extended the ideas in the solution to the general case, or I showed how this problem relates to other problems, mathematical ideas, or applications.

Presentation

① The presentation of my solution and reasoning is unclear to others.

②

③ The presentation of my solution and reasoning is clear in most places, but others may have trouble understanding parts of it.

④

⑤ The presentation of my solution and reasoning is clear and can be understood by others.

Copyright © by McDougal Littell Inc. All rights reserved.

Math Thematics, Book 1 **5-53**

MODULE 5

SOLUTION GUIDE TEXTBOOK E²

A Weighty Question (E² on textbook page 340)

All of the *Math Thematics* Assessment Scales should be used to assess student work.

Partial Solution

I drew a picture of how you would weigh a mass of 34 kilograms with a balance scale and the 1-kilogram, 3-kilogram, 9-kilogram, and 27-kilogram weights. The equation to describe this weighing is 27 + 9 + 1 = 34 + 3.

I used tables to show that any whole kilogram mass from 1 to 40 could be measured using the 1-kilogram, 3-kilogram, 9-kilogram, and 27-kilogram weights. The mass that is to be found is in heavier type.

1 = **1**	9 + 3 = **11** + 1	27 + 3 = **21** + 9	27 + 3 + 1 = **31**
3 = **2** + 1	9 + 3 = **12**	27 + 3 + 1 = **22** + 9	27 + 9 = **32** + 3 + 1
3 = **3**	9 + 3 + 1 = **13**	27 = **23** + 3 + 1	27 + 9 = **33** + 3
3 + 1 = **4**	27 = **14** + 9 + 3 + 1	27 = **24** + 3	27 + 9 + 1 = **34** + 3
9 = **5** + 3 + 1	27 = **15** + 9 + 3	27 + 1 = **25** + 3	27 + 9 = **35** + 1
9 = **6** + 3	27 + 1 = **16** + 9 + 3	27 = **26** + 1	27 + 9 = **36**
9 + 1 = **7** + 3	27 = **17** + 9 + 1	27 = **27**	27 + 9 + 1 = **37**
9 = **8** + 1	27 = **18** + 9	27 + 1 = **28**	27 + 9 + 3 = **38** + 1
9 = **9**	27 + 1 = **19** + 9	27 + 3 = **29** + 1	27 + 9 + 3 = **39**
9 + 1 = **10**	27 + 3 = **20** + 9 + 1	27 + 3 = **30**	27 + 9 + 3 + 1 = **40**

After I wrote all the combinations, I noticed that the weights are all powers of 3 (3^0, 3^1, 3^2, 3^3). If I only used the 1-kilogram weight I would only be able to measure one mass. With a 1-kilogram and a 3-kilogram weight I could measure objects with a mass of 1, 2, 3, or 4 kilograms. Adding a 9-kilogram weight means that I can weigh objects from 1 to 13 kilograms. The pattern can be written as $3^0 + 3^1 + 3^2 + 3^3 + \cdots + 3^{n-1}$, where *n* is the *n*th weight. So if this balance set had a 3^4-kilogram weight, I should be able to measure objects from 1 to $3^0 + 3^1 + 3^2 + 3^3 + 3^4 = 1 + 3 + 9 + 27 + 81 = 121$ kilograms.

Other Considerations

- **Connections** Students can explore whether other powers can be used to weigh an object with a mass in whole kilograms. For example, powers of 2 (1, 2, 4, 8, ...) can be used to weigh an object, but powers of 4 (1, 4, 16, 64, ...) cannot.

MODULE 5

ALTERNATE E²

What's the Combination

The Situation
There are 10 lockers along a wall. The janitor opens every locker. A student walks by and closes the second locker, and every second locker after it. The secretary goes to the third locker, closes it if it is open, and opens it if it is closed. The secretary does the same for every third locker after it. The principal then goes to the fourth locker, closes it if it is open, and opens it if it is closed. This pattern continues as someone opens (or closes) the 5th, 6th, 7th, 8th, 9th, and then 10th lockers.

The Problem
- At the end, which lockers are open? Which are closed?
- Were any lockers never closed? If so, which one(s)?
- Which lockers were opened initially, closed, and never opened again?

Something to Think About
- What problem solving strategies could you use to solve this problem?
- Suppose there were 20 lockers in a row and the same procedure is used. Would your answers for the first 10 lockers change? Why?

Present Your Results
Describe what you did to solve this problem. What strategies did you use? Show any drawings, diagrams, charts, or tables you used to solve the problem. How did you check your solution?

MODULE 5

SOLUTION GUIDE ALTERNATE E²

What's the Combination?

There is only one answer for this E², but the approach and representations used in this problem will vary. You should also see connections made to other problems or mathematics. All of the *Math Thematics* Assessment Scales should be used to assess students' work.

The sample responses below do not show complete solutions. Since students explored factors in Module 4, we would expect most students to make a connection to factors.

Partial Solution

I used a table to determine if a locker was open or closed. (X = closed; O = open.)

	\multicolumn{10}{c	}{Locker Number}
	1	2	3	4	5	6	7	8	9	10
1st pass	O	O	O	O	O	O	O	O	O	O
2nd pass	O	X	O	X	O	X	O	X	O	X
3rd pass	O	X	X	X	O	O	O	X	X	X
4th pass	O	X	X	O	O	O	O	O	X	X
5th pass	O	X	X	O	X	O	O	O	X	O
6th pass	O	X	X	O	X	X	O	O	X	O
7th pass	O	X	X	O	X	X	X	O	X	O
8th pass	O	X	X	O	X	X	X	X	X	O
9th pass	O	X	X	O	X	X	X	X	O	O
10th pass	O	X	X	O	X	X	X	X	O	X

Partial Solution

I tried to think of another way to figure out if a locker was open or not. If the pass number was a factor of the locker number, then the locker would be changed (either opened or closed). For example, on the 5th pass, lockers 5 and 10 are changed because 5 is a factor of 5 and 10. Then I wrote the factors of each number and noticed that if the locker number had an odd number of factors, it would be open. If the locker number had an even number of factors it would be closed. See my table.

	1	2	3	4	5	6	7	8	9	10
10th pass	O	X	X	O	X	X	X	X	O	X
Factors of the locker number	1	1, 2	1, 3	1, 2, 4	1, 5	1, 2, 3, 6	1, 7	1, 2, 4, 8	1, 3, 9	1, 2, 5, 10
Number of factors	1	2	2	3	2	4	2	4	3	4

Other Considerations

- **Mathematical Language** Students should discuss how the factors of a locker number could be used to determine if the locker is open or not.
- **Connections** Students may show that this problem is similar to the *30 Pennies in a Row* problem, extend the pattern for 100 lockers or to the general case, or identify number patterns using factors or primes. Students may notice that every open locker is a perfect square.

5-56 Math Thematics, Book 1

MODULE 5 SECTION 1 — **WARM-UPS**

Replace each __?__ with >, <, or =.

1. $\frac{4}{3}$ __?__ 1
2. $\frac{3}{4}$ __?__ 1
3. $\frac{1}{12}$ __?__ $\frac{11}{12}$
4. $\frac{6}{3}$ __?__ 2
5. $\frac{5}{2}$ __?__ $\frac{2}{5}$
6. $\frac{9}{1}$ __?__ 9

MODULE 5 SECTION 1 — **QUICK QUIZ**

1. Write the fractions in order from least to greatest.
$\frac{1}{2}, \frac{5}{4}, \frac{5}{7}, \frac{3}{9}, \frac{4}{11}, \frac{4}{3}$

2. Use number sense to compare the fractions. Replace each __?__ with >, <, or = .

   a. $\frac{46}{47}$ __?__ $\frac{211}{212}$
   b. $\frac{3}{11}$ __?__ $\frac{3}{13}$

3. Use a common denominator to compare the fractions. Replace each __?__ with >, <, or = .

   a. $\frac{8}{11}$ __?__ $\frac{2}{3}$
   b. $\frac{14}{24}$ __?__ $\frac{21}{36}$

4. Use decimals to compare. Replace each __?__ with >, <, or = .

   a. $\frac{4}{38}$ __?__ $\frac{11}{94}$
   b. $\frac{10}{53}$ __?__ $\frac{42}{200}$

5. Eight out of 23 students in Ms. Silver's class got an A on their midterm exam. Ten out of 27 students in Mr. Gold's class got an A on the exam. Which class had the greater fraction of A's on the midterm exam?

ANSWERS

Warm-Ups: 1. > 2. < 3. < 4. = 5. > 6. =

Quick-Quiz: 1. $\frac{3}{9}, \frac{4}{11}, \frac{1}{2}, \frac{5}{7}, \frac{5}{4}, \frac{4}{3}$ 2. a. < b. > 3. a. > b. =
4. a. < b. < 5. Mr. Gold's class

MODULE 5 SECTION 2 — WARM-UPS

Would you use inches, feet, yards, or miles to estimate each length?

1. distance around your wrist
2. a football field
3. your height
4. cloth or material
5. the length of a piece of paper
6. distance from home to school

MODULE 5 SECTION 2 — QUICK QUIZ

1. If you could measure the wingspan of an airplane, what customary unit of length would you use?
2. Replace each ___?___ with the number that makes the statement true.
   a. 18 yd = ___?___ ft
   b. 114 in. = ___?___ ft
   c. 3960 ft = ___?___ mi
3. Write each measurement as a fraction of a foot.
   a. 4 in.
   b. $2\frac{1}{2}$ in.
   c. 69 in.
4. Jose jogged 2160 yd, then after resting jogged 1800 yd more. How many miles did he jog in all?
5. Monica had 12 ft 8 in. of a favorite decorative edging. She used $2\frac{1}{2}$ yd of the edging to make a craft project. How many feet of edging does she have left?

ANSWERS

Warm-Ups: Samples are given. **1.** inches **2.** yards **3.** feet, inches, or both **4.** feet or yards **5.** inches **6.** miles

Quick-Quiz: 1. ft or yd **2. a.** 54 **b.** 9.5 **c.** 0.75 **3. a.** $\frac{1}{3}$ ft **b.** $\frac{5}{24}$ ft **c.** $\frac{23}{4}$ ft or $5\frac{3}{4}$ ft **4.** $2\frac{1}{4}$ mi **5.** $5\frac{1}{6}$ ft

5-58 Math Thematics, Book 1

MODULE 5 SECTION 3 — WARM-UPS

Find the GCF of each set of numbers.

1. 4 and 10
2. 88 and 33
3. 114 and 36
4. 13 and 51
5. 18 and 90
6. 204 and 252

MODULE 5 SECTION 3 — QUICK QUIZ

1. Find each sum. Write each answer in lowest terms.

   a. $\dfrac{3}{14} + \dfrac{4}{7}$
   b. $\dfrac{5}{10} + \dfrac{1}{10} + \dfrac{1}{5}$
   c. $\dfrac{1}{8} + \dfrac{3}{16} + \dfrac{10}{32}$

2. Find each difference. Write each answer in lowest terms.

   a. $\dfrac{5}{9} - \dfrac{2}{5}$
   b. $\dfrac{3}{4} - \dfrac{2}{3}$
   c. $\dfrac{6}{7} - \dfrac{1}{3}$

3. Your rain gauge showed that it rained $\dfrac{1}{4}$ in. on Tuesday, $\dfrac{5}{16}$ in. on Wednesday, and $\dfrac{3}{8}$ in. on Thursday. How much rain fell during the three-day period?

4. During a survey, $\dfrac{5}{9}$ of the people surveyed said they preferred orange juice. Only $\dfrac{1}{6}$ of the people preferred tomato juice. What fraction of the people surveyed preferred neither orange juice nor tomato juice?

ANSWERS

Warm-Ups: 1. 2   2. 11   3. 6   4. 1   5. 18   6. 12

Quick-Quiz: 1. a. $\dfrac{11}{14}$ b. $\dfrac{4}{5}$ c. $\dfrac{5}{8}$ 2. a. $\dfrac{7}{45}$ b. $\dfrac{1}{12}$ c. $\dfrac{11}{21}$ 3. $\dfrac{15}{16}$ in.   4. $\dfrac{5}{18}$

| MODULE 5   SECTION 4 | WARM-UPS |

Write an equivalent fraction with the given denominator.

1. $\dfrac{1}{3} = \dfrac{?}{9}$

2. $\dfrac{?}{100} = \dfrac{17}{25}$

3. $\dfrac{4}{8} = \dfrac{?}{10}$

4. $\dfrac{?}{15} = \dfrac{8}{20}$

5. $\dfrac{44}{11} = \dfrac{?}{1}$

6. $\dfrac{?}{80} = \dfrac{9}{16}$

| MODULE 5   SECTION 4 | QUICK QUIZ |

1. Find each sum. Write each answer in lowest terms.

   a. $2\dfrac{3}{7} + 3\dfrac{6}{7}$

   b. $1\dfrac{3}{5} + 3\dfrac{7}{10}$

2. Find each difference. Write each answer in lowest terms.

   a. $4\dfrac{2}{9} - 1\dfrac{2}{3}$

   b. $10\dfrac{7}{10} - 4\dfrac{3}{5}$

3. Carmen needs $18\dfrac{1}{2}$ yd of material to make costumes for a play. She has $5\dfrac{2}{3}$ yd already. How much more does she need to buy?

4. Seth ran $6\dfrac{1}{2}$ mi on Monday, $4\dfrac{2}{5}$ mi on Wednesday, and $8\dfrac{7}{10}$ mi on Friday. How far did he run during these three days?

5. Estimate $1\dfrac{23}{42} + 3\dfrac{61}{78}$ by rounding to the nearest half.

ANSWERS

Warm-Ups: 1. 3   2. 68   3. 5   4. 6   5. 4   6. 45

Quick-Quiz: 1. a. $6\dfrac{2}{7}$ b. $5\dfrac{3}{10}$ 2. a. $2\dfrac{5}{9}$ b. $6\dfrac{1}{10}$ 3. $12\dfrac{5}{6}$ yd   4. $19\dfrac{3}{5}$ mi   5. $5\dfrac{1}{2}$

MODULE 5 SECTION 5 — WARM-UPS

Write each mixed number as a fraction.

1. $1\frac{2}{5}$
2. $3\frac{3}{4}$
3. $9\frac{6}{7}$
4. $4\frac{1}{2}$
5. $11\frac{3}{8}$

MODULE 5 SECTION 5 — QUICK QUIZ

1. Replace each __?__ with the number that makes the statement true.
   a. 18 pt = __?__ qt
   b. 40 c = __?__ gal
   c. 50 fl oz = __?__ c

2. Find each product. Write each answer in lowest terms.
   a. $4\frac{1}{2} \cdot 1\frac{2}{3}$
   b. $3\frac{1}{4} \cdot \frac{7}{13}$
   c. $2\frac{3}{4} \cdot 1\frac{5}{8}$

3. Theo needs $2\frac{3}{4}$ c of flour to make 1 batch of cookies. How many cups of flour does he need to make 5 batches?

4. Write the reciprocal of each number.
   a. $2\frac{3}{11}$
   b. $\frac{7}{9}$
   c. $3\frac{1}{3}$

ANSWERS

Warm-Ups: 1. $\frac{7}{5}$ 2. $\frac{15}{4}$ 3. $\frac{69}{7}$ 4. $\frac{9}{2}$ 5. $\frac{91}{8}$

Quick-Quiz: 1. a. 9 b. 2.5 c. 6.25 2. a. $7\frac{1}{2}$ b. $1\frac{3}{4}$ c. $4\frac{15}{32}$ 3. $13\frac{3}{4}$ c 4. a. $\frac{11}{25}$ b. $\frac{9}{7}$ c. $\frac{3}{10}$

MODULE 5 SECTION 6 — WARM-UPS

Multiply.

1. $\dfrac{1}{2} \cdot \dfrac{1}{4}$
2. $\dfrac{3}{4} \cdot \dfrac{5}{7}$
3. $\dfrac{8}{5} \cdot \dfrac{1}{4}$
4. $\dfrac{9}{10} \cdot \dfrac{10}{8}$
5. $\dfrac{13}{16} \cdot \dfrac{2}{3}$
6. $\dfrac{6}{9} \cdot \dfrac{3}{2}$

MODULE 5 SECTION 6 — QUICK QUIZ

1. How many $\dfrac{3}{4}$ in. strips can you cut from a piece of paper that is 15 in. wide?

2. First decide whether each quotient will be *greater than 1* or *less than 1*. Then find each quotient. Write each answer in lowest terms.

   a. $\dfrac{1}{4} \div \dfrac{3}{5}$
   b. $\dfrac{2}{3} \div \dfrac{1}{10}$

3. How many $\dfrac{3}{4}$ c servings of juice can you get from a 64 fl oz container of juice?

4. Find each quotient. Write each answer in lowest terms.

   a. $2\dfrac{3}{4} \div \dfrac{8}{9}$
   b. $4\dfrac{2}{5} \div \dfrac{11}{15}$

5. In a relay race $6\dfrac{1}{2}$ times around the track, each of the 4 runners ran an equal distance. How many laps did each runner run?

ANSWERS

Warm-Ups: 1. $\dfrac{1}{8}$ 2. $\dfrac{15}{28}$ 3. $\dfrac{8}{20}$ or $\dfrac{2}{5}$ 4. $\dfrac{90}{80}$ or $\dfrac{9}{8}$ or $1\dfrac{1}{8}$ 5. $\dfrac{26}{48}$ or $\dfrac{13}{24}$ 6. $\dfrac{18}{18}$ or 1

Quick-Quiz: 1. 20 strips 2. a. < 1; $\dfrac{5}{12}$ b. > 1; $6\dfrac{2}{3}$ 3. $10\dfrac{2}{3}$ servings 4. a. $3\dfrac{3}{32}$ b. 6 5. $1\dfrac{5}{8}$ laps around the track

5-62 Math Thematics, Book 1

MODULE 5 SECTION 1 — PRACTICE AND APPLICATIONS

For use with Exploration 1

1. Write an inequality that compares each fraction with $\frac{1}{2}$.

   a. $\frac{3}{8}$ b. $\frac{11}{12}$ c. $\frac{5}{8}$

   d. $\frac{3}{4}$ e. $\frac{5}{6}$ f. $\frac{1}{5}$

   g. $\frac{2}{9}$ h. $\frac{41}{50}$ i. $\frac{19}{90}$

2. Write the fractions in order from least to greatest.

   a. $\frac{3}{4}, \frac{3}{25}, \frac{3}{10}, \frac{3}{8}, \frac{3}{11}$ b. $\frac{1}{50}, \frac{1}{10}, \frac{1}{3}, \frac{1}{100}$

   c. $\frac{7}{12}, \frac{7}{8}, \frac{7}{10}, \frac{7}{100}, \frac{7}{9}$ d. $\frac{8}{9}, \frac{24}{25}, \frac{9}{10}, \frac{3}{4}, \frac{99}{100}$

   e. $\frac{2}{5}, \frac{1}{10}, \frac{7}{9}, \frac{5}{8}$ f. $\frac{29}{60}, \frac{12}{99}, \frac{19}{20}, \frac{15}{19}$

3. Replace each __?__ with >, <, or =.

   a. $\frac{5}{9}$? $\frac{5}{11}$ b. $\frac{47}{48}$? $\frac{48}{49}$ c. $\frac{12}{25}$? $\frac{10}{12}$

   d. $\frac{24}{25}$? $\frac{8}{9}$ e. $\frac{14}{25}$? $\frac{14}{27}$ f. $\frac{9}{16}$? $\frac{13}{18}$

   g. $\frac{2}{3}$? $\frac{1}{5}$ h. $\frac{1}{2}$? $\frac{15}{30}$ i. $\frac{2}{9}$? $\frac{3}{4}$

   j. $\frac{3}{11}$? $\frac{5}{9}$ k. $\frac{7}{15}$? $\frac{7}{8}$ l. $\frac{1}{6}$? $\frac{1}{10}$

4. a. The inequality $x > \frac{1}{3}$ is true for every number greater than $\frac{1}{3}$. Give two values for *x* that are fractions and that make the inequality a true statement.

   b. The inequality $x < \frac{5}{8}$ is true for every number less than $\frac{5}{8}$. Give two values for *x* that are fractions and that make the inequality a true statement.

5. Sonya and Ivan each eat a piece of pie that is $\frac{1}{8}$ of the pie. How is it possible for Ivan to eat more pie than Sonya?

(continued)

MODULE 5 SECTION 1 **PRACTICE AND APPLICATIONS**

For use with Exploration 2

6. Use a common denominator to compare the fractions. Replace each __?__ with >, <, or =.

a. $\frac{2}{3}$ __?__ $\frac{5}{8}$ b. $\frac{3}{8}$ __?__ $\frac{2}{5}$ c. $\frac{5}{12}$ __?__ $\frac{3}{4}$

d. $\frac{7}{12}$ __?__ $\frac{2}{3}$ e. $\frac{4}{12}$ __?__ $\frac{8}{24}$ f. $\frac{11}{30}$ __?__ $\frac{7}{15}$

g. $\frac{5}{8}$ __?__ $\frac{11}{24}$ h. $\frac{3}{14}$ __?__ $\frac{9}{28}$ i. $\frac{5}{6}$ __?__ $\frac{11}{24}$

7. Use decimals to compare. Replace each __?__ with >, <, or =.

a. $\frac{75}{90}$ __?__ $\frac{128}{185}$ b. $\frac{78}{165}$ __?__ $\frac{13}{35}$ c. $\frac{86}{255}$ __?__ $\frac{48}{125}$

d. $\frac{134}{305}$ __?__ $\frac{79}{200}$ e. $\frac{23}{25}$ __?__ $\frac{218}{225}$ f. $\frac{315}{408}$ __?__ $\frac{94}{115}$

g. $\frac{23}{65}$ __?__ $\frac{138}{390}$ h. $\frac{72}{95}$ __?__ $\frac{150}{187}$ i. $\frac{18}{35}$ __?__ $\frac{23}{48}$

8. Replace each __?__ with >, <, or =.

a. 60% __?__ $\frac{3}{5}$ b. $\frac{1}{3}$ __?__ 28% c. 72% __?__ $\frac{3}{4}$

d. 81% __?__ $\frac{4}{5}$ e. $\frac{1}{4}$ __?__ 23% f. 69% __?__ $\frac{2}{3}$

g. 42% __?__ $\frac{5}{8}$ h. $\frac{2}{5}$ __?__ 25% i. 18% __?__ $\frac{9}{50}$

9. Use mental math, paper and pencil, or a calculator to compare the fractions. Replace each __?__ with >, <, or =.

a. $\frac{23}{25}$ __?__ $\frac{3}{5}$ b. $\frac{48}{205}$ __?__ $\frac{185}{315}$ c. $\frac{32}{125}$ __?__ $\frac{102}{212}$

d. $\frac{19}{50}$ __?__ $\frac{7}{20}$ e. $\frac{15}{51}$ __?__ $\frac{150}{521}$ f. $\frac{65}{97}$ __?__ $\frac{520}{776}$

g. $\frac{13}{26}$ __?__ $\frac{39}{52}$ h. $\frac{5}{9}$ __?__ $\frac{55}{99}$ i. $\frac{20}{81}$ __?__ $\frac{1}{4}$

j. $\frac{55}{102}$ __?__ $\frac{99}{200}$ k. $\frac{26}{75}$ __?__ $\frac{1}{3}$ l. $\frac{304}{512}$ __?__ $\frac{120}{200}$

10. To pass inspection in the machine shop, the width of a widget must be between $\frac{1}{8}$ cm and $\frac{3}{16}$ cm. Will a widget that is $\frac{7}{64}$ cm wide pass the inspection? Explain.

5-64 Math Thematics, Book 1

Name _____ Date _____

MODULE 5 SECTION 2   **PRACTICE AND APPLICATIONS**

For use with Exploration 1

1. For each situation, name an appropriate customary unit or combination of units for measuring.

   a. checking that the perimeter of the goalie box meets regulations in soccer

   b. finding the distance across town

   c. measuring the length of your arm

2. Use a standard ruler to measure the length of the crayon to the nearest $\frac{1}{2}$ in., the nearest $\frac{1}{4}$ in. and the nearest $\frac{1}{8}$ in.

For use with Exploration 2

3. Replace each __?__ with the number that makes the statement true.

   a. 6 yd = __?__ ft   **b.** 26,400 yd = __?__ mi   **c.** $6\frac{1}{3}$ yd = __?__ in.

   d. 39 in. = __?__ ft   **e.** $5\frac{3}{4}$ ft = __?__ in.   **f.** 14 ft = __?__ yd

4. Write each measurement as a fraction of a yard.

   a. 24 in.   **b.** 8 ft   **c.** 10 ft

5. Add or subtract. Simplify when possible.

   a.   2 yd 1 ft
       + 5 yd 2 ft

   b.   6 yd 1 ft
       − 4 yd 2 ft

   c.   3536 ft
       + 1744 ft

   d.   7 ft 8 in.
       − 2 ft 10 in.

   e.   4 ft 7 in.
       + 6 ft 8 in.

   f.   6 yd
       − 2 yd 1 ft

6. A carpenter has a 12 ft long piece of lumber. He cuts a section off that is $6\frac{3}{4}$ ft long. How long (in yd, ft, and in.) is the remaining piece of lumber?

Name _____ Date _____

| MODULE 5 SECTION 3 | PRACTICE AND APPLICATIONS |

For use with Exploration 1

1. Find each sum. Write each answer in lowest terms.

   a. $\dfrac{1}{4} + \dfrac{3}{5}$ b. $\dfrac{5}{8} + \dfrac{1}{4}$ c. $\dfrac{5}{12} + \dfrac{3}{8}$

   d. $\dfrac{3}{8} + \dfrac{5}{6}$ e. $\dfrac{5}{6} + \dfrac{3}{5}$ f. $\dfrac{5}{12} + \dfrac{8}{9}$

2. Find each difference. Write each answer in lowest terms.

   a. $\dfrac{7}{10} - \dfrac{3}{5}$ b. $\dfrac{8}{9} - \dfrac{5}{12}$ c. $\dfrac{7}{8} - \dfrac{1}{2}$

   d. $\dfrac{15}{16} - \dfrac{3}{8}$ e. $\dfrac{5}{6} - \dfrac{5}{12}$ f. $\dfrac{5}{8} - \dfrac{2}{5}$

3. Find each sum or difference. Write each answer in lowest terms.

   a. $\dfrac{1}{2} + \dfrac{4}{5}$ b. $\dfrac{11}{12} - \dfrac{5}{8}$ c. $\dfrac{4}{15} + \dfrac{2}{3}$

   d. $\dfrac{3}{4} - \dfrac{2}{7}$ e. $\dfrac{7}{16} + \dfrac{3}{4}$ f. $\dfrac{2}{3} - \dfrac{4}{9}$

4. Find the value of each expression. Write each answer in lowest terms.

   a. $\dfrac{7}{9} - \dfrac{3}{18}$ b. $\dfrac{3}{7} + \dfrac{4}{5}$ c. $\dfrac{8}{9} - \dfrac{3}{4}$

   d. $\dfrac{3}{4} - \dfrac{1}{2} + \dfrac{5}{8}$ e. $\dfrac{2}{3} + \dfrac{1}{6} + \dfrac{2}{5}$ f. $\dfrac{9}{16} + \dfrac{1}{4} - \dfrac{3}{8}$

   g. $\dfrac{5}{9} - \dfrac{1}{3} + \dfrac{5}{6}$ h. $\dfrac{7}{10} - \dfrac{1}{4} + \dfrac{1}{8}$ i. $\dfrac{3}{8} + \dfrac{5}{16} + \dfrac{1}{4}$

5. Lana has 48 rocks in her rock collection. Of the rocks, $\dfrac{3}{8}$ are quartz and $\dfrac{1}{3}$ are granite. How many of Lana's rocks are quartz or granite?

6. Ryan has $\dfrac{7}{8}$ c oil. He uses $\dfrac{3}{4}$ c oil to make a cake. He needs $\dfrac{1}{3}$ c oil to make some brownies. How much more oil does Ryan need to make the brownies?

Name _____ Date _____

MODULE 5 SECTION 4 — **PRACTICE AND APPLICATIONS**

For use with Exploration 1

1. Estimate each sum by first rounding each mixed number to the nearest whole number and then adding.

   a. $4\frac{7}{8} + 2\frac{1}{4}$ **b.** $5\frac{1}{6} + 3\frac{1}{5}$ **c.** $2\frac{1}{9} + 3\frac{5}{6}$

   d. $5\frac{7}{9} + 1\frac{2}{7}$ **e.** $2\frac{11}{12} + 4\frac{8}{9}$ **f.** $6\frac{3}{10} + 2\frac{6}{7}$

   g. $2\frac{1}{5} + 4\frac{1}{8}$ **h.** $1\frac{7}{8} + 2\frac{1}{3}$ **i.** $2\frac{2}{7} + 1\frac{1}{10}$

   j. $4\frac{4}{5} + 3\frac{1}{7}$ **k.** $2\frac{3}{10} + 1\frac{2}{3}$ **l.** $4\frac{1}{12} + 1\frac{9}{10}$

2. Find each sum. Write each answer in lowest terms.

   a. $1\frac{2}{3} + 2\frac{1}{4}$ **b.** $3\frac{1}{5} + 4\frac{2}{3}$ **c.** $6\frac{1}{4} + 2\frac{5}{8}$

   d. $3\frac{4}{5} + 1\frac{1}{4}$ **e.** $6\frac{1}{2} + 2\frac{2}{3}$ **f.** $2\frac{5}{9} + 1\frac{1}{6}$

   g. $2\frac{1}{6} + 3\frac{2}{3}$ **h.** $3\frac{3}{8} + 4\frac{3}{4}$ **i.** $5\frac{1}{6} + 7\frac{1}{2}$

   j. $4\frac{2}{9} + 6\frac{1}{2}$ **k.** $7\frac{2}{3} + 4\frac{5}{9}$ **l.** $8\frac{3}{10} + 5\frac{4}{5}$

   m. $6\frac{3}{8} + 1\frac{5}{6}$ **n.** $2\frac{5}{6} + 5\frac{3}{5}$ **o.** $7\frac{5}{12} + 3\frac{8}{9}$

3. Christy has a rectangular vegetable garden that is $8\frac{1}{2}$ ft long and $6\frac{3}{4}$ ft wide. How much fencing will Christy need to enclose her garden?

4. George makes a tail for his kite by sewing two pieces of fabric together. One piece is $2\frac{3}{5}$ m long. The other piece is $3\frac{7}{10}$ m long. How long is the kite tail?

5. A chef uses $8\frac{1}{2}$ c flour for his cakes, $9\frac{3}{4}$ c flour for his pies, and $25\frac{2}{3}$ c flour for his breads.

   a. How much flour does he use altogether?

   b. Will he have any flour left from a 50 pound bag of flour?

(continued)

Name _____ Date _____

MODULE 5 SECTION 4 — PRACTICE AND APPLICATIONS

For use with Exploration 2

6. Use mental math to find each difference.

    a. $7\frac{1}{4} - 2$ **b.** $9 - \frac{2}{3}$ **c.** $8\frac{7}{8} - 3$

    d. $9\frac{1}{3} - 5\frac{2}{3}$ **e.** $6\frac{3}{4} - 2\frac{1}{2}$ **f.** $15 - 4\frac{7}{12}$

    g. $6\frac{1}{2} - 5\frac{1}{4}$ **h.** $10 - 7\frac{1}{3}$ **i.** $3\frac{1}{2} - 2\frac{2}{5}$

7. Find each difference. Write each answer in lowest terms.

    a. $4\frac{1}{2} - 2\frac{1}{6}$ **b.** $6\frac{4}{5} - 2\frac{3}{10}$ **c.** $9\frac{5}{8} - 6\frac{1}{4}$

    d. $8\frac{2}{3} - \frac{3}{12}$ **e.** $10\frac{5}{9} - 4\frac{1}{6}$ **f.** $15\frac{1}{2} - 8\frac{3}{4}$

    g. $9\frac{3}{4} - 5\frac{1}{5}$ **h.** $19\frac{1}{3} - 6\frac{1}{2}$ **i.** $8\frac{3}{5} - 4\frac{3}{4}$

    j. $15\frac{1}{2} - 12\frac{7}{8}$ **k.** $18\frac{5}{8} - 12\frac{1}{2}$ **l.** $23\frac{1}{8} - 10\frac{2}{3}$

8. Find each sum or difference. Write each answer in lowest terms.

    a. $3\frac{2}{3} + 1\frac{5}{9}$ **b.** $6\frac{2}{3} - 4\frac{2}{5}$ **c.** $48\frac{1}{3} - 26\frac{1}{2}$

    d. $6\frac{3}{4} + 9\frac{5}{6}$ **e.** $6\frac{3}{4} - 2\frac{1}{2}$ **f.** $15 - 4\frac{7}{12}$

    g. $78\frac{1}{2} - 24\frac{3}{4}$ **h.** $12\frac{1}{2} + 8\frac{7}{10}$ **i.** $18\frac{5}{6} - 4\frac{3}{5}$

    j. $16\frac{2}{3} - 5\frac{3}{4}$ **k.** $10\frac{1}{3} + 45\frac{7}{8}$ **l.** $98\frac{1}{2} - 32\frac{2}{3}$

9. To make costumes for a school play, the costume designer needs $25\frac{5}{8}$ yd of fabric.

    a. She has $18\frac{2}{3}$ yd of fabric. How many more yards of fabric does she need?

    b. A parent donates $5\frac{1}{2}$ yards of fabric to use for the costumes. How many more yards of fabric will the costume designer need now?

    c. How much fabric will the costume designer have left if she buys 2 yards of fabric to complete the costumes? Is it more or less than $\frac{1}{2}$ yard of fabric?

Name _____ Date _____

| MODULE 5 SECTION 5 | PRACTICE AND APPLICATIONS |

For use with Exploration 1

1. Replace each __?__ with the number that makes the statement true.

   a. __?__ qt = 64 fl oz
   b. __?__ qt = 12 pt
   c. $3\frac{1}{2}$ c = __?__ fl oz

   d. __?__ pt = 3 gal
   e. 2 gal = __?__ fl oz
   f. __?__ qt = 1 pt

   g. 40 fl oz = __?__ pt
   h. $\frac{1}{2}$ gal = __?__ c
   i. 20 c = __?__ pt

2. Students in a sixth grade class drink 18 pints of milk for lunch. How many gallons of milk do they drink?

For use with Exploration 2

3. Use the distributive property and mental math to find each product. Write each answer in lowest terms.

   a. $2 \cdot 6\frac{1}{3}$
   b. $4\frac{1}{4} \cdot 3$
   c. $3\frac{1}{6} \cdot 6$

   d. $3\frac{1}{8} \cdot 8$
   e. $3\frac{1}{2} \cdot 4$
   f. $10 \cdot 2\frac{1}{5}$

4. Find each product. Write each answer in lowest terms.

   a. $6 \cdot 2\frac{1}{8}$
   b. $3 \cdot 5\frac{3}{4}$
   c. $2\frac{3}{5} \cdot 4$

   d. $\frac{5}{7} \cdot \frac{2}{5}$
   e. $3\frac{1}{2} \cdot \frac{4}{5}$
   f. $\frac{5}{8} \cdot \frac{8}{5}$

   g. $2\frac{1}{3} \cdot 4\frac{1}{2}$
   h. $3\frac{1}{4} \cdot 2\frac{2}{5}$
   i. $3\frac{1}{4} \cdot 4\frac{3}{8}$

5. Write the reciprocal of each number.

   a. $\frac{1}{9}$
   b. $2\frac{5}{6}$
   c. 28
   d. $\frac{6}{7}$
   e. $3\frac{3}{5}$
   f. $\frac{5}{6}$

6. Use mental math to find each product by first multiplying pairs of reciprocals.

   a. $8 \cdot \frac{2}{3} \cdot \frac{1}{4} \cdot \frac{3}{2} \cdot 5$
   b. $4 \cdot \frac{3}{8} \cdot \frac{1}{6} \cdot \frac{4}{5} \cdot \frac{5}{4} \cdot \frac{8}{3} \cdot \frac{1}{4}$

7. A recipe for chocolate pudding calls for $3\frac{1}{2}$ c milk. How much milk would you need to make $2\frac{1}{2}$ times the original recipe?

MODULE 5 SECTION 6 PRACTICE AND APPLICATIONS

For use with Exploration 1

1. Find each quotient. Write each answer in lowest terms.

   a. $1 \div \frac{1}{3}$ b. $8 \div \frac{1}{4}$ c. $4 \div \frac{2}{3}$

   d. $4 \div \frac{1}{5}$ e. $14 \div \frac{7}{12}$ f. $6 \div \frac{3}{5}$

   g. $9 \div \frac{3}{5}$ h. $12 \div \frac{3}{4}$ i. $10 \div \frac{5}{6}$

   j. $8 \div \frac{4}{7}$ k. $4 \div \frac{2}{5}$ l. $20 \div \frac{10}{11}$

   m. $15 \div \frac{1}{2}$ n. $16 \div \frac{4}{5}$ o. $20 \div \frac{5}{9}$

2. Find each quotient. Write each answer in lowest terms.

   a. $2 \div \frac{3}{4}$ b. $1 \div \frac{3}{5}$ c. $6 \div \frac{4}{7}$

   d. $4 \div \frac{5}{6}$ e. $3 \div \frac{4}{3}$ f. $2 \div \frac{5}{9}$

   g. $1 \div \frac{6}{7}$ h. $2 \div \frac{5}{8}$ i. $4 \div \frac{6}{5}$

   j. $5 \div \frac{3}{8}$ k. $1 \div \frac{5}{9}$ l. $3 \div \frac{2}{5}$

   m. $4 \div \frac{7}{4}$ n. $8 \div \frac{3}{2}$ o. $2 \div \frac{3}{4}$

   p. $2 \div \frac{4}{5}$ q. $6 \div \frac{5}{12}$ r. $4 \div \frac{7}{8}$

3. Julie has a 20 ft long piece of crepe paper. She wants to make streamers that are $\frac{5}{8}$ ft long from the paper.

   a. How many streamers can Julie make?

   b. Will there be any crepe paper left over? If so, how much?

4. The art teacher has 50 oz of clay. He divides the clay into $\frac{3}{4}$ oz pieces for his classes.

   a. How many pieces of clay does he have for his classes?

   b. Is there any clay left over? If so, how much?

(continued)

Name	Date

MODULE 5 SECTION 6   **PRACTICE AND APPLICATIONS**

For use with Exploration 2

5. Find each quotient. Write each answer in lowest terms.

   a. $\frac{3}{4} \div \frac{3}{8}$ **b.** $\frac{18}{5} \div \frac{3}{8}$ **c.** $\frac{5}{12} \div \frac{3}{4}$

   d. $2\frac{1}{5} \div \frac{1}{5}$ **e.** $2\frac{3}{4} \div \frac{1}{3}$ **f.** $5\frac{2}{3} \div 1\frac{3}{5}$

   g. $4\frac{2}{7} \div 2$ **h.** $3\frac{1}{4} \div 1\frac{1}{2}$ **i.** $8 \div \frac{4}{5}$

   j. $6\frac{1}{2} \div 1\frac{3}{4}$ **k.** $16 \div \frac{8}{9}$ **l.** $4\frac{2}{3} \div 2\frac{1}{3}$

   m. $3\frac{1}{6} \div 1\frac{2}{3}$ **n.** $5\frac{1}{2} \div 3\frac{3}{4}$ **o.** $6\frac{1}{4} \div 2\frac{2}{5}$

   p. $8\frac{1}{2} \div \frac{5}{8}$ **q.** $6 \div 3\frac{3}{4}$ **r.** $2\frac{1}{3} \div 1\frac{1}{2}$

   s. $3\frac{1}{5} \div 2\frac{1}{4}$ **t.** $5\frac{3}{5} \div \frac{9}{10}$ **u.** $4 \div \frac{3}{4}$

   v. $4\frac{3}{8} \div 2$ **w.** $3\frac{5}{8} \div \frac{1}{2}$ **x.** $3\frac{3}{4} \div \frac{1}{3}$

6. The pizza maker at the pizza parlor uses $1\frac{3}{4}$ c flour for each small pizza he makes. He uses $2\frac{1}{3}$ c flour for every large pizza he makes. He always makes the same number of small and large pizzas.

   a. How much flour does he use for one small and one large pizza?

   b. How many pizzas can he make from 26 c of flour? How many large? How many small?

   c. Is there any flour left over?

7. Carter wants to paint a long banner with different strips of color. He cuts a piece of paper that is $3\frac{3}{5}$ m long.

   a. If he makes each color section $\frac{3}{8}$ m long, how many different color sections can Carter make?

   b. Carter wants to have some room left to fold over the edges of the paper after each section is painted. Will he have some room to do this? If so, how much?

Name _____   Date _____

MODULE 5 SECTIONS 1–6   PRACTICE AND APPLICATIONS

For use with Section 1

1. Write the fractions in order from least to greatest.

   a. $\dfrac{74}{75}, \dfrac{12}{25}, \dfrac{1}{50}, \dfrac{99}{100}, \dfrac{1}{3}$

   b. $\dfrac{5}{6}, \dfrac{3}{5}, \dfrac{1}{8}, \dfrac{3}{4}, \dfrac{1}{9}$

2. Replace each ___?___ with >, <, or =.

   a. $\dfrac{4}{5}$ __?__ $\dfrac{4}{15}$ **b.** $\dfrac{7}{8}$ __?__ $\dfrac{8}{9}$ **c.** $\dfrac{2}{5}$ __?__ $\dfrac{2}{3}$

   d. $\dfrac{8}{15}$ __?__ $\dfrac{64}{120}$ **e.** $\dfrac{11}{12}$ __?__ $\dfrac{23}{27}$ **f.** $\dfrac{19}{37}$ __?__ $\dfrac{41}{95}$

For use with Section 2

3. Replace each ___?___ with the number that makes the statement true.

   a. 7 yd = __?__ ft   **b.** 15,840 yd = __?__ ft   **c.** $3\dfrac{2}{3}$ yd = __?__ in.

   d. 57 in. = __?__ ft   **e.** $8\dfrac{1}{2}$ ft = __?__ in.   **f.** 10 ft = __?__ yd

4. Add or subtract. Simplify when possible.

   a. 3 yd 2 ft
          + 1 yd 2 ft

   b. 3 ft 8 in.
          − 1 ft 10 in.

   c. 6 ft
          − 3 ft 3 in.

For use with Section 3

5. Find each sum or difference. Write each answer in lowest terms.

   a. $\dfrac{3}{8} + \dfrac{2}{5}$ **b.** $\dfrac{7}{12} - \dfrac{3}{8}$ **c.** $\dfrac{3}{5} + \dfrac{1}{2}$

   d. $\dfrac{7}{9} - \dfrac{2}{3}$ **e.** $\dfrac{5}{6} + \dfrac{3}{4}$ **f.** $\dfrac{8}{9} - \dfrac{1}{8}$

6. Find the value of each expression. Write each answer in lowest terms.

   a. $\dfrac{7}{8} - \dfrac{3}{4} + \dfrac{1}{2}$ **b.** $\dfrac{2}{3} - \dfrac{1}{6} + \dfrac{1}{4}$ **c.** $\dfrac{3}{5} + \dfrac{2}{3} + \dfrac{7}{10}$

7. Roger ran $2\dfrac{1}{2}$ mi on Monday and $3\dfrac{3}{4}$ mi on Wednesday. How many more miles must Roger run if he wants to run 10 miles by Friday?

(continued)

Name _____ Date _____

MODULE 5 SECTIONS 1–6 — PRACTICE AND APPLICATIONS

For use with Section 4

8. Estimate each sum by first rounding each mixed number to the nearest whole number and then adding.

    a. $3\frac{7}{9} + 2\frac{1}{8}$ **b.** $4\frac{1}{6} + 1\frac{1}{4}$ **c.** $2\frac{5}{6} + 2\frac{11}{12}$

9. Find each sum. Write each answer in lowest terms.

    a. $5\frac{1}{6} + 2\frac{3}{8}$ **b.** $1\frac{4}{7} + 2\frac{2}{3}$ **c.** $3\frac{7}{12} + 1\frac{7}{8}$

10. Use mental math to find each difference.

    a. $8\frac{6}{7} - 3$ **b.** $4 - 1\frac{3}{8}$ **c.** $12\frac{3}{8} - 5\frac{1}{4}$

11. Find each sum or difference. Write each answer in lowest terms.

    a. $4\frac{1}{2} + 3\frac{5}{9}$ **b.** $8\frac{2}{3} - 1\frac{5}{9}$ **c.** $4\frac{2}{5} - 1\frac{3}{4}$

    d. $3\frac{1}{6} + 2\frac{7}{9}$ **e.** $4\frac{7}{8} - 2\frac{1}{2}$ **f.** $20 - 12\frac{3}{5}$

For use with Section 5

12. Replace each __?__ with the number that makes the statement true.

    a. __?__ qt = 96 fl oz   **b.** __?__ qt = 18 pt   **c.** $3\frac{1}{2}$ c = __?__ fl oz

    d. __?__ pt = 5 gal   **e.** $1\frac{1}{2}$ gal = __?__ fl oz   **f.** __?__ qt = 5 pt

13. Find each product. Write each answer in lowest terms.

    a. $4 \cdot 2\frac{1}{6}$ **b.** $5 \cdot 2\frac{1}{4}$ **c.** $6\frac{3}{4} \cdot 4$

    d. $\frac{5}{7} \cdot \frac{7}{5}$ **e.** $2\frac{3}{5} \cdot 1\frac{3}{8}$ **f.** $1\frac{3}{4} \cdot \frac{2}{3}$

For use with Section 6

14. Find each quotient. Write each answer in lowest terms.

    a. $8 \div \frac{5}{6}$ **b.** $3\frac{1}{4} \div 1\frac{3}{4}$ **c.** $6 \div 1\frac{5}{9}$

    d. $9 \div \frac{3}{8}$ **e.** $2\frac{5}{6} \div \frac{1}{3}$ **f.** $2\frac{4}{9} \div \frac{2}{3}$

Name _____   Date _____

| MODULE 5 SECTION 1 | STUDY GUIDE |

Paper Folding   Comparing Fractions

GOAL   **LEARN HOW TO:** • use number sense to compare fractions
• use common denominators to write equivalent fractions
• choose a method to compare fractions

AS YOU: • fold fraction strips
• explore lists of numbers

Exploration 1: Fraction Number Sense

Using Number Sense to Compare Fractions

An **inequality** is a statement that uses the symbol > (*is greater than*) or < (*is less than*) to compare two numbers. You will be writing inequalities as you compare fractions.

Using Number Sense to Compare Fractions

There are three basic techniques that use number sense to compare fractions.

1. See if the numerators or the denominators are the same.

   $\frac{2}{5} > \frac{2}{9}$, since the numerators are the same and fifths are greater than ninths.

   $\frac{5}{7} < \frac{6}{7}$, since the denominators are the same and $5 < 6$.

2. See if one fraction is greater than $\frac{1}{2}$ and the other is less than $\frac{1}{2}$.

   $\frac{7}{8} > \frac{2}{5}$, since $\frac{7}{8} > \frac{1}{2}$ and $\frac{2}{5} < \frac{1}{2}$.

3. See if both fractions are one part less than a whole.

   $\frac{10}{11} > \frac{4}{5}$, since $\frac{10}{11}$ is just $\frac{1}{10}$ less than a whole while $\frac{4}{5}$ is $\frac{1}{5}$ less than a whole, and $\frac{1}{11} < \frac{1}{5}$.

Exploration 2: Common Denominators

Using a Common Denominator to Compare Fractions

When two fractions have different denominators, you can compare them more easily by rewriting them as equivalent fractions with a **common denominator**.

Math Thematics, Book 1

Name _____ Date _____

MODULE 5 SECTION 1 — STUDY GUIDE

Example

Compare the fractions $\frac{5}{6}$ and $\frac{3}{4}$.

Sample Response

Examine the two denominators looking for their least common multiple, also called the **least common denominator**.

multiples of 6: 6, 12, 18, …   multiples of 4: 4, 8, 12, …

12 is the least common denominator of 6 and 4.

Rewrite the fractions as equivalent fractions using the least common denominator.

$$\frac{5}{6} = \frac{5 \cdot 2}{6 \cdot 2} = \frac{10}{12} \qquad \frac{3}{4} = \frac{3 \cdot 3}{4 \cdot 3} = \frac{9}{12}$$

Since the fractions have the same denominator, look at the numerators to compare them.

Since $\frac{10}{12} > \frac{9}{12}$, therefore $\frac{5}{6} > \frac{3}{4}$.

Using Decimals to Compare Fractions

When the least common denominator of two fractions is too difficult to find, you can use a calculator to rewrite the fractions as decimals in order to compare them.

Example

Compare $\frac{7}{9}$ and $\frac{8}{13}$.

Sample Response

Step 1 Use division to rewrite each fraction as a decimal.

[7] [÷] [9] [=] [0.77777777]

[8] [÷] [1] [3] [=] [0.61538462]

Step 2 Compare the decimals.

Since $0.77777777 > 0.61538462$, therefore $\frac{7}{9} > \frac{8}{13}$.

MODULE 5 SECTION 1 — PRACTICE & APPLICATION EXERCISES — STUDY GUIDE

Exploration 1

Write an inequality that compares each fraction with $\frac{1}{2}$.

1. $\frac{5}{7}$
2. $\frac{6}{13}$
3. $\frac{358}{1000}$
4. $\frac{13}{9}$

Write the fractions in order from least to greatest.

5. $\frac{4}{7}, \frac{4}{13}, \frac{4}{100}, \frac{4}{3}, \frac{4}{5}$

6. $\frac{12}{13}, \frac{11}{12}, \frac{4}{5}, \frac{2}{3}, \frac{8}{9}$

Mental Math For Exercises 7–10, use number sense to compare the fractions. Replace each __?__ with >, <, or =.

7. $\frac{8}{11}$ __?__ $\frac{8}{9}$
8. $\frac{38}{39}$ __?__ $\frac{37}{38}$
9. $\frac{58}{120}$ __?__ $\frac{80}{110}$
10. $\frac{21}{43}$ __?__ $\frac{19}{43}$

11. **Writing** Jill filled a bag with $\frac{1}{2}$ kg of rocks and Jack filled a bag with $\frac{1}{2}$ kg of feathers. Jill said her bag of rocks was heavier than Jack's bag of feathers. Do you agree? Explain.

Exploration 2

Use a common denominator to compare the fractions. Replace each __?__ with >, <, or =.

12. $\frac{5}{6}$ __?__ $\frac{7}{12}$
13. $\frac{11}{16}$ __?__ $\frac{17}{32}$
14. $\frac{4}{7}$ __?__ $\frac{3}{5}$
15. $\frac{13}{20}$ __?__ $\frac{41}{50}$

For Exercises 16–19, use decimals to compare. Replace each __?__ with >, <, or =.

16. $\frac{9}{10}$ __?__ $\frac{17}{20}$
17. $\frac{71}{100}$ __?__ $\frac{333}{400}$
18. $\frac{103}{153}$ __?__ $\frac{178}{200}$
19. $\frac{387}{492}$ __?__ $\frac{58}{73}$

20. **Algebra Connection** The compound inequality $\frac{1}{2} < x < \frac{7}{8}$ means that x represents any number greater than $\frac{1}{2}$ and less than $\frac{7}{8}$. Give two values for x that are fractions and that make the inequality true.

Spiral Review

21. The mean of five scores has the same value as the median. If the sum of the scores is 445, what is the sum of all the scores except the median? (Module 3, pp. 196–198)

22. Let S be the set 0, 2, 3, 5. How many different whole numbers are there between 10 and 100 that contain only the digits from set S? Explain your strategies. (Module 1, pp. 30–34)

Name _____ Date _____

| MODULE 5 SECTION 2 | STUDY GUIDE |

Building the Great Wall   Customary Units of Length

GOAL **LEARN HOW TO:** • develop benchmarks for inch, foot, and yard
• find fractional measures on a ruler
• convert between customary units of length
• add and subtract lengths

AS YOU: • find the lengths of objects
• explore the dimensions of objects

Exploration 1: Investigating Benchmarks

Measuring Length in Customary Units

Parts of your body or common objects make good benchmarks for estimating lengths in inches, feet, yards, or miles. For instance, on the hand of an average-sized adult, the distance from the knuckle of the thumb to the end of the thumb is about 1 inch.

Some measurements are given using a combination of units. For example, on a high school football field, the distance between the uprights on the goal posts is 23 ft 4 in.

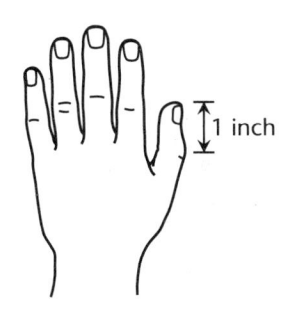

Exploration 2: Converting Customary Units of Length

The customary units of length are related in the following ways.

  1 ft = 12 in.   1 yd = 3 ft = 36 in.   1 mi = 1760 yd = 5280 ft

To convert from a larger unit to a smaller unit, you multiply. To convert from a smaller unit to a larger unit, you divide.

Example

Convert 4 mi to feet.

  1 mi =   5280 ft
  × 4   ×   4
  4 mi = 21,120 ft

Convert 72 in. to yards.

Since 36 in. = 1 yd, divide 72 by 36:

$36\overline{)72}$ gives 2   So, 72 in. = 2 yd.

Adding and Subtracting Lengths in Customary Units

When adding and subtracting customary measurements, you may need to regroup units. For example, 8 ft 9 in. + 5 ft 6 in. = 14 ft 3 in.

Name _____ Date _____

| MODULE 5 SECTION 2 | PRACTICE & APPLICATION EXERCISES | STUDY GUIDE |

Exploration 1

Use your benchmarks to estimate each measure.

1. the height of your classroom, to the nearest yard

2. the distance from your knee to your ankle, to the nearest foot

For each situation in Exercises 3 and 4, name an appropriate customary unit or combination of units for measuring.

3. measuring the length of the route you travel from home to school

4. finding the altitude (height above sea level) of the city in which you live

5. What is the length of the segment to the nearest

   a. inch? b. $\frac{1}{2}$ inch?

   c. $\frac{1}{4}$ inch? d. $\frac{1}{8}$ inch?

Exploration 2

For Exercises 6–8, replace each __?__ with the number that makes the statement true.

6. 18 yd = __?__ ft   7. 34,320 ft = __?__ mi   8. 114 in. = __?__ ft

9. **Social Studies** Some units of measurement can be traced to the Middle Ages.

   a. The *furlong* was originally a "furrow long," the length of a plowed strip of land in the division of medieval manors. If 8 furlongs = 1 mi, how many feet are in 1 furlong?

   b. The *rod* originated from the length of the pole used by a plowman to measure a furrow. If 40 rods = 1 furlong, how many feet are in 1 rod?

Find each sum or difference. Simplify answers when possible.

10. 6 mi 5176 ft
    + 10 mi 943 ft

11. 14 ft 8 in.
    − 8 ft 10 in.

12. 10 yd 1 ft
    + 4 yd 2 ft

Spiral Review

Write the prime factorization of each number. (Module 4, pp. 252–253)

13. 128   14. 600   15. 1440   16. 9000

Find the value of each expression. (Module 4, pp. 255–256)

17. 4^5 18. 5^4 19. 3^2 20. 6^3

5-78 Math Thematics, Book 1

MODULE 5 SECTION 3	STUDY GUIDE

Over and Under   Addition and Subtraction of Fractions

GOAL   **LEARN HOW TO:** • add and subtract fractions
AS YOU: • explore measurements in patterns

Exploration 1: Adding and Subtracting Fractions

Adding Fractions

To add fractions, follow these steps:

Step 1 Rewrite the fractions using a common denominator.

Step 2 Add the numerators and write the sum over the common denominator.

Add: $\frac{3}{5} + \frac{2}{7}$

The least common denominator is 35.

$$\frac{3 \cdot 7}{5 \cdot 7} + \frac{2 \cdot 5}{7 \cdot 5} = \frac{21}{35} + \frac{10}{35}$$
$$= \frac{21 + 10}{35}$$
$$= \frac{31}{35}$$

Subtracting Fractions

To subtract fractions, follow these steps:

Step 1 Rewrite the fractions using a common denominator.

Step 2 Subtract the numerators and write the difference over the common denominator.

Step 3 Write the answer in lowest terms.

Subtract: $\frac{11}{6} - \frac{1}{3}$

The least common denominator is 6.

$$\frac{11}{6} - \frac{1 \cdot 2}{3 \cdot 2} = \frac{11}{6} - \frac{2}{6}$$
$$= \frac{11 - 2}{6}$$
$$= \frac{9}{6}$$
$$= \frac{3}{2} \text{ or } 1\frac{1}{2}$$

MODULE 5 SECTION 3 | PRACTICE & APPLICATION EXERCISES | STUDY GUIDE

Exploration 1

Find each sum. Write each answer in lowest terms.

1. $\frac{1}{2} + \frac{2}{3}$
2. $\frac{3}{5} + \frac{3}{10}$
3. $\frac{5}{6} + \frac{3}{11}$
4. $\frac{4}{27} + \frac{1}{3} + \frac{5}{9}$

For Exercises 5–8, find each difference. Write each answer in lowest terms.

5. $\frac{7}{9} - \frac{3}{5}$
6. $\frac{3}{4} - \frac{5}{16}$
7. $\frac{4}{5} - \frac{1}{3}$
8. $\frac{12}{7} - \frac{2}{3}$

9. The first step in refining coal tar is a distillation process used to obtain three different liquid parts called *fractions* of the coal tar and an undistillable residue called *pitch*. The table gives data about the fractions of the coal tar that are distillable. What part of the unrefined coal tar is pitch?

Name of fraction	Size of fraction
light oil	$\frac{1}{20}$
middle oil	$\frac{17}{100}$
heavy oil	$\frac{4}{25}$

10. **Displaying Data** The circle graph shows the distribution of the production of passenger cars in the U.S. in 1996.

    a. About what fraction was produced by General Motors? by foreign-owned companies?

    b. Compare Ford's production to Chrysler's.

    c. Write a fraction for Ford's part of the total production.

    U.S. Production of 1996 Passenger Cars

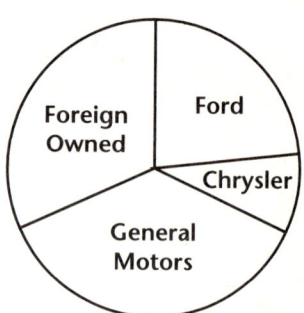

    Source: 1998 Information Please Almanac

Spiral Review

For Exercises 11–14, find the least common multiple of each set of numbers. (Module 4, p. 296)

11. 10 and 45
12. 12 and 60
13. 9, 18, and 27
14. 25, 50, and 75

15. If this spinner is spun once, what is the theoretical probability that it will land on a letter that is not a vowel?
    (Module 4, pp. 239–241)

| MODULE 5 SECTION 4 | STUDY GUIDE |

Masks Addition and Subtraction of Mixed Numbers

GOAL   **LEARN HOW TO:** • add mixed numbers using paper and pencil and mental math
• subtract mixed numbers

AS YOU: • determine amounts of materials needed for design projects

Exploration 1: Adding Mixed Numbers

Using Estimation

One way to estimate the sum of two mixed numbers is to round each number to the nearest whole number. For example, the sum $6\frac{1}{3} + 3\frac{3}{4}$ is about $6 + 4$, or 10.

Using Paper and Pencil

To add mixed numbers, add the whole numbers and the fractions separately.

Example

To add: Use a common denominator.

$$6\frac{1}{3} \rightarrow 6\frac{1 \cdot 4}{3 \cdot 4} \rightarrow 6\frac{4}{12}$$
$$+ 3\frac{3}{4} \rightarrow 3\frac{3 \cdot 3}{3 \cdot 4} \rightarrow + 3\frac{9}{12}$$
$$9\frac{13}{12} \rightarrow 9 + 1\frac{1}{12} = 10\frac{1}{12}$$

Exploration 2: Subtracting Mixed Numbers

Using Paper and Pencil

To subtract mixed numbers, subtract the fractions first and then the whole numbers, regrouping if necessary.

Example

To subtract: Use a common denominator.   Regroup.

$$6\frac{1}{3} \rightarrow 6\frac{4}{12} \rightarrow 5 + \frac{12}{12} + \frac{4}{12} \rightarrow 5\frac{16}{12}$$
$$-3\frac{3}{4} \rightarrow -3\frac{9}{12} \rightarrow -3\frac{9}{12} \rightarrow -3\frac{9}{12}$$
$$2\frac{7}{12}$$

MODULE 5 SECTION 4 — PRACTICE & APPLICATION EXERCISES — STUDY GUIDE

Exploration 1

Estimate each sum by first rounding each mixed number to the nearest whole number and then adding.

1. $7\frac{2}{9} + 11\frac{5}{6}$
2. $10\frac{1}{3} + 18\frac{7}{17}$
3. $14\frac{7}{11} + 3\frac{16}{19}$
4. $20\frac{60}{128} + 16\frac{200}{412}$

Find each sum. Write each answer in lowest terms.

5. $6\frac{2}{5} + 13\frac{3}{10}$
6. $3\frac{1}{2} + 7\frac{2}{5}$
7. $6\frac{1}{3} + 5\frac{3}{4}$
8. $7\frac{2}{3} + 6\frac{5}{8}$

For Exercises 9–11, use compatible numbers to find each sum. Look for fraction parts with a sum of 1.

9. $5\frac{5}{6} + 9\frac{1}{8} + 3\frac{1}{6}$
10. $12\frac{2}{3} + 4\frac{7}{9} + 14\frac{1}{3}$
11. $6\frac{1}{5} + 7\frac{3}{7} + 4\frac{4}{5} + 2\frac{4}{7}$

Estimate each sum by first rounding each mixed number to the nearest half.

12. $7\frac{3}{5} + 8\frac{9}{11}$
13. $23\frac{5}{8} + 7\frac{7}{12}$
14. $16\frac{5}{9} + 30\frac{5}{13}$
15. $100\frac{17}{20} + 200\frac{27}{40}$

Exploration 2

Find each difference. Write each answer in lowest terms.

16. $8\frac{2}{3} - 4\frac{1}{5}$
17. $4\frac{7}{12} - 1\frac{3}{8}$
18. $3\frac{1}{6} - 1\frac{3}{4}$
19. $12\frac{2}{5} - 3\frac{3}{4}$

Use mental math to find each difference. Explain what you did.

20. $10 - 4\frac{2}{5}$
21. $16 - 9\frac{7}{9}$
22. $13\frac{3}{7} - 8$
23. $29 - 11\frac{5}{12}$

Use the table to answer Exercises 24 and 25.

24. Which of the horses covered the greatest distance in one race?

25. What was the difference in distances covered by Silver Charm in the two races he won?

1997 Winners in Races for 3-Year Old Horses

Race	Distance (mi)	Winner
Kentucky Derby	$1\frac{1}{4}$	Silver Charm
Preakness Stakes	$1\frac{3}{16}$	Silver Charm
Belmont Stakes	$1\frac{1}{2}$	Touch Gold

Spiral Review

26. Draw the next two terms of the sequence. (Module 1, pp. 3–5)

27. Draw a parallelogram with two consecutive sides congruent. What special type of parallelogram have you drawn? (Module 2, p. 83)

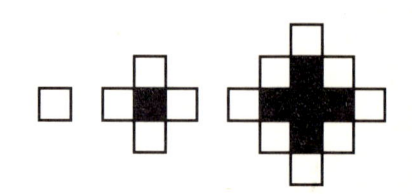

Name _____ Date _____

| MODULE 5 SECTION 5 | STUDY GUIDE |

Recipe for Success   Capacity and Mixed Number Multiplication

GOAL   **LEARN HOW TO:** • use benchmarks for customary units of capacity
• convert between customary units of capacity
• use the distributive property to multiply mixed numbers
As You: • estimate the capacity of containers and increase a recipe

Exploration 1: Customary Units of Capacity

The **capacity** of a container is the amount it can hold. The customary units of capacity are related in the following ways.

1 cup (c) = 8 fluid ounces (fl oz)   1 pint (pt) = 2 c
1 quart (qt) = 2 pt   1 gallon (gal) = 4 qt

To convert from a larger unit of capacity to a smaller unit, you multiply. The conversion of 6 gal to quarts is shown at the right.

$$\begin{array}{r} 1 \text{ gal} = 4 \text{ qt} \\ \times 6 = \times 6 \\ \hline 6 \text{ gal} = 24 \text{ qt} \end{array}$$

Exploration 2: Multiplying Mixed Numbers

The Distributive Property

Recall that you use the distributive property to multiply a sum by a number. This property tells you to multiply the number by each term of the sum.

$6 \cdot (5 + 2) = 6 \cdot 5 + 6 \cdot 2$
$ = 30 + 12$
$ = 42$

Multiplying Mixed Numbers

To multiply a mixed number by a whole number, write the mixed number as a sum and apply the distributive property.

$6 \cdot 5\frac{1}{2} = 6 \cdot \left(5 + \frac{1}{2}\right)$
$\phantom{6 \cdot 5\frac{1}{2}} = (6 \cdot 5) + \left(6 \cdot \frac{1}{2}\right)$
$\phantom{6 \cdot 5\frac{1}{2}} = 30 + 3 = 33$

To multiply two mixed numbers, first rewrite each of them as a fraction. Then multiply.

$7\frac{1}{2} \cdot 1\frac{3}{4} = \frac{15}{2} \cdot \frac{7}{4}$
$\phantom{7\frac{1}{2} \cdot 1\frac{3}{4}} = \frac{15 \cdot 7}{2 \cdot 4}$
$\phantom{7\frac{1}{2} \cdot 1\frac{3}{4}} = \frac{105}{8} \text{ or } 13\frac{1}{8}$

Reciprocals

Two numbers whose product is 1 are called **reciprocals**. The reciprocal of a mixed number is found by writing it as a fraction and then interchanging the numerator and denominator.

Name _____ Date _____

| MODULE 5 SECTION 5 | PRACTICE & APPLICATION EXERCISES | STUDY GUIDE |

Exploration 1

Which customary unit would be the most convenient for measuring the capacity of each item?

1. a can of soup
2. a tank of gasoline
3. a single-serving milk container

For Exercises 4–6, replace each __?__ with the number that makes the statement true.

4. $1\frac{1}{2}$ gal = __?__ pt
5. 288 fl oz = __?__ qt
6. 160 c = __?__ gal

7. Get Well Pharmacy pays $7.99 for 1 gal of cough syrup. The syrup is then repackaged into 8 fl oz bottles and sold for $1.39 each. How much profit does the pharmacy make on 1 gal of the syrup?

Exploration 2

Mental Math Use the distributive property and mental math to find each product. Write each answer in lowest terms.

8. $8 \cdot 3\frac{1}{4}$
9. $12 \cdot 5\frac{1}{2}$
10. $6\frac{1}{3} \cdot 6$
11. $10\frac{1}{5} \cdot 15$

Find each product. Write each answer in lowest terms.

12. $5\frac{3}{5} \cdot 1\frac{3}{10}$
13. $7\frac{5}{8} \cdot 3\frac{2}{3}$
14. $4\frac{4}{5} \cdot 7\frac{2}{3}$
15. $3\frac{5}{6} \cdot 2\frac{7}{12}$

16. **Geometry** Mrs. Gold had her students use pipe cleaners to construct a cube and then dip it into a bubble solution to observe how the bubbles clung to the pipe cleaners. The recipe for bubble solution is 1 c dishwashing liquid, $\frac{1}{2}$ c glycerin, and 2 c water. This recipe makes enough solution for 2 groups working together. If Mrs. Gold wanted enough solution for 8 groups, how much glycerin did she need?

Write the reciprocal of each number.

17. $\frac{4}{5}$
18. 15
19. $\frac{12}{7}$
20. $9\frac{2}{3}$

Spiral Review

21. Write $\frac{4}{5}$ as a decimal and as a percent. (Module 3, pp. 174–175)

Apply the rule "multiply by 3 and then add 10" to each given input number. Write each input and output as an ordered pair. (Modules 4 and 5, pp. 282–284, 342–343)

22. 8
23. 0
24. $\frac{4}{9}$
25. $7\frac{1}{6}$

Name _____   Date _____

MODULE 5 SECTION 6   **STUDY GUIDE**

Dividing the Puzzle   Division with Fractions

GOAL **LEARN HOW TO:** • divide a whole number by a fraction
                          • divide by fractions and mixed numbers
         AS YOU: • investigate geometric puzzle pieces and lengths on a ruler

Exploration 1: Dividing by a Fraction

To divide by a fraction, you can multiply by its reciprocal.

Example

$12 \div \frac{1}{2} = 12 \cdot \frac{2}{1} = \frac{24}{1}$, or 24

Exploration 2: Dividing Fractions and Mixed Numbers

Using Number Sense in Division

When you divide a number by a smaller number, the quotient is greater than 1.

Divide $\frac{5}{6} \div \frac{1}{3}$.

Multiply by the reciprocal of the divisor. $\frac{5}{6} \div \frac{1}{3} = \frac{5}{6} \cdot \frac{3}{1}$

$= \frac{15}{6}$ or $2\frac{1}{2}$

The quotient is greater than 1. ⎯⎯⎯⎯↑

When you divide a number by a larger number, the quotient is less than 1.

Divide $\frac{1}{3} \div \frac{5}{6}$.

Multiply by the reciprocal of the divisor. $\frac{1}{3} \div \frac{5}{6} = \frac{1}{3} \cdot \frac{6}{5}$

$= \frac{6}{15}$ or $\frac{2}{5}$

The quotient is less than 1. ⎯⎯⎯⎯↑

Dividing by a Mixed Number

When dividing a mixed number by another mixed number, first write each mixed number as a fraction. Then multiply by the reciprocal of the divisor.

Example

To divide $2\frac{5}{6} \div 5\frac{1}{2}$, follow these steps:

Step 1 Write each mixed number as a fraction. $2\frac{5}{6} \div 5\frac{1}{2} = \frac{17}{6} \div \frac{11}{2}$

Step 2 Multiply by the reciprocal of the divisor. $= \frac{17}{6} \cdot \frac{2}{11}$

Step 3 Reduce to lowest terms, if possible. $= \frac{34}{66}$, or $\frac{17}{33}$

Name _____ Date _____

MODULE 5 SECTION 6 | PRACTICE & APPLICATION EXERCISES | STUDY GUIDE

Exploration 1

For Exercises 1–4, find each quotient. Write each answer in lowest terms.

1. $6 \div \dfrac{2}{3}$
2. $16 \div \dfrac{3}{4}$
3. $20 \div \dfrac{4}{5}$
4. $18 \div \dfrac{3}{2}$

5. Mr. Tomkins wants to put a "No Trespassing" sign in the middle of every $\dfrac{1}{4}$ mi section of a 3 mi long fence on his farm. How many signs will he need?

6. A jogging trail is $\dfrac{5}{8}$ mi long. How many times must Rachel run the trail in order to run a total of 20 mi?

Exploration 2

For Exercises 7–10, find each quotient. Write each answer in lowest terms.

7. $\dfrac{3}{4} \div \dfrac{1}{8}$
8. $\dfrac{14}{35} \div \dfrac{2}{7}$
9. $3\dfrac{1}{3} \div 5\dfrac{1}{2}$
10. $6\dfrac{7}{8} \div 1\dfrac{2}{3}$

11. **Aerodynamics** The largest helicopter ever built has a rotor diameter of $219\dfrac{5}{6}$ ft, while the smallest helicopter ever built has a rotor diameter of just $14\dfrac{3}{4}$ ft. About how many times greater is the larger rotor diameter?

12. Paco has a board $4\dfrac{1}{2}$ ft long. He wants to cut it into pieces that are each $1\dfrac{1}{2}$ ft long.

   a. Draw a diagram showing where he should cut the board.
   b. How many pieces will he have?
   c. What quotient does your diagram model?

Spiral Review

13. If you draw both diagonals of each square, how many triangles (of any size) are formed? **(Module 2, pp. 81–82)**

14. The *proper divisors* of a number are all of its factors except the number itself. Write a rule that relates the sum of the proper divisors of a power of 2 to the number itself. **(Module 1, pp. 6–7)**

Number = Power of 2	Proper Divisors
$2 = 2^1$	1
$4 = 2^2$	1, 2
$8 = 2^3$	1, 2, 4

MODULE 5 — TECHNOLOGY

For Use with Section 2

Here is a program for the TI-80 that allows you to add or subtract measures involving feet and inches. The numbers on the left side are for reference and are not part of the program itself.

1. PROGRAM: FEET
2. LBL 2
3. INPUT "ADD 1, SUBT 2=",X
4. DISP "FIRST NUMB"
5. INPUT "FEET=",A
6. INPUT "INCHES=",B
7. DISP "SECOND NUMB"
8. INPUT "FEET=",C
9. INPUT "INCHES=",D
10. 12*A+B→E
11. 12*C+D→F
12. IF X=1
13. THEN
14. E+F→G
15. GOTO 1
16. END
17. E-F→G
18. LBL 1
19. INT(G/12)→H
20. G-H*12→J
21. DISP "ANS"
22. DISP "FT",H
23. DISP "IN",J
24. GOTO 2

Notice that line 1 gives the title of the program: "Feet". Line 3 asks you to tell the calculator whether you want to add or subtract the two measurements that you enter. In lines 4 through 9, you input each of the two measures in feet and inches. If the first measurement is 7 feet 4 inches, then A = 7 and B = 4.

1. If the second measurement is 6 feet 9 inches,
C = _____ and D = _____ .

Name _____   **Date** _____

MODULE 5   TECHNOLOGY

In line 10, the first measurement is converted to inches only. The resulting number of inches is called E.

2. What is the value of E if the first measurement is 7 feet 4 inches?
_____

3. In line 11, the letter F represents the value in inches of the second measurement. What is F if the second measurement is 6 feet 9 inches?
_____

In line 14, the two inch measurements E and F are added and the answer in inches is called G.

4. What is G for the two measurements given above? _____

In lines 19 and 20, the measure G is converted from inches to feet and inches.

H is the name given to the whole-number part of the quotient of G divided by 12.

5. What is the value of H in the example above? _____

6. In line 20, J is given the value of G−H*12. What is the value of J?
_____

7. What part does J play in the final answer of the addition problem?
_____

If the two numbers are subtracted, then line 17 is used and lines 12 through 16 are passed over.

Name _____   Date _____

MODULE 5 QUIZ — MID-MODULE

Write the fractions in order from least to greatest.

1. $\frac{3}{7}, \frac{2}{3}, \frac{4}{9}, \frac{6}{7}$

2. $\frac{1}{4}, \frac{5}{12}, \frac{6}{16}, \frac{4}{8}$

3. $\frac{10}{11}, \frac{7}{9}, \frac{2}{3}, \frac{10}{22}$

Use mental math to compare each fraction with $\frac{3}{4}$. Then replace each ? with >, <, or =.

4. $\frac{4}{6}$ ___?___ $\frac{31}{40}$

5. $\frac{79}{100}$ ___?___ $\frac{8}{13}$

6. $\frac{108}{140}$ ___?___ $\frac{37}{52}$

Use mental math, paper and pencil, or a calculator to compare the fractions. Replace each with >, <, or =.

7. $\frac{40}{41}$ ___?___ $\frac{108}{109}$

8. $\frac{2}{7}$ ___?___ $\frac{13}{49}$

9. $\frac{14}{38}$ ___?___ $\frac{22}{53}$

10. In Mr. Fernandez's class, 10 out of 32 students turned in their projects early. In Ms. Chan's class, 9 out of 24 turned their projects in early. In which class did a greater fraction of the class turn their projects in ahead of schedule? How can you tell without using a calculator?

11. What is the length of this nail to the nearest 1 in.? the nearest $\frac{1}{2}$ in.? the nearest $\frac{1}{4}$ in.?

Replace each ? with the number that makes the statement true.

12. 150 in. = __?__ ft

13. 18 yd = __?__ ft

14. 2 yd 2 ft = __?__ in.

Find each sum or difference.

15. 1 mi 800 yd 2 ft
   +   1200 yd 12 ft

16. 18 yd 11 in.
   +   24 ft

17. 8 ft 4 in.
   − 4 ft 7 in.

Find each sum or difference. Write each answer in lowest terms.

18. $\frac{4}{9} + \frac{1}{3} + \frac{1}{6}$

19. $\frac{1}{2} + \frac{6}{15}$

20. $\frac{7}{12} - \frac{1}{3}$

21. $\frac{9}{20} - \frac{1}{6}$

22. $\frac{5}{22} + \frac{1}{2} + \frac{4}{11}$

23. $\frac{12}{13} - \frac{23}{39}$

Name _____ Date _____

MODULE 5 TEST   FORM A

Write the fractions in order from least to greatest.

1. $\frac{2}{9}, \frac{3}{4}, \frac{1}{5}, \frac{3}{10}$

2. $\frac{4}{11}, \frac{5}{6}, \frac{7}{8}, \frac{52}{100}$

Measure the length of the pencil as described.

3. to the nearest inch

4. to the nearest $\frac{1}{2}$ inch

5. to the nearest $\frac{1}{4}$ inch

Replace each ___?___ with the number that makes the statement true.

6. $4\frac{2}{9}$ yd = ___?___ in.

7. 70 in. = ___?___ ft

8. $6\frac{1}{3}$ ft = ___?___ in.

9. 31 ft = ___?___ yd

10. 2 mi 80 yd 5 ft = ___?___ yd

11. 8000 ft = ___?___ mi

Find each sum. Write each sum in lowest terms.

12. $\frac{11}{12} + \frac{7}{12}$

13. $\frac{6}{7} + \frac{1}{4}$

14. $\frac{13}{6} + \frac{7}{3}$

15. $5\frac{4}{7} + 1\frac{1}{2}$

16. Angela needed 12 ft 7 in. of wood for one carpentry project and 18 ft 9 in. for another. How many feet of wood does she need altogether for the two projects?

Use mental math or paper and pencil to find each sum or difference.

17. $\frac{5}{6} + 1\frac{1}{3} + 2\frac{2}{3}$

18. $6\frac{9}{10} - 1\frac{4}{5}$

19. $16\frac{1}{3} - 4\frac{7}{9}$

20. Eric's family has picked $3\frac{1}{2}$ bushels of apples. His mother uses $1\frac{7}{8}$ bushels to make applesauce. How many bushels of apples do they have left?

5-90   Math Thematics, Book 1

MODULE 5 TEST

FORM A

Find each difference. Write each difference in lowest terms.

21. $\frac{7}{9} - \frac{1}{3}$ **22.** $7\frac{3}{4} - 2\frac{1}{8}$ **23.** $6 - 2\frac{3}{5}$ **24.** $\frac{7}{11} - \frac{1}{4}$

25. Your family drinks $3\frac{1}{2}$ gallons of milk per week. Which of the following is not an equivalent measure?

    a. 56 c   **b.** 28 pt   **c.** 440 fl oz   **d.** 14 qt

Find each product. Write each product in lowest terms.

26. $3\frac{2}{3} \cdot 1\frac{1}{2}$ **27.** $1\frac{1}{5} \cdot 1\frac{2}{3}$ **28.** $2\frac{2}{5} \cdot 3\frac{1}{3}$

29. Arne has $31\frac{1}{2}$ cups of orange juice for a party. The large glasses that he plans to use will hold $1\frac{1}{2}$ cups of juice. How many glasses of orange juice can he serve using the amount of juice that he has?

Find each quotient. Write each quotient in lowest terms.

30. $4\frac{1}{2} \div \frac{3}{4}$ **31.** $6 \div \frac{1}{5}$ **32.** $\frac{7}{11} \div \frac{7}{9}$

| Name | Date |

MODULE 5 TEST FORM B

Write the fractions in order from least to greatest.

1. $\dfrac{6}{7}, \dfrac{1}{3}, \dfrac{3}{4}, \dfrac{9}{13}$

2. $\dfrac{5}{9}, \dfrac{5}{12}, \dfrac{65}{99}, \dfrac{2}{3}$

Measure the length of the paper clip as described.

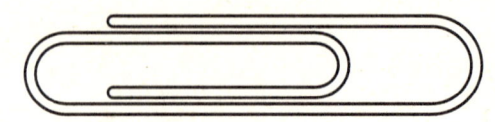

3. to the nearest inch

4. to the nearest $\dfrac{1}{2}$ inch

5. to the nearest $\dfrac{1}{4}$ inch

Replace each __?__ with the number that makes the statement true.

6. $3\dfrac{5}{6}$ yd = __?__ in.

7. 90 in. = __?__ ft

8. $5\dfrac{1}{4}$ ft = __?__ in.

9. 42 ft = __?__ yd

10. 1 mi 42 yd 6 ft = __?__ yd

11. 7500 ft = __?__ mi

Find each sum. Write each sum in lowest terms.

12. $\dfrac{6}{7} + \dfrac{4}{7}$

13. $\dfrac{3}{8} + \dfrac{2}{3}$

14. $\dfrac{11}{5} + \dfrac{13}{10}$

15. $6\dfrac{5}{6} + \dfrac{1}{2}$

16. The stepladder is 9 ft 10 in. Carl can reach 6 ft 4 in. if he stretches his arm up. How many feet will Carl be able to reach up the side of the house if he stands on the top of the stepladder?

Use mental math or paper and pencil to find each sum or difference.

17. $1\dfrac{3}{8} + \dfrac{1}{4} + 5\dfrac{5}{8}$

18. $10\dfrac{1}{2} - 5\dfrac{3}{4}$

19. $8\dfrac{7}{12} - 2\dfrac{3}{4}$

20. Oscar jumped $10\dfrac{2}{3}$ ft in the long jump. Elmo jumped $2\dfrac{11}{12}$ ft. How many feet farther did Oscar jump than Elmo? how many inches?

Name   Date

MODULE 5 TEST   FORM B

Find each difference. Write each difference in lowest terms.

21. $\frac{11}{15} - \frac{2}{5}$ **22.** $6\frac{4}{5} - 1\frac{7}{10}$ **23.** $5 - 3\frac{4}{7}$ **24.** $5\frac{2}{9} - \frac{5}{9}$

25. For the road race the race director told the volunteers to have at least 400 oz of water at each water stop. Which of the following is not an equivalent measure?

   a. 50 c   **b.** $12\frac{1}{2}$ qt   **c.** $3\frac{1}{4}$ gal   **d.** 25 pt

Find each product. Write each product in lowest terms.

26. $2\frac{1}{4} \cdot 2\frac{1}{3}$ **27.** $5\frac{1}{3} \cdot \frac{3}{4}$ **28.** $4\frac{9}{10} \cdot \frac{5}{7}$

29. Delia has $12\frac{2}{3}$ yd of ribbon. She needs $\frac{2}{3}$ yd of ribbon to make one ornament. How many ornaments does she have enough ribbon to make?

Find each quotient. Write each quotient in lowest terms.

30. $5\frac{1}{3} \div \frac{4}{5}$ **31.** $7 \div \frac{1}{4}$ **32.** $\frac{4}{13} \div \frac{4}{7}$

MODULE 5 — STANDARDIZED ASSESSMENT

1. Which answer correctly lists the fractions in order from least to greatest?

a. $\frac{8}{10}, \frac{6}{8}, \frac{7}{8}, \frac{6}{7}$ b. $\frac{6}{7}, \frac{6}{8}, \frac{7}{8}, \frac{8}{10}$

c. $\frac{7}{8}, \frac{6}{7}, \frac{8}{10}, \frac{6}{8}$ d. $\frac{6}{8}, \frac{8}{10}, \frac{6}{7}, \frac{7}{8}$

2. Which of the following lengths is *not* equivalent to the other three?

a. $\frac{1}{5}$ mi b. 352 yd

c. 1046 ft d. 12,672 in.

3. How many feet are there in $\frac{3}{8}$ mi?

a. 1980 ft b. 1880 ft

c. 660 ft d. 1260 ft

4. Find $4\frac{2}{5} + 2\frac{2}{3}$ and express the answer in lowest terms.

a. $6\frac{1}{15}$ b. $7\frac{1}{15}$

c. $7\frac{1}{3}$ d. $7\frac{1}{2}$

5. On a weekend bike trip Chloe rode $6\frac{1}{4}$ h on Saturday and $5\frac{2}{3}$ h on Sunday. How many hours did she ride in all?

a. 12 h b. $11\frac{11}{12}$ h

c. $11\frac{3}{4}$ h d. $12\frac{1}{6}$ h

6. Find $5\frac{3}{10} - 3\frac{4}{5}$ and express the answer in lowest terms.

a. $1\frac{9}{10}$ b. $1\frac{3}{5}$

c. $2\frac{3}{10}$ d. $1\frac{1}{2}$

7. The world record for the 100 mi run is approximately $11\frac{1}{2}$ h. How many hours faster could a car cover the same distance if it was travelling at 60 mi/h?

a. $8\frac{5}{6}$ b. $9\frac{1}{6}$

c. $9\frac{5}{6}$ d. 10

8. Which of the following is not equivalent to $2\frac{3}{4}$ gallons?

a. 22 pt b. 10 qt

c. 352 fl oz d. 44 c

9. How many $2\frac{3}{8}$ inch strips can you cut from a piece of paper that is 1 yd wide?

a. 15 b. 16

c. 17 d. 18

10. Find $3\frac{1}{3} \cdot 2\frac{5}{8}$.

a. $6\frac{5}{24}$ b. $7\frac{17}{24}$

c. $8\frac{3}{4}$ d. $9\frac{5}{11}$

11. Find $10\frac{2}{3} \div 2\frac{1}{2}$.

a. $4\frac{1}{6}$ b. $5\frac{3}{4}$

c. $5\frac{1}{6}$ d. $4\frac{4}{15}$

12. A restaurant serves a bowl of cereal with $\frac{2}{3}$ c of milk. How many bowls of cereal can be served using 1 gallon of milk?

a. 10 b. 16

c. 24 d. 28

5-94 Math Thematics, Book 1

MODULE 5

MODULE PERFORMANCE ASSESSMENT

A farmer called the veterinarian because she had 5 sick animals—a 2 lb rabbit, a 7 lb cat, a 30 lb lamb, a 100 lb goat, and the family's pet dog. The vet prescribed the same medicine for each animal in similar doses. Each animal was to take $\frac{2}{3}$ fluid ounce per pound.

Unfortunately, the vet had driven all the way out to the farm without his containers for measuring the doses. The farmer, however, was not worried. She went to the barn and quickly returned with 8 old containers. Container A was marked $1\frac{2}{3}$ oz, container B was marked 3 oz, and container C was marked $3\frac{2}{3}$ oz. Containers D, E, F, and G were each $16\frac{1}{3}$ oz, and container H held exactly $109\frac{1}{3}$ oz.

"Just fill the container H up to the brim. That's all I'll need," the farmer told the vet. The astonished vet did as she said and then sat down to watch as the farmer gave exactly the correct amount of medicine to each of her sick animals. There were no additional markings on the containers, she did not pour any onto the ground, nor did she return any to container H. When she was done with the first four animals, she had exactly the right amount for the dog. How did she do it?

How much did the dog weigh?

Answers

PRACTICE AND APPLICATIONS

Module 5, Section 1

1. a. $\frac{3}{8} < \frac{1}{2}$ b. $\frac{11}{12} > \frac{1}{2}$ c. $\frac{5}{8} > \frac{1}{2}$ d. $\frac{3}{4} > \frac{1}{2}$ e. $\frac{5}{6} > \frac{1}{2}$
f. $\frac{1}{5} < \frac{1}{2}$ g. $\frac{2}{9} < \frac{1}{2}$ h. $\frac{41}{50} > \frac{1}{2}$ i. $\frac{19}{90} < \frac{1}{2}$
2. a. $\frac{3}{25}, \frac{3}{11}, \frac{3}{10}, \frac{3}{8}, \frac{3}{4}$ b. $\frac{1}{100}, \frac{1}{50}, \frac{1}{10}, \frac{1}{3}$
c. $\frac{7}{100}, \frac{7}{12}, \frac{7}{10}, \frac{7}{9}, \frac{7}{8}$ d. $\frac{3}{4}, \frac{8}{9}, \frac{9}{10}, \frac{24}{25}, \frac{99}{100}$
e. $\frac{1}{10}, \frac{2}{5}, \frac{5}{8}, \frac{7}{9}$ f. $\frac{12}{99}, \frac{29}{60}, \frac{15}{19}, \frac{19}{20}$
3. a. > b. < c. < d. > e. > f. < g. > h. = i. < j. < k. < l. >
4. a. Sample Response: $\frac{1}{2}, \frac{3}{4}$
b. Sample Response: $\frac{1}{2}, \frac{1}{4}$
5. His pie is larger.
6. a. > b. < c. < d. < e. = f. < g. > h. < i. >
7. a. > b. > c. < d. < e. < f. < g. = h. < i. >
8. a. = b. > c. < d. < e. > f. > g. < h. > i. =
9. a. > b. < c. < d. > e. > f. = g. < h. = i. <
j. > k. > l. <
10. No; $\frac{7}{64} < \frac{1}{8}$

Module 5, Section 2

1. a. feet b. miles c. inches
2. $3\frac{1}{2}$ in., $3\frac{3}{4}$ in., $3\frac{5}{8}$ in.
3. a. 18 b. 15 c. 228 d. $3\frac{1}{4}$ e. 69 f. $4\frac{2}{3}$
4. a. $\frac{2}{3}$ yd b. $2\frac{2}{3}$ yd c. $3\frac{1}{3}$ yd
5. a. 8 yd b. 1 yd 2 ft c. 1 mi d. 1 yd 1 ft 10 in.
e. 3 yd 2 ft 3 in. f. 3 yd 2 ft
6. 1 yd 2 ft 3 in.

Module 5, Section 3

1. a. $\frac{17}{20}$ b. $\frac{7}{8}$ c. $\frac{19}{24}$ d. $\frac{29}{24}$ or $1\frac{5}{24}$ e. $\frac{43}{30}$ or $1\frac{13}{30}$
f. $\frac{47}{36}$ or $1\frac{11}{36}$
2. a. $\frac{1}{10}$ b. $\frac{17}{36}$ c. $\frac{3}{8}$ d. $\frac{9}{16}$ e. $\frac{5}{12}$ f. $\frac{9}{40}$
3. a. $\frac{13}{10}$ or $1\frac{3}{10}$ b. $\frac{7}{24}$ c. $\frac{14}{15}$ d. $\frac{13}{28}$ e. $\frac{19}{16}$ or $1\frac{3}{16}$ f. $\frac{2}{9}$
4. a. $\frac{11}{18}$ b. $\frac{43}{35}$ or $1\frac{8}{35}$ c. $\frac{5}{36}$ d. $\frac{7}{8}$ e. $\frac{37}{30}$ or $1\frac{7}{30}$ f. $\frac{7}{16}$
g. $\frac{19}{18}$ or $1\frac{1}{18}$ h. $\frac{23}{40}$ i. $\frac{15}{16}$
5. 34 rocks
6. $\frac{5}{24}$ c

Module 5, Section 4

1. a. about 7 b. about 8 c. about 6 d. about 7
e. about 8 f. about 9 g. about 6 h. about 4
i. about 3 j. about 8 k. about 4 l. about 6
2. a. $3\frac{11}{12}$ b. $7\frac{13}{15}$ c. $8\frac{7}{8}$ d. $5\frac{1}{20}$ e. $9\frac{1}{6}$ f. $3\frac{13}{18}$ g. $5\frac{5}{6}$
h. $8\frac{1}{8}$ i. $12\frac{2}{3}$ j. $10\frac{13}{18}$ k. $12\frac{2}{9}$ l. $14\frac{1}{10}$ m. $8\frac{5}{24}$
n. $8\frac{13}{30}$ o. $11\frac{11}{36}$
3. $30\frac{1}{2}$ ft
4. $6\frac{3}{10}$ m
5. a. $43\frac{11}{12}$ c b. Yes.
6. a. $5\frac{1}{4}$ b. $8\frac{1}{3}$ c. $5\frac{7}{8}$ d. $3\frac{2}{3}$ e. $4\frac{1}{4}$ f. $10\frac{5}{12}$ g. $1\frac{1}{4}$
h. $2\frac{2}{3}$ i. $1\frac{1}{10}$
7. Find each difference. Write each answer in lowest terms.
a. $2\frac{1}{3}$ b. $4\frac{1}{2}$ c. $3\frac{3}{8}$ d. $8\frac{5}{12}$ e. $6\frac{7}{18}$ f. $6\frac{3}{4}$ g. $4\frac{11}{20}$
h. $12\frac{5}{6}$ i. $3\frac{17}{20}$ j. $2\frac{5}{8}$ k. $6\frac{1}{8}$ l. $12\frac{11}{24}$
8. a. $5\frac{2}{9}$ b. $2\frac{4}{15}$ c. $21\frac{5}{6}$ d. $16\frac{7}{12}$ e. $4\frac{1}{4}$ f. $10\frac{5}{12}$
g. $53\frac{3}{4}$ h. $21\frac{1}{5}$ i. $14\frac{7}{30}$ j. $10\frac{11}{12}$ k. $56\frac{5}{24}$ l. $65\frac{5}{6}$
9. a. $6\frac{23}{24}$ yd b. $1\frac{11}{24}$ yd c. $\frac{13}{24}$ yd; more

Module 5, Section 5

1. a. 2 b. 6 c. 28 d. 24 e. 256 f. $\frac{1}{2}$ g. $2\frac{1}{2}$ h. 8
i. 10
2. $2\frac{1}{4}$ gal
3. a. $12\frac{2}{3}$ b. $12\frac{3}{4}$ c. 19 d. 25 e. 14 f. 22
4. a. $12\frac{3}{4}$ b. $17\frac{1}{4}$ c. $10\frac{2}{5}$ d. $\frac{2}{7}$ e. $2\frac{4}{5}$ f. 1 g. $10\frac{1}{2}$
h. $7\frac{4}{5}$ i. $14\frac{7}{32}$
5. a. 9 b. $\frac{6}{17}$ c. $\frac{1}{28}$ d. $\frac{7}{6}$ e. $\frac{5}{18}$ f. $\frac{6}{5}$
6. a. 10 b. $\frac{1}{6}$
7. $8\frac{3}{4}$ c

Module 5, Section 6

1. a. 3 b. 32 c. 6 d. 20 e. 24 f. 10 g. 15 h. 16
i. 12 j. 14 k. 10 l. 22 m. 30 n. 20 o. 36
2. a. $2\frac{2}{3}$ b. $1\frac{2}{3}$ c. $10\frac{1}{2}$ d. $4\frac{4}{5}$ e. $2\frac{1}{4}$ f. $3\frac{3}{5}$ g. $1\frac{1}{6}$
h. $3\frac{1}{5}$ i. $3\frac{1}{3}$ j. $13\frac{1}{3}$ k. $1\frac{4}{5}$ l. $7\frac{1}{2}$ m. $2\frac{2}{7}$ n. $5\frac{1}{3}$ o. $2\frac{2}{3}$
p. $2\frac{1}{2}$ q. $14\frac{2}{5}$ r. $4\frac{4}{7}$

3. a. 32 streamers **b.** No.
4. a. 66 **b.** Yes; $\frac{2}{3}$ oz
5. a. 2 **b.** $9\frac{3}{5}$ **c.** $\frac{5}{9}$ **d.** 11 **e.** $8\frac{1}{4}$ **f.** $3\frac{13}{24}$ **g.** $2\frac{1}{7}$ **h.** $2\frac{1}{6}$
i. 10 **j.** $3\frac{5}{7}$ **k.** 18 **l.** 2 **m.** $1\frac{9}{10}$ **n.** $1\frac{7}{15}$ **o.** $2\frac{29}{48}$
p. $13\frac{3}{5}$ **q.** $1\frac{3}{5}$ **r.** $1\frac{5}{9}$ **s.** $1\frac{19}{45}$ **t.** $6\frac{2}{9}$ **u.** $5\frac{1}{3}$ **v.** $2\frac{3}{16}$
w. $7\frac{1}{4}$ **x.** $11\frac{1}{4}$
6. a. $4\frac{1}{12}$ c **b.** 12 pizzas; 6 large pizzas; 6 small pizzas **c.** Yes.
7. a. 9 color sections **b.** Yes; $\frac{3}{5}$ m

Module 5, Sections 1–6
1. a. $\frac{1}{50}, \frac{1}{3}, \frac{12}{25}, \frac{74}{75}, \frac{99}{100}$ **b.** $\frac{1}{9}, \frac{1}{8}, \frac{3}{5}, \frac{3}{4}, \frac{5}{6}$
2. a. > **b.** < **c.** < **d.** = **e.** > **f.** >
3. a. 21 **b.** 47,520 **c.** 132 **d.** $4\frac{3}{4}$ **e.** 102 **f.** $3\frac{1}{3}$
4. a. 5 yd 1 ft **b.** 1 ft 10 in. **c.** 2 ft 9 in.
5. a. $\frac{31}{40}$ **b.** $\frac{5}{24}$ **c.** $1\frac{1}{10}$ **d.** $\frac{1}{9}$ **e.** $1\frac{7}{12}$ **f.** $\frac{55}{72}$
6. a. $\frac{5}{8}$ **b.** $\frac{3}{4}$ **c.** $1\frac{29}{30}$
7. $3\frac{3}{4}$ mi
8. a. about 6 **b.** about 5 **c.** about 6
9. a. $7\frac{13}{24}$ **b.** $4\frac{5}{21}$ **c.** $5\frac{11}{24}$
10. a. $5\frac{6}{7}$ **b.** $2\frac{5}{8}$ **c.** $7\frac{1}{8}$
11. a. $8\frac{1}{18}$ **b.** $7\frac{1}{9}$ **c.** $2\frac{13}{20}$ **d.** $5\frac{17}{18}$ **e.** $2\frac{3}{8}$ **f.** $7\frac{2}{5}$
12. a. 3 **b.** 9 **c.** 28 **d.** 40 **e.** 192 **f.** $2\frac{1}{2}$
13. a. $8\frac{2}{3}$ **b.** $11\frac{1}{4}$ **c.** 27 **d.** 1 **e.** $3\frac{23}{40}$ **f.** $1\frac{1}{6}$
14. a. $9\frac{3}{5}$ **b.** $1\frac{6}{7}$ **c.** $3\frac{6}{7}$ **d.** 24 **e.** $8\frac{1}{2}$ **f.** $3\frac{2}{3}$

STUDY GUIDE

Module 5, Section 1
1. $\frac{5}{7} > \frac{1}{2}$
2. $\frac{6}{13} < \frac{1}{2}$
3. $\frac{358}{1000} < \frac{1}{2}$
4. $\frac{13}{9} > \frac{1}{2}$
5. $\frac{4}{100}, \frac{4}{13}, \frac{4}{7}, \frac{4}{5}, \frac{4}{3}$
6. $\frac{2}{3}, \frac{4}{5}, \frac{8}{9}, \frac{11}{12}, \frac{12}{13}$
7. <
8. >
9. <
10. >

11. No; Sample Response: Even though one rock may be heavier than one feather, $\frac{1}{2}$ kg of each material weighs the same amount.
12. >
13. >
14. <
15. <
16. >
17. <
18. <
19. <
20. Sample Response: $\frac{5}{8}, \frac{6}{8}$
21. 356
22. 12 (20, 22, 23, 25, 30, 32, 33, 35, 50, 52, 53, 55); Sample Response: Make a list.

Module 5, Section 2
1. Sample Response: 3 yd
2. Sample Response: 1 ft
3. Sample Response: miles
4. Sample Response: feet
5. a. 2 in. **b.** $1\frac{1}{2}$ in. or 2 in. **c.** $1\frac{3}{4}$ in.
d. $1\frac{3}{4}$ in.
6. 54
7. 6.5
8. 9.5
9. a. 660 ft
b. 16.5 ft
10. 17 mi 839 ft
11. 5 ft 10 in.
12. 15 yd
13. 2^7
14. $2^3 \cdot 3 \cdot 5^2$
15. $2^5 \cdot 3^2 \cdot 5$
16. $2^3 \cdot 3^2 \cdot 5^3$
17. 1024
18. 625
19. 9
20. 216

Module 5, Section 3
1. $\frac{7}{6}$ or $1\frac{1}{6}$
2. $\frac{9}{10}$
3. $\frac{73}{66}$ or $1\frac{7}{66}$
4. $\frac{28}{27}$ or $1\frac{1}{27}$
5. $\frac{8}{45}$
6. $\frac{7}{16}$
7. $\frac{7}{15}$
8. $\frac{22}{21}$ or $1\frac{1}{21}$

9. $\frac{62}{100}$ or $\frac{31}{50}$

10. a. Sample Response: $\frac{1}{3}$; $\frac{1}{3}$
b. Sample Response: Ford's production was almost 3 times Chrysler's.
c. Sample Response: $\frac{2}{9}$

11. 90
12. 60
13. 54
14. 150
15. $\frac{2}{4}$ or $\frac{1}{2}$

Module 5, Section 4
1. about 19
2. about 28
3. about 19
4. about 36
5. $19\frac{7}{10}$
6. $10\frac{9}{10}$
7. $12\frac{1}{12}$
8. $14\frac{7}{24}$
9. $18\frac{1}{8}$
10. $31\frac{7}{9}$
11. 21
12. about $16\frac{1}{2}$
13. about 31
14. about 47
15. about $301\frac{1}{2}$
16. $4\frac{7}{15}$
17. $3\frac{5}{24}$
18. $1\frac{5}{12}$
19. $8\frac{13}{20}$
20. $5\frac{3}{5}$; Sample Response: work backward: $4\frac{2}{5} + \frac{3}{5} = 5$, so $4\frac{2}{5} + 5\frac{3}{5} = 10$
21. $6\frac{2}{9}$; Sample Response: work backward: $9\frac{7}{9} + \frac{2}{9} = 10$, so $9\frac{7}{9} + 6\frac{2}{9} = 16$
22. $5\frac{3}{7}$; Sample Response: $13 - 8 = 5$, so $13\frac{3}{7} - 8 = 5\frac{3}{7}$
23. $17\frac{7}{12}$; Sample Response: work backward: $11\frac{5}{12} + \frac{7}{12} = 12$, so $11\frac{5}{12} + 17\frac{7}{12} = 29$
24. Touch Gold
25. $\frac{1}{16}$ mi

26. Sample Response:

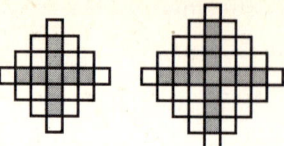

27. rhombus

Module 5, Section 5
1. Sample Response: fluid ounce
2. gallon
3. Sample Response: pint
4. 12
5. 9
6. 10
7. $14.25
8. 26
9. 66
10. 38
11. 153
12. $\frac{182}{25}$ or $7\frac{7}{25}$
13. $\frac{671}{24}$ or $27\frac{23}{24}$
14. $\frac{184}{5}$ or $36\frac{4}{5}$
15. $\frac{713}{72}$ or $9\frac{65}{72}$
16. 2 c
17. $\frac{5}{4}$
18. $\frac{1}{15}$
19. $\frac{7}{12}$
20. $\frac{3}{29}$
21. 0.8; 80%
22. (8, 34)
23. (0, 10)
24. $\left(\frac{4}{9}, 11\frac{1}{3}\right)$
25. $\left(7\frac{1}{6}, 31\frac{1}{2}\right)$

Module 5, Section 6
1. 9
2. $\frac{64}{3}$ or $21\frac{1}{3}$
3. 25
4. 12
5. 12 signs
6. 32 times
7. 6
8. $\frac{7}{5}$ or $1\frac{2}{5}$
9. $\frac{20}{33}$
10. $\frac{33}{8}$ or $4\frac{1}{8}$

11. about 15 times greater
12. a.

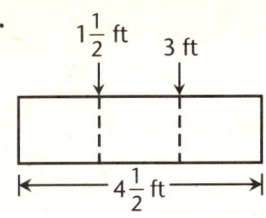

   $1\frac{1}{2}$ ft   3 ft

   $4\frac{1}{2}$ ft

   b. 3 pieces c. $4\frac{1}{2} \div 1\frac{1}{2} = 3$
13. 18 triangles
14. sum of proper divisors = number − 1

TECHNOLOGY

Module 5
1. C=6, D=9
2. 88
3. 81
4. 169
5. 14
6. 1
7. It is the number of inches in the final answer.

ASSESSMENT

Mid-Module 5 Quiz
1. $\frac{3}{7}, \frac{4}{9}, \frac{2}{3}, \frac{6}{7}$
2. $\frac{1}{4}, \frac{6}{16}, \frac{5}{12}, \frac{4}{8}$
3. $\frac{10}{22}, \frac{2}{3}, \frac{7}{9}, \frac{10}{11}$
4. <
5. >
6. >
7. <
8. >
9. <
10. Ms. Chan's class; Sample Response: compare each fraction, $\frac{10}{32}$ and $\frac{9}{24}$, to $\frac{1}{3}$. Since $\frac{9}{24} > \frac{1}{3}$ and $\frac{1}{3} > \frac{10}{32}$, you can conclude that $\frac{9}{24} > \frac{10}{32}$.
11. 3 in., $3\frac{1}{2}$ in., $3\frac{1}{4}$ in.
12. $12\frac{1}{2}$
13. 54
14. 96
15. 2 mi 244 yd 2 ft
16. 26 yd 11 in.
17. 3 ft 9 in.
18. $\frac{17}{18}$
19. $\frac{9}{10}$
20. $\frac{1}{4}$
21. $\frac{17}{60}$
22. $1\frac{1}{11}$
23. $\frac{1}{3}$

Module 5 Test (Form A)
1. $\frac{1}{5}, \frac{2}{9}, \frac{3}{10}, \frac{3}{4}$
2. $\frac{4}{11}, \frac{52}{100}, \frac{5}{6}, \frac{7}{8}$
3. 4 in.
4. $3\frac{1}{2}$ in.
5. $3\frac{3}{4}$ in.
6. 152
7. $5\frac{5}{6}$
8. 76
9. $10\frac{1}{3}$
10. $3601\frac{2}{3}$
11. $1\frac{17}{33}$
12. $1\frac{1}{2}$
13. $1\frac{3}{28}$
14. $4\frac{1}{2}$
15. $7\frac{1}{14}$
16. $31\frac{1}{3}$ ft
17. $4\frac{5}{6}$
18. $5\frac{1}{10}$
19. $11\frac{5}{9}$
20. $1\frac{5}{8}$
21. $\frac{4}{9}$
22. $5\frac{5}{8}$
23. $3\frac{2}{5}$
24. $\frac{17}{44}$
25. c
26. $5\frac{1}{2}$
27. 2
28. 8
29. 21 glasses
30. 6
31. 30
32. $\frac{9}{11}$

Module 5 Test (Form B)
1. $\frac{1}{3}, \frac{9}{13}, \frac{3}{4}, \frac{6}{7}$

2. $\frac{5}{12}, \frac{5}{9}, \frac{65}{99}, \frac{2}{3}$
3. 2 in.
4. $2\frac{1}{2}$ in.
5. $2\frac{2}{4}$ in., or $2\frac{1}{2}$ in.
6. 138
7. $7\frac{1}{2}$
8. 63
9. 14
10. 1804
11. $1\frac{37}{88}$
12. $1\frac{3}{7}$
13. $1\frac{1}{24}$
14. $3\frac{1}{2}$
15. $7\frac{1}{3}$
16. $16\frac{1}{6}$ ft
17. $7\frac{1}{4}$
18. $4\frac{3}{4}$
19. $5\frac{5}{6}$
20. $7\frac{3}{4}$ ft; 93 in.
21. $\frac{1}{3}$
22. $5\frac{1}{10}$
23. $1\frac{3}{7}$
24. $4\frac{2}{3}$
25. c
26. $5\frac{1}{4}$
27. 4
28. $3\frac{1}{2}$
29. 19
30. $6\frac{2}{3}$
31. 28
32. $\frac{7}{13}$

STANDARDIZED ASSESSMENT

Module 5
1. d
2. c
3. a
4. b
5. b
6. d
7. c

8. b
9. a
10. c
11. d
12. c

MODULE PERFORMANCE ASSESSMENT

Module 5
1. Determine the correct dose for each animal.

   2 lb rabbit × $\frac{2}{3}$ oz/lb = $1\frac{1}{3}$ oz

   7 lb cat × $\frac{2}{3}$ oz/lb = $4\frac{2}{3}$ oz

   30 lb lamb × $\frac{2}{3}$ oz/lb = 20 oz

   100 lb goat × $\frac{2}{3}$ oz/lb = $66\frac{2}{3}$ oz

   The dog's weight is unknown.

2. To medicate the rabbit, fill container B, then fill container A from container B. Medicate the rabbit with the amount remaining in container B.

   $3 - 1\frac{2}{3} = 1\frac{1}{3}$ oz for the rabbit

3. Then, to medicate the cat, refill container B, and then give the amounts in container A and container B to the cat.

   $1\frac{2}{3} + 3 = 4\frac{2}{3}$ oz for the cat

4. To medicate the lamb, fill container C and container D and give the amounts to the lamb.

   $3\frac{2}{3} + 16\frac{1}{3} = 20$ oz for the lamb

5. To medicate the goat, fill containers D, E, F, G, and B. Fill container A from container B. Then give containers D, E, F, G, and B to the goat.

   $\left(4 \times 16\frac{1}{3}\right) + 1\frac{1}{3} = 66\frac{2}{3}$ oz for the goat

6. Dose for dog = Total amount of medicine − Total used to medicate other animals

   $= 109\frac{1}{3} - \left(1\frac{1}{3} + 4\frac{2}{3} + 20 + 66\frac{2}{3}\right)$

   $= 109\frac{1}{3} - 92\frac{2}{3}$

   $= 16\frac{2}{3}$ oz for the dog

7. Dose for dog ÷ Dose per pound = Weight of dog

   $16\frac{2}{3}$ oz ÷ $\frac{2}{3}$ oz/lb = 25 lb dog

BOOK 1
TEACHER'S RESOURCES FOR MODULE 6

MIDDLE GRADES MATHThematics

MODULE 6: Comparisons and Predictions

- Planning and Teaching Suggestions, p. 6-8
- Labsheets, p. 6-49
- Extended Explorations, p. 6-59
- Blackline Masters, p. 6-62

6-1

MODULE 6: COMPARISONS and PREDICTIONS

Module Overview

Situations from nature, literature, sports, and the news provide opportunities for students to build an understanding of ratios, proportions, and percent, and to solve problems involving comparisons and predictions. Models, graphs, and tables are used to explore and represent relationships. Students also look at congruent and similar figures.

Module Objectives

Section	Objectives	NCTM Standards
1	◆ Use ratios to compare quantities. ◆ Express a ratio three ways: using the word *to*, a colon, or fraction form. ◆ Recognize and write equivalent ratios.	1, 2, 3, 4, 5
2	◆ Find unit rates and use them to make predictions. ◆ Make a table to represent a rate, and use patterns in the data to make predictions.	1, 2, 3, 4, 8
3	◆ Use ratio as a tool for investigating measurements. ◆ Write the decimal form of a ratio to make comparisons. ◆ Find and use a "nice" fraction form of a ratio to describe data and make predictions. ◆ Make a scatter plot. ◆ Fit a line to data in a scatter plot and use it to make predictions.	1, 2, 3, 4, 10, 13
4	◆ Use cross products to find the missing term in a proportion. ◆ Write and use proportions to solve problems and make predictions. ◆ Explore when using a proportion is or is not appropriate.	1, 2, 3, 4, 7, 9
5	◆ Identify similar figures and their corresponding parts. ◆ Understand characteristics that make figures similar. ◆ Identify congruent figures. ◆ Apply similarity to solving problems involving scale drawings, scale models, and map scales. ◆ Measure and draw angles using a protractor.	1, 2, 3, 4, 12, 13
6	◆ Use a "nice" fraction and mental math to find the percent of a number. ◆ Use a "nice" fraction to estimate a percent or percent of a number. ◆ Apply the percent equivalents for thirds. ◆ Construct a tree diagram to list all the outcomes of an experiment. ◆ Use a tree diagram to determine and compare probabilities.	1, 2, 3, 4, 7, 11

Topic Spiraling

Section	Connections to Prior and Future Concepts
1	Section 1 explores ratios and defines equivalent ratios. Equivalent fractions are applied.
2	Section 2 presents rates. Tables are used to see the patterns formed by equivalent rates. Predictions are made using unit rates or a table. Rates are revisited in Book 2 Module 5.
3	In Section 3 students use scatter plots and several forms of ratios to compare and predict. Mean, fraction/decimal equivalents, and coordinate graphing are applied, and work with graph scales is extended. Scatter plots are used in Module 7 and revisited in Book 2 Module 5.
4	In Section 4 students solve proportions and, as appropriate, use proportions to solve problems. Equations formed from cross products are solved intuitively using the idea of number fact families. Students use equations in Module 7 and use proportions to find percent in Module 8.
5	Section 5 explores the relationship between corresponding parts of similar figures. Proportions are applied to solve problems involving scale. Congruence from Module 2 and angles from Module 1 are revisited and a protractor is introduced. Book 2 Modules 4 and 6 treat similarity.
6	Section 6 extends common fraction/percent equivalents from Module 3 and probability from Module 4. Students use fractions and mental math to find or estimate a percent of a number. Tree diagrams for two-stage experiments and the concept of a fair game are introduced. In Module 8 students find a percent of a number using decimals and find geometric probabilities.

Integration

Mathematical Connections	1	2	3	4	5	6
algebra (including patterns and functions)		**389–396***	402–404, 406, 408	**414–412**	427–428, 433–437	447
geometry	380–387		402–412	421	**423–437***	446, 447
data analysis, probability, discrete math	388	394, 395	**397–412**	413, 420	434	**438–449**
Interdisciplinary Connections and Applications						
social studies and geography		389, 394	407, 409		433–436	
reading and language arts	380, 386		397, 406			
science	387	394–396	407, 410, 413	421	435–436	449
arts				420	423–424, 427–435	
health, physical education, and sports	386			417		438–440, 445–446
design, gliders, oceanography, Spanish	385		409, 412		436	

*** Bold page numbers** *indicate that a topic is used throughout the section.*

Guide for Assigning Homework

Regular Scheduling (45 min class period)

			exercises to note		
Section/ P&A Pages	Core Assignment	Extended Assignment	Additional Practice/Review	Open-ended Problems	Special Problems
1 pp. 385–388	**Day 1:** 1–8, 9a, 10, ROS 13, SR 14–25	1–9, Chal 12, ROS 13, SR 14–25	Sec 1 Ex Prac, p. 388; P&A 11	ROS 13	Mod Proj 1–2
2 pp. 393–396	**Day 1:** 1–9 (odd), 10, 11–17 (odd), 18, 20, ROS 21, SR 22–28	1–9 (odd), 10, 11–17 (odd), 18, 20, ROS 21, SR 22–28, Ext 29	Sec 2 Ex Prac, p. 396; P&A 2–8 (even), 12, 14, 19	P&A 16	P&A 16
3 pp. 406-412	**Day 1:** 1a, 2–7, SR 21–24	1–7, SR 21–24	Sec 3 Ex Prac, p. 411; TB, p. 597; P&A 8		P&A 1b
	Day 2: 8–14	8–14	P&A 15	P&A 15	Mod Proj 3–6
	Day 3: 16–18, *ROS 20, SR 25–30	16–18, ROS 20, SR 25–30	P&A 19	Std Test, p. 411; E^2, p. 412	E^2, p. 412
4 pp. 419–422	**Day 1:** 1–11, SR 19–24	1–11, SR 19–24	Sec 4 Ex Prac, p. 422		
	Day 2: 12, 13, 15–17, *ROS 18	12, 13, Chal 14, 15–17, *ROS 18			
5 pp. 432–437	**Day 1:** 1–6, 8, 9, SR 31–33	1–6, 8, 9, SR 31–33	Sec 5 Ex Prac, p. 437; P&A 7		
	Day 2: 10–18 (even), 19, SR 34–36	10–18 (even), 19, Chal 20, SR 34–36	P&A 11–17 (odd)		Career 41–42
	Day 3: 22, 24–26, 28, ROS 30, SR 37–40	22, 24–26, 28, ROS 30, SR 37–40	P&A 21, 23, 27, 29	Std Test, p. 437	Std Test, p. 437; Mod Proj 7–9
6 pp. 445– 449	**Day 1:** 2–16 (even), 17, 18, SR 29–32	2–16 (even), 17, 18, Chal 19, SR 29–32	Sec 6 Ex Prac, p. 448; P&A 1–15 (odd)		Mod Proj 10–13
	Day 2: 20–25, 27, ROS 28	20–25, Chal 26, 27, ROS 28			
Review/ Assess	Review and Assess (PE), Quick Quizzes (TRB), Mid-Module Quiz (TRB), Module Tests— Forms A and B (TRB), Standardized Assessment (TRB) Cumulative Test (TRB)				Allow 6 days
Enrich/ Assess	E^2 (PE) and Alternate E^2 (TRB), Module Project (PE), Module Performance Assessment (TRB)				
Yearly Pacing	**Mod 6:** 18 days	**Mods 1–6:** 107 days	**Remaining:** 33 days		**Total:** 140 days

Key: P&A = Practice & Application; ROS = Reflecting on the Section; SR = Spiral Rev; TB = Toolbox; Ex Prac= Extra Skill Practice; Ext = Extension; * more time

Block Scheduling (90 min class period)

	Day 1	Day 2	Day 3	Day 4	Day 5	Day 6	
Teach	Sec 1 Expl 1; Sec 2 Expl 1	Sec 3 Expl 1–2	Sec 3 Expl 3; Sec 4 Expl 1	Sec 4 Expl 2; Sec 5 Expl 1	Sec 5 Expl 2–3	Sec 6	Allow 3 days review/assess/projects
Apply/ Assess (P&A)	Sec 1: 1–10, ROS 13, SR 14–25; Sec 2: 2–8, 9–12, 14, 15, 17, 18, ROS 21, SR 22–28	Sec 3: 1a, 2, 4, 6, 9–12, SR 21–24	Sec 3: 14, 16–19, *ROS 20, SR 25–30; Sec 4: 1–11, SR 19–24	Sec 4: 12, 13, 15, 16, 17, *ROS 18; Sec 5: 2–6, 8, 9, SR 31–33	Sec 5: 10–18 (even), 19, 22, 24, 25, 26, 28, ROS 30, SR 34–40	Sec 6: 2–18 (even), 20–25, 27, ROS 28, SR 29–32	
Yearly Pacing	**Mod 6:** 9 days		**Mods 1–6:** 53 days		**Remaining:** 17 days		**Total:** 70 days

6-4

Materials List

Section	Materials
1	pennies, 1 in. squares, metric ruler, chalk or large newsprint with marker
2	object to represent a sandbag, watch or clock to time seconds, tape measure, Labsheet 2A, ruler, calculator (optional), graph paper
3	scissors, string, metric ruler, Labsheets 3A and 3B, uncooked spaghetti (or clear plastic ruler), graph paper, graphing software (optional); for E^2: ruler, string
4	no materials required
5	Labsheets 5A and 5B, pattern blocks, metric ruler, tracing paper, ruler, protractor, compass or round object, tape measure
6	Labsheets 6A–6C, paper clip; for R and A: protractor

Support Materials in this Resource Book

Section	Practice	Study Guide	Assessment	Enrichment
1	Section 1	Section 1	Quick Quiz	
2	Section 2	Section 2	Quick Quiz	
3	Section 3	Section 3	Quick Quiz, Mid-Module Quiz	Technology Activity, Alternate Extended Exploration
4	Section 4	Section 4	Quick Quiz	
5	Section 5	Section 5	Quick Quiz	
6	Section 6	Section 6	Quick Quiz	
Review/ Assess	Sections 1–6		Module Tests Forms A and B Standardized Assessment Module Performance Assessment Cumulative Test Modules 5–6	

Classroom Ideas

Bulletin Boards:
- diagram of Gulliver showing body ratios
- pictures of dinosaurs and their tracks
- M.C. Escher's artwork
- sports statistics with photographs

Student Work Displays:
- completed labsheets
- scatter plots from body ratios
- chair designs from the E^2

Interest Centers:
- skeleton to label with body ratios
- maps with cards to write real to scaled distance ratios
- spinners for playing *Dueling Spinners*

Visitors/Field Trips:
- artist, architect, cartographer, paleontologist

Technology:
- Module 6 Technology Activity in TRB for PE, p. 404
- graphing software
- *McDougal Littell Mathpack: Stats!*, CD-ROM/disks, Mac/Win

Home Involvement

The Math Gazette
Comparisons and Predictions

Sneak Preview!

Over the next four weeks in our mathematics class, we will be using ratios to compare measures, exploring rates and unit rates, using graphs to make predictions, solving proportions, comparing similar figures, measuring angles, and using percents for probabilities, while completing a thematic unit on Comparisons and Predictions. Some of the topics we will be discussing are:

✗ what it would be like to be one inch tall

✗ the Mississippi River flood of 1993

✗ record long jumps

✗ *Gulliver's Travels*

✗ the art of M. C. Escher

✗ probabilities related to sports events

Ask Your Student

What is a unit rate? (Sec. 2)

If two ratios are equivalent, what is true of their cross products? (Sec. 4)

How do you measure an angle with a protractor? (Sec. 5)

A softball player had 6 hits in 18 at-bats. About what percent is this? (Sec. 6)

Connections

Literature:
Students will read the poem, *One Inch Tall*, from *Where the Sidewalk Ends*, by Shel Silverstein. The poem describes some of the consequences of being one inch tall. Students may be interested in writing about being a different size, such as one foot tall, or twice as tall as they are now.

Students will also read an excerpt from *Gulliver's Travels*, by Jonathon Swift. The story describes Lemuel Gulliver's stay among the Lilliputians.

Social Studies:
Students will learn about teen volunteers who helped sandbag during the Mississippi River flood of 1993. They may be interested in finding out more about relief efforts for this flood or for the Red River flood of 1997. Possible resources include *the Reader's Guide to Periodical Literature* and the Internet.

Art:
Students will examine the geometry of drawings by M. C. Escher. They may be interested in creating their own Escher-like designs.

E² Project

Following Section 3, students will have about one week to complete the E² project, *The Ideal Chair*. Students will collect and use data to design the ideal classroom chair for students at their grade level.

Comparisons and Predictions

Section Title	Mathematics Your Student Will Be Learning	Activities
1: Mr. Tall and Mr. Short	♦ using ratios to make comparisons ♦ writing equivalent ratios	♦ use pennies and squares to measure and compare the heights of figures ♦ begin work on the Module Project, *Mystery Tracks*
2: The Sandbag Brigade	♦ using rates to make predictions ♦ finding unit rates	♦ collect and graph data while simulating a sandbag brigade
3: Body Ratios	♦ writing a ratio as a decimal ♦ using ratios to describe data ♦ fitting a line to data in a scatter plot	♦ compare students' measurements to body ratios described in *Gulliver's Travels* ♦ collect and analyze other body ratio data ♦ use graphing software to make a scatter plot ♦ continue work on the Module Project ♦ design a classroom chair
4: Jumping Ability	♦ using cross products ♦ solving proportions	♦ analyze data about jump lengths
5: Very Similar	♦ identifying similar and congruent figures ♦ using proportions to find unknown lengths ♦ measuring and drawing angles	♦ use pattern blocks to make similar polygons ♦ use a protractor to measure and draw angles ♦ continue work on the Module Project
6: Playing the Percentages	♦ using fractions to find and estimate percents ♦ making a tree diagram to find probabilities	♦ play the game *Dueling Spinners* ♦ draw tree diagrams ♦ complete the Module Project

MODULE 6

Activities to do at Home

♦ Look for rates and unit rates around the home. Examine food and cleanser labels, gas and electric meters, and cookbooks. (After Sec. 2)

♦ Choose and measure a body ratio, such as the length of a person's stride when walking to the person's height. Measure the ratio for several people; then create a rule that will predict a person's height, given the stride length. (After Sec. 3)

♦ Make a scale drawing of a household object. Start with a small object and make a scale drawing that is larger than the object. (After Sec. 5)

Related Topics

You may want to discuss these related topics with your student:

Design

Optical illusions

Blueprints

Olympic results

6-7

Section 1 Exploring Ratios

Section Planner

DAYS FOR MODULE 6
1 2 3 4 5 6 7 8 9 10 11 12

SECTION 1

First Day
Setting the Stage, p. 380
Exploration 1, pp. 381–383
Key Concepts, p. 384

Block Schedule

Day 1
Setting the Stage, Exploration 1, Key Concepts
(Day 1 continues in Sec. 2.)

RESOURCE ORGANIZER

Teaching Resources
- Practice and Applications, Sec. 1
- Study Guide, Sec. 1
- Warm-Up, Sec. 1
- Quick Quiz, Sec. 1

Section Overview

Section 1 will introduce students to the concepts of ratios and equivalent ratios, important foundations for the proportion topics that will follow this section. Students will use physical models to compare two quantities, the heights of two fictitious characters. They will write their comparison as a ratio. By manipulating the models they will discover that there are many equivalent forms of a ratio. For this reason, they will recognize how ratios can be used to make predictions. The students will also learn to write a ratio in three different ways.

Though equivalent ratios is a new topic, students will recognize their relationship to equivalent fractions, which they studied in Module 2. Should any students need to refresh their understanding of equivalent fractions, they can do so by referring to the discussion on page 114 in Module 2.

SECTION OBJECTIVES

Exploration 1
- use ratios to compare quantities
- express a ratio three ways: using the word *to*, a colon, or fraction form
- recognize and write equivalent ratios

ASSESSMENT OPTIONS

Checkpoint Questions
- Question 5 on p. 382
- Question 12 on p. 383

Embedded Assessment
- For a list of embedded assessment exercises see p. 6-11.

Performance Task/Portfolio
- Exercise 11 on p. 386 (language arts)
- ★ Exercise 12 on p. 386 (challenge)
- Exercise 13 on p. 386 (research)
- Module Project on p. 387

★ = a problem solving task that can be assessed using the Assessment Scales

SECTION 1 MATERIALS

Exploration 1
- pennies
- one-inch squares

Module Project on page 387
- metric ruler
- chalk or large newsprint and marker

Teacher Support for Pupil Pages 380–381

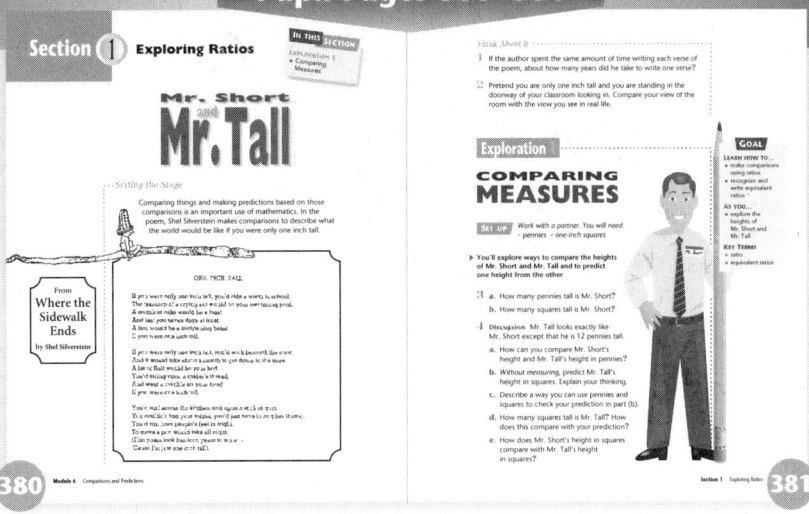

Setting the Stage

MOTIVATE

The reading on page 380 should be done in class, either individually or in groups. You may want to have students read the poem out loud to better enjoy its rhythm and rhyme. **Question 2** is a good question for the class to discuss together. If time allows, students could take turns standing at the classroom door and squatting down to help them imagine what it would be like to actually view the world from the "one inch" level. You could also have students pretend their height is just 1 in. less than the height of the room and predict the view of the classroom from 1 in. below the ceiling. Students could then compare and discuss the different views.

Exploration 1

PLAN

Classroom Management
Exploration 1 should be completed with students working in pairs. This exploration builds on students' previous understanding of equivalent fractions, so you may want to briefly review this topic before beginning the exploration. Each pair of students will need at least 20 pennies and 15 one-inch squares. It may be helpful to count out the number of pennies and one-inch squares into resealable bags so they can be distributed and collected more easily.

GUIDE

Developing Math Concepts
As students learn to make comparisons using ratios, you may want to present some real life examples to help students realize that this is a common and useful way to relate two quantities. Some examples are: My teacher is 3 times as old as me; my younger brother takes twice as long to get dressed in the mornings as I do; Anna only walks half as far to school as Luke. Invite students to share other everyday situations where they might use ratios to make comparisons.

Common Error When first working with ratios, students may incorrectly want to use addition or subtraction to compare. After working through the exploration, students should understand why these approaches are incorrect. Students may also write the order of the numbers in the ratio incorrectly. When explaining this concept, you may want to focus on the ratios written as fractions to help students better understand how the order of the numbers makes a difference.

Discussion In *Question 4(a)*, some students may compare by adding or subtracting—Mr. Tall is 4 pennies taller than Mr. Short. By the time they get to *Question 4(e)*, students should begin to see that they need to compare the heights using multiplication or division—Mr. Tall's height is $1\frac{1}{2}$ times the height of Mr. Short, or Mr. Short's height is $\frac{2}{3}$ the height of Mr. Tall.

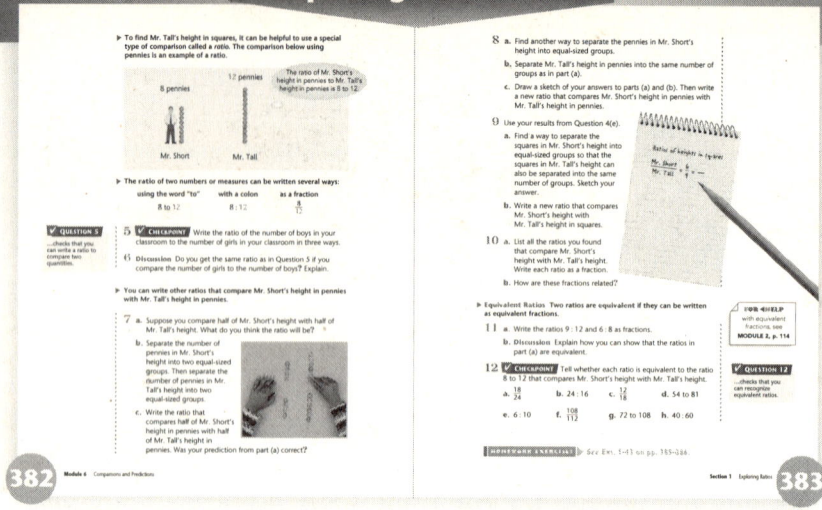

Exploration 1 continued

Classroom Examples
On a local television station, there are 12 min of commercials for every 18 min of programming. Write the ratio of the number of minutes of commercials to the number of minutes of programming in three different ways.

Answer: 12 to 18, 12 : 18, $\frac{12}{18}$

Checkpoint In *Question 5*, check to make sure students write the number of boys first in the ratio (as the numerator in the ratio written as a fraction). This is important for the class discussion in *Question 6*.

Discussion Students should realize that the numbers used in the comparisons must be written in the correct order when recording the ratios, and that a different ratio results in *Question 6* when they write the number of girls first.

Checkpoint For *Question 12*, students should use the methods discussed in *Question 11* to determine if the ratios are equivalent. Note that if students write 24 : 16 (part b) incorrectly as $\frac{16}{24}$, they will mistakenly think this ratio is equivalent to $\frac{8}{12}$.

HOMEWORK EXERCISES

See the Suggested Assignment for Day 1 on page 6-11. For Exercise Notes, see page 6-11.

CLOSE

Closure Question Why is it important to know how to use ratios and equivalent ratios? What is important about the numbers in ratios?

Sample Response: Ratios and equivalent ratios allow you to compare numbers or measures. The order that the numbers appear in a ratio is important.

Customizing Instruction

Second Language Learners In addition to the key terms *ratio* and *equivalent ratios*, you will want to make sure all students understand the meaning of the words *compare* and *predict* since they are used throughout the exploration.

Visual Learners Visual learners will find that sketching the various ratios is especially helpful in visualizing the comparisons. Encourage these students to sketch their answers if needed, even though the question may not ask them to do so.

Background Information Shel Silverstein's work ranges from amusing and whimsical to poignant and touching. Students who are interested in reading more of Shel Silverstein's works can look for *A Giraffe and a Half, Lafcadio The Lion Who Shot Back, The Missing Piece, A Light in the Attic,* and *The Giving Tree.*

Teacher Support for Pupil Pages 384–385

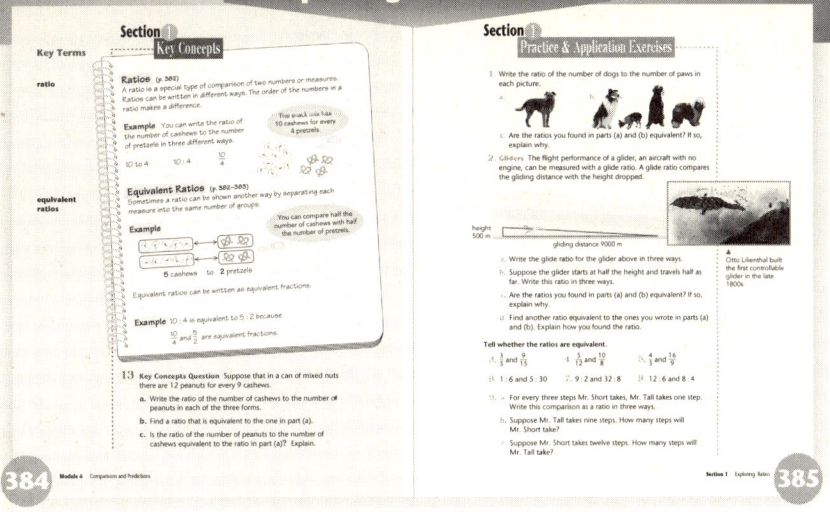

SUGGESTED ASSIGNMENT

Core Course
Day 1: Exs. 1–8, 9a, 10, 13–25

Extended Course
Day 1: Exs. 1–9, 12–25

Block Schedule
Day 1: Exs. 1–10, 13–25; Sec. 2, Exs. 2–12, 14, 15, 17, 18, 21–28

EMBEDDED ASSESSMENT

These section objectives are tested by the exercises listed.

Use ratios to compare quantities.
Exercises 1a, 1b, 9a

Express a ratio three ways: using the word *to*, a colon, or fraction form.
Exercises 2a, 2b

Recognize and write equivalent ratios.
Exercises 3–5

Practice & Application
EXERCISE NOTES

Technology For *Exs. 3–8*, students could use a calculator to write the ratios as decimals in order to check their equivalence.

Customizing Instruction

Home Involvement Those helping students at home will find the Key Concepts on page 384 a handy reference to the key ideas, terms, and skills of Section 1.

Absent Students For students who were absent for all or part of this section, the blackline Study Guide for Section 1 may be used to present the ideas, concepts, and skills of Section 1.

Extra Help For students who need additional practice, the blackline Practice and Applications for Section 1 provides additional exercises that may be used to confirm the skills of Section 1. The Extra Skill Practice on page 388 also provides additional exercises.

6-11

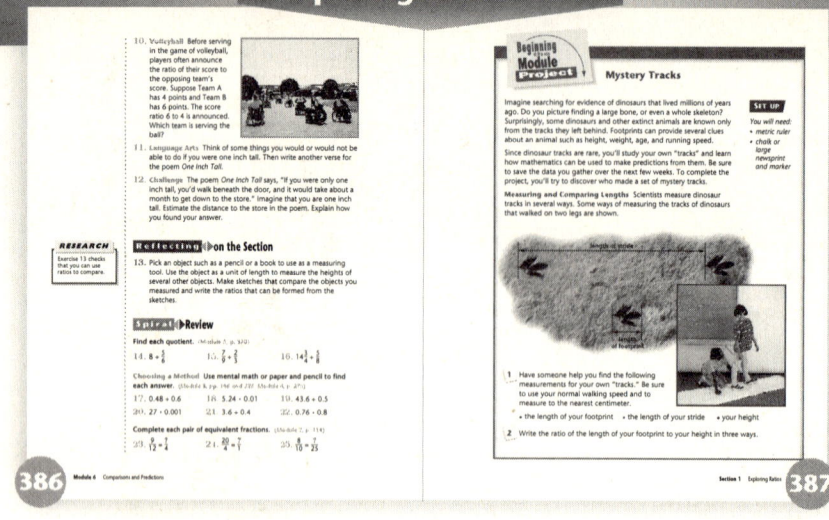

Practice & Application

Language Arts For *Ex. 11*, you may want to work with a Language Arts teacher at your school so your students write their verse with the same rhythmic pattern (called *meter*) as used in the poem.

Ongoing Assessment Students may want to save their answers to the Reflecting on the Section exercise *(Ex. 13)* for their portfolio to show their understanding of using ratios to make comparisons.

Beginning the Module Project

Students will need a partner as they begin working on the Module Project. You will want to decide ahead of time whether the measurements will be taken with or without students' shoes on. Enough floor space is needed so that students can walk several normal strides. Suggestions for ways to take the stride and footprint measurements include marking with chalk on the floor or using a marker on large sheets of newspaper. If it is convenient, you could measure outside on an asphalt or concrete surface by having students wet the bottom of their feet before walking. Their footprints will show up well on the pavement. Remind students to take and record the measurements carefully since they will be used as the data for several activities throughout this module.

Closing the Section

In this section, students have learned to write equivalent ratios and to make comparisons using ratios. Students can use what they have learned about ratios to draw a picture of Mr. Tall. Make sure that the lengths of his arms, legs, and body are all correct. Have students explain how they determined the various body measurements.

QUICK QUIZ ON THIS SECTION

1. A certain trail mix contains 12 peanuts for every 20 raisins. Write the ratio of raisins to peanuts in each of three ways.

2. Which pair of ratios is equivalent?
   A. 2 : 7 and 6 : 14
   B. $\frac{4}{11}$ and $\frac{12}{33}$
   C. 2 to 3 and 4 to 9

3. What is the ratio of vowels to consonants in the word MATHEMATICS?

4. An animal shelter has 12 dogs, 20 cats, and 4 other animals. What is the ratio of dogs to all of the animals at the shelter?

5. What is the ratio of the number of vertices of a polygon to its number of sides?

For answers, see Quick Quiz blackline on p. 6-62.

Section 2: Rates

Section Planner

DAYS FOR MODULE 6
1 **2** 3 4 5 6 7 8 9 10 11 12

SECTION 2

First Day
Setting the Stage, *p. 389*
Exploration 1, *pp. 390–391*
Key Concepts, *p. 393*

Block Schedule

Day 1 continued
Setting the Stage, Exploration 1, Key Concepts

RESOURCE ORGANIZER

Teaching Resources
- Practice and Applications, Sec. 2
- Study Guide, Sec. 2
- Warm-Up, Sec. 2
- Quick Quiz, Sec. 2

Section Overview

In Section 2, students will act out a problem involving rates. They will base their understanding of rates on ratios, which they studied in the previous section. Because they have learned to make predictions using ratios, they will be able to solve problems involving predictions based on a rate. Students will learn why a rate is a special type of ratio by identifying the units used to measure the quantities in their rates. They will describe how one measure depends on the other measure in a rate. Rate and unit rate, both key terms, are defined in this section. Students will also apply their understanding of equivalent ratios to find a unit rate.

In Module 4, students learned how to graph ordered pairs on a coordinate grid. In Exercise 18 of this section, they will plot the equivalent ratio data from the Setting the Stage activity on a coordinate grid. They will use the resulting graph to make predictions. For a review of graphing on a coordinate grid, refer students to page 288 in Module 4.

SECTION OBJECTIVES

Exploration 1
- find unit rates and use them to make predictions
- make a table to represent a rate and use patterns in the data to make predictions

ASSESSMENT OPTIONS

Checkpoint Questions
- Question 7 on p. 391
- Question 12 on p. 392

Embedded Assessment
- For a list of embedded assessment exercises see p 6-16.

Performance Task/Portfolio
- Exercise 16 on p. 394 (research)
- Exercise 20 on p. 395 (writing)
- Exercise 21 on p. 395 (journal)

SECTION 2 MATERIALS

Setting the Stage
- object to represent a sandbag
- watch or clock to time seconds
- tape measure

Practice & Application Exercises
- Labsheet 2A
- your classes brigade data
- ruler
- calculator
- graph paper

6-13

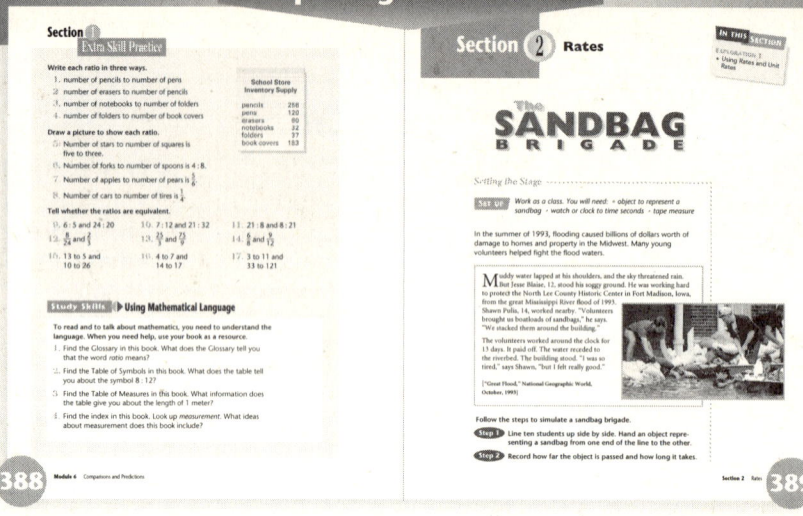

Setting the Stage

MOTIVATE

The reading on page 389 should be done in class, either individually or in groups. You will need to create plenty of floor space to conduct the brigade activity. To set up the sandbag brigade, have 10 students line up side by side spaced one arm's length apart. Use a tape measure to measure (in feet) the length of the brigade in feet. One alternative procedure is to measure out a 25 ft line on the floor and have 10 students space themselves equally along the line. This will give students easier numbers to work with in Practice & Application *Ex. 18*, which uses data from this activity. To actively involve all students in your class, divide them into groups and have each group do the activity independently.

Each group would then use their own data for *Questions 1–3* and *Ex. 18*. You could also have all the students form a single brigade line. In either case, be sure that students write the appropriate number under "Number of students" in the table on Labsheet 2A when completing *Ex. 18*. To time the brigade, start timing when the first person lifts the "sandbag," and stop timing when the last person in line places the "sandbag" on the floor. To be sure all students understand the instructions, you may wish to do a trial run of the brigade activity before you actually start timing. Any easily-handled object can be used to simulate the sandbag. Suggestions include a textbook or notebook, a backpack, or a 5 lb bag of potatoes.

Exploration 1

PLAN

Classroom Management After completing the sandbag brigade activity as a class, students should work on Exploration 1 in groups of 2 to 4. You may want to remind students that the ratio they record in *Question 3(c)* will be used in *Ex. 18*. Be sure all students record this ratio correctly.

Managing Time If the sandbag activity is done as a quick demonstration, you should be able to cover the Section in one day. If you spend more time on this activity, you could take two days to complete the Section. If so, you may wish to spend time in class on comparison shopping (see *Ex. 16* on p. 394) or on using a graph to make predictions (see *Ex. 18* on p.394).

Teacher Support for Pupil Pages 390–391

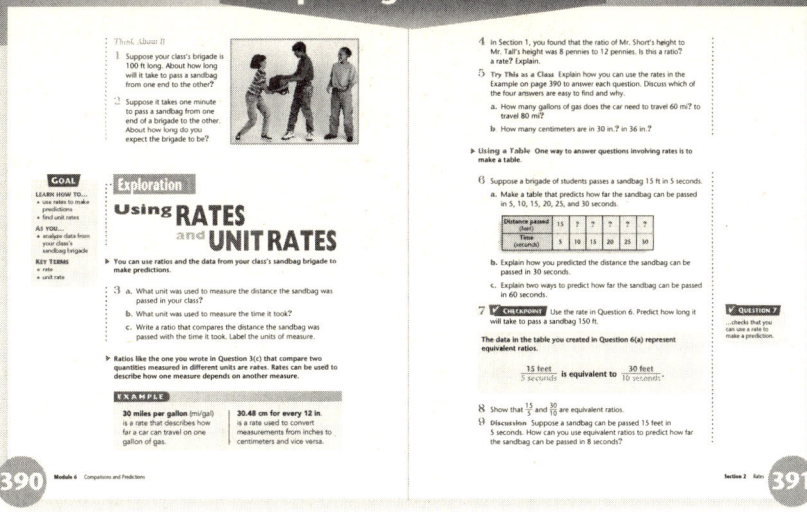

Exploration 1 continued

GUIDE

Developing Math Concepts In using rates to make predictions, you will want to remind students of their work with equivalent fractions. Though the concept of unit rate is not formally defined until after *Question 9*, some students may intuitively know how to find and use a unit rate to solve problems. When setting up equivalent ratios, remind students that it is still important to write the numbers in the ratios in the correct order, paying close attention to the units.

Common Error Students may set up the equivalent ratios incorrectly, especially if they fail to write the units beside the numbers. Remind students that to set up a correct equivalence, the units in both numerators must be the same and the units in the denominators must be the same. Stress to students that they will make this error less frequently if they always write in the units.

Try This as a Class *Question 5* gives students the opportunity to think about ways to use rates to solve problems before being shown these methods later. Students should realize that the easiest answers to find are the first one in part (a) and the second one in part (b) since they can be found using the given rate.

Checkpoint In *Question 7*, students can use equivalent fractions or multiplication to make their predictions. Some students may extend the table to find the answer, while others may think to find and use the unit rate.

Discussion By the time students reach *Question 9* in the exploration, they should be able to set up equivalent ratios and use equivalent ratio patterns to make the prediction. Some students may find and use the unit rate to make the prediction. If so, ask them to share their thinking with the class since unit rate is developed next in *Questions 10* and *11* on page 392.

Customizing Instruction

Alternative Approach 1 If it is not possible for students to actually do the sandbag brigade, a reasonable time for 10 students to pass the "sandbag" is about 9 s. Students who finish the exploration with extra time may wish to try the Extension problem (*Ex. 29*) on page 395.

Alternative Approach 2 To answer *Ex. 18*, students will need to use the class's sandbag brigade data from the beginning of the section. It may be a good idea to display the data on the board or overhead to be sure all students use the correct information, and to provide the information to students who may have been absent for this part of the exploration.

MODULE 6 ◆ SECTION 2

6-15

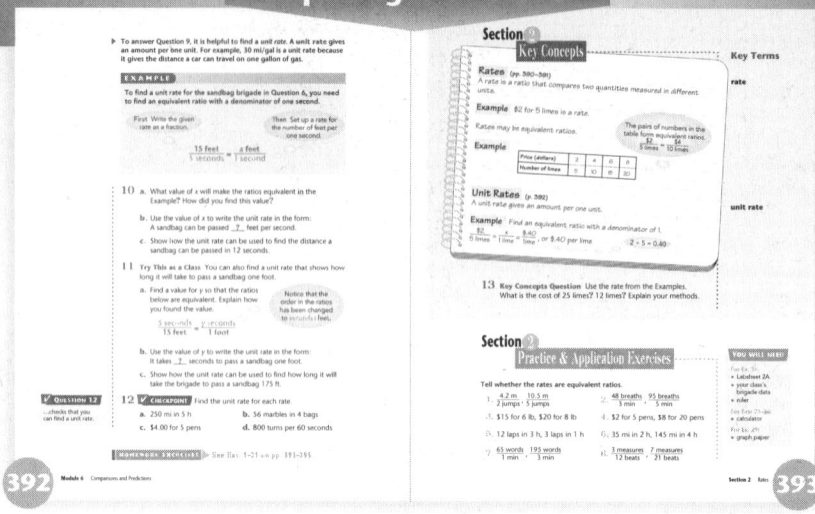

Exploration 1 continued

Classroom Examples
Suppose the rate in Question 6 was 12 ft in 5 s rather than 15 ft in 5 s. Find the unit rate.

Answer:
$\frac{12 \text{ ft}}{5 \text{ s}} = \frac{2.4 \text{ ft}}{1 \text{ s}}$, or 2.4 ft/s

Checkpoint In *Question 12*, encourage students to use mental math to find the unit rate for parts (a–c).

HOMEWORK EXERCISES

See the Suggested Assignment for Day 1 on page 6-16. For Exercise Notes, see page 6-16.

CLOSE

Closure Question How are ratios, rates, and unit rates alike? How are they different?

Sample Response: Ratios, rates, and unit rates are all comparisons between two numbers or measures. A ratio compares two numbers that are not measured or are measured with the same units, a rate compares two numbers measured with different units, and a unit rate compares two numbers with different units but gives its answer per one unit.

SUGGESTED ASSIGNMENT

Core Course
Day 1: Exs. 1–9 odd, 10, 11–17 odd, 18, 20–28

Extended Course
Day 1: Exs. 1–9 odd, 10, 11–17 odd, 18, 20–29

Block Schedule
Day 1: Sec. 1, Exs. 1–10, 13–25; Exs. 2–12, 14, 15, 17, 18, 21–28

Customizing Instruction

Home Involvement Those helping students at home will find the Key Concepts on page 393 a handy reference to the key ideas, terms, and skills of Section 2.

Absent Students For students who were absent for all or part of this section, the blackline Study Guide for Section 2 may be used to present the ideas, concepts, and skills of Section 2.

Extra Help For students who need additional practice, the blackline Practice and Applications for Section 2 provides additional exercises that may be used to confirm the skills of Section 2. The Extra Skill Practice on page 396 also provides additional exercises.

Teacher Support for Pupil Pages 394–395

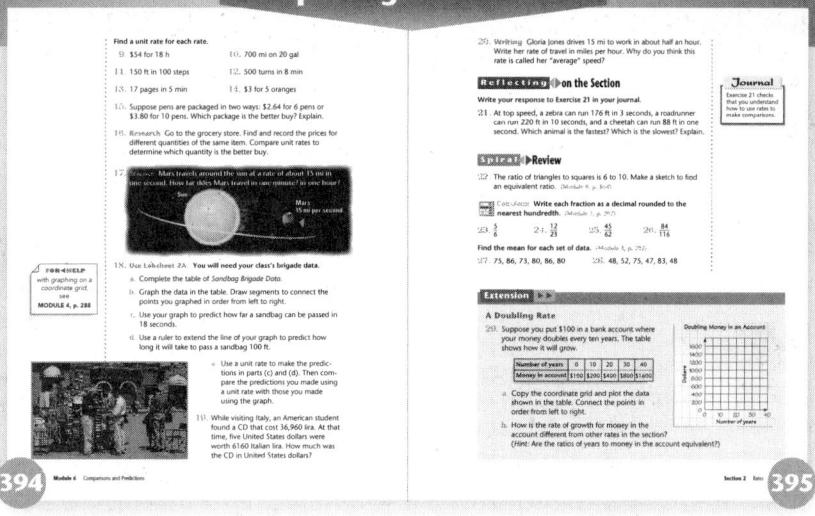

EMBEDDED ASSESSMENT

These section objectives are tested by the exercises listed.

Find unit rates and use them to make predictions.
Exercises 9, 11, 15, 18e

Make a table to represent a rate, and use patterns in the data to make predictions.
Exercise 18a

Practice & Application

EXERCISE NOTES

Developing Math Concepts
For *Exs. 9–14*, rates such as dollars per hour, miles per gallon, feet per step, and so on are preferable, while hours per dollar, gallons per mile, and so on are acceptable. In *Ex. 16*, if some students are unable to visit a grocery store, an alternative would be to bring in grocery store advertisements from different stores that show the prices of various items. Students could find the unit rates from the advertisements and then determine the better buy.

Research Rate of exchange is a useful application of unit rate, especially for those traveling to other countries. For *Ex. 19*, you may want to have students do research on the current rate of exchange between the U.S. dollar and the currency of various countries and present their findings to the class. All students could then determine the cost of various items in these countries based on the rate of exchange.

Ongoing Assessment You may want to have students save their answers to *Ex. 21* for their portfolio to show their understanding of how to use rates to make comparisons.

Closing the Section

While analyzing data from the sandbag brigade activity, students have learned how to find unit rates and to use rates to make predictions. Students will be able to reflect on these understandings while answering the Reflecting on the Section exercise (*Ex. 21*). You may wish to have students share their answers to this exercise with the class.

QUICK QUIZ ON THIS SECTION

1. Are the rates equivalent ratios?
   a. 120 mi in 2 h, 210 mi in 3 h
   b. $10 for 50 lb, $25 for 125 lb

2. Find a unit rate for each rate.
   a. 1000 m in 5 min
   b. $120 for 15 h

3. Which is the better buy, 5 lb of flour for $1.69 or 12 lb of flour for $4.25?

4. If Eric can read 130 pages in 2 h, how long will it take him to read a 325 page novel?

5. It takes $\frac{1}{3}$ c of sugar to make 12 muffins. Complete the table.

Cups of sugar	Number of muffins
$\frac{2}{3}$	?
1	?
2	?
3	?

For answers, see Quick Quiz blackline on p. 6-63.

6-17

Section 3: Using Ratios

Section Planner

DAYS FOR MODULE 6
1 2 **3** 4 5 **6** 7 8 9 10 11 12

SECTION 3

First Day
Setting the Stage, p. 397
Exploration 1, pp. 398–399

Second Day
Exploration 2, pp. 400–401

Third Day
Exploration 3, pp. 402–403
Key Concepts, p. 405

Block Schedule

Day 2
Setting the Stage, Exploration 1, Exploration 2

Day 3
Exploration 3, Key Concepts
(Day 3 continues in Sec. 4.)

RESOURCE ORGANIZER

Teaching Resources
- Practice and Applications, Sec. 3
- Study Guide, Sec. 3
- Mid-Module Quiz
- Technology Activity, Sec. 3
- Warm-Up, Sec. 3
- Quick Quiz, Sec. 3

Section Overview

In Section 3, students will act out a problem involving body ratios, then record data and use ratios to make predictions based on the data. Key terms introduced in this section are *"nice" fraction*, *scatter plot*, and *fitted line*. Students will write ratios as decimals, just as they wrote fractions as decimals in Module 3. As they organize their body ratios in a table, the students will, where possible, use "nice" fractions to describe the mean of the ratios. In Explorations 1 and 2, they will use their body ratio data to make predictions. In Exploration 3, students will use a scatter plot to make their predictions. Instructions are given on the technology activity (page 404) for making a scatter plot and drawing a fitted line using computer software. Possible areas of review for this section include writing a fraction as a decimal and plotting points. The decimal review can be found in Module 3 on page 202 and a review of plotting points can be found in Module 4 on page 288.

SECTION OBJECTIVES

Exploration 1
- use ratio as a tool for investigating measurements
- write the decimal form of a ratio to make comparisons

Exploration 2
- find and use a "nice" fraction form of a ratio to describe data and make predictions

Exploration 3
- make a scatter plot
- fit a line to data in a scatter plot and use it to make predictions

ASSESSMENT OPTIONS

Checkpoint Questions
- Question 8 on p. 399
- Question 14 on p. 401
- Question 21 on p. 403

Embedded Assessment
- For a list of embedded assessment exercises see p. 6-23.

Performance Task/Portfolio
- Exercise 1b on p. 406 (create your own)
- Exercise 15 on p. 408 (home involvement)
- Exercises 17, 18 (writing)
- Module Project on p. 410
- Standardized Testing on p. 411
- ★ Extended Exploration on p. 412

★ = a problem solving task that can be assessed using the Assessment Scales

---

SECTION 3 MATERIALS

Exploration 1
- scissors
- string
- metric ruler

Exploration 2
- Labsheet 3A
- scissors
- string
- metric ruler

Exploration 3
- completed Labsheet 3A
- Labsheet 3B
- uncooked spaghetti
- graph paper

Teacher Support for Pupil Pages 396–397

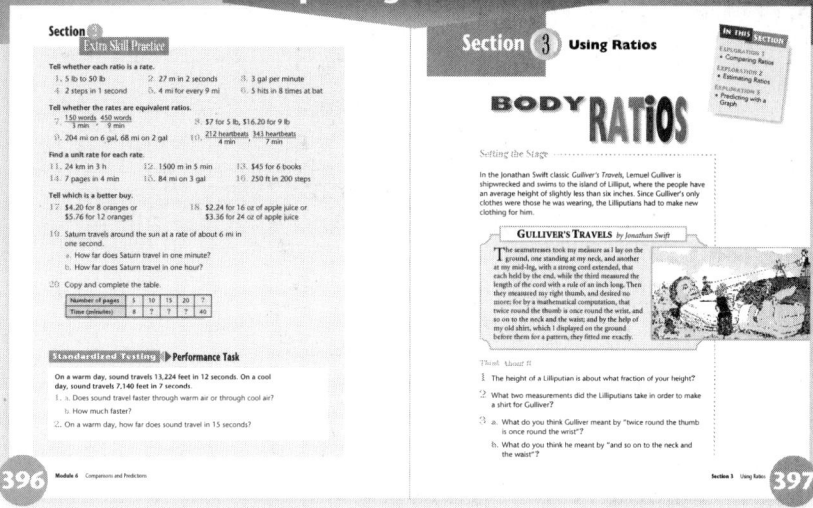

Setting the Stage

MOTIVATE

The reading on page 397 should be done in class, either individually or in groups. To help students get an idea of the size of things on the island of Lilliput, you may wish to present some other mathematical facts from the story. Based on knowing that a Lilliputian is about 6 in. tall, you could have students estimate the following: the length of a Lilliputian's sword (3 in.), the tallest trees in their land (7 ft), the height of their horses $\left(4\frac{1}{2} \text{ in.}\right)$, the capacity of one of their large barrels (less than half a pint), the number of their beds put together that it took to make a bed for Gulliver (600), the number of tailors it took to make Gulliver's clothes (300), and the number of Lilliputians it would take to equal the length of Gulliver's sword (5 Lilliputian men). Students may enjoy making their estimates in small groups or with a partner, then sharing their estimates with the class.

Exploration 1

PLAN

Classroom Management
Exploration 1 is best performed in groups of 2 to 4. Students should work with a partner to measure around their wrist and thumb. When measuring around the thumb, caution students to be sure they wrap the string around the base of the thumb so that the measurements are comparable. Also, be sure to use regular string as opposed to yarn which will stretch during use.

Organizing Groups Although mixed groupings are suggested for most cooperative work, you may want to consider grouping girls and boys separately for this exploration (and also for Exploration 2). Some students may feel uncomfortable taking measurements of classmates of the opposite gender.

6-19

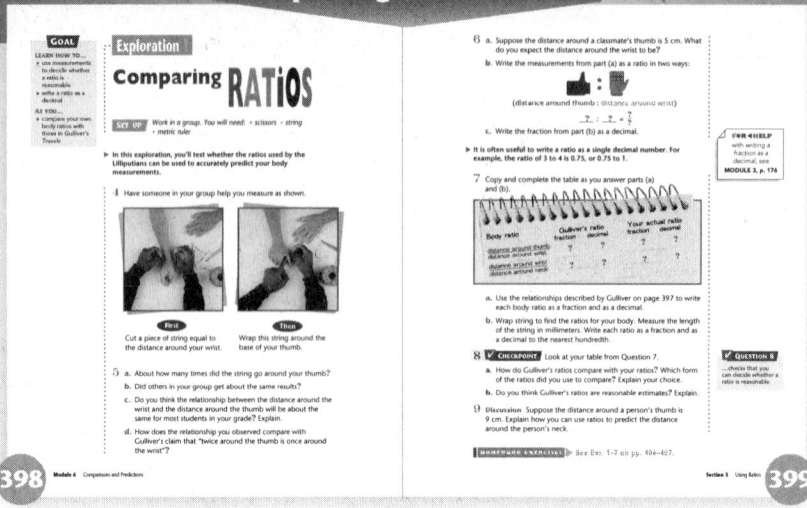

Exploration 1 continued

GUIDE

Developing Math Concepts
You may want to remind students to think back to their work comparing fractions in Section 1 as they learn to compare ratios by writing them as decimals. You might also encourage students to use number sense to compare the ratios whenever possible. It is important that students have a good understanding of writing ratios as decimals before moving on to Explorations 2 and 3 where they will use both forms of a ratio to make predictions. Students will need to round their decimals to the nearest hundredth in *Question 7(b)*.

Checkpoint As students think about their answers to *Question 8*, you may want to have them share information from their completed tables from *Question 7*. Knowing some of the other ratios that were found should help them realize that the decimal form of a ratio is often the better form for making comparisons. The shared results could also help them decide in part (b) if Gulliver's ratios are reasonable estimates to use.

Discussion In *Question 9*, it may be helpful to suggest that students look back at their answers to *Question 3* to remind them of the relationships between the thumb, wrist, and neck measurements. Point out how setting up equivalent ratios can help students predict the distance around the person's neck. Students might also be able to observe the relationship between the thumb, wrist, and neck measurements by looking at their completed table from *Question 7*.

HOMEWORK EXERCISES

See the Suggested Assignment for Day 1 on page 6-23. For Exercise Notes, see page 6-23.

Customizing Instruction

Alternative Approach If available, students could also use metric tape measures to take the measurements for their thumb, wrist, and neck. Students would simply wrap the tape measure around once and record the number of millimeters. They could then look at their recorded measures to determine the 1 to 2 ratio.

Second Language Learners Some students may need extra help understanding the sentence structure in the reading from *Gulliver's Travels*. The second sentence in the reading may be easier to understand if you explain it as if it were three separate sentences, pausing at each semicolon to clarify the complete thought. You may wish to have the students explain the meaning of each sentence back to you in his or her own words to check their understanding.

Background Information Though Jonathan Swift (1667–1745) never left England or Ireland, he wrote some of the world's most famous travel stories. *Gulliver's Travels*, written in 1726, has been read for over 200 years in countries around the world. It is the best-known of Swift's skillful satires.

Teacher Support for Pupil Pages 400–401

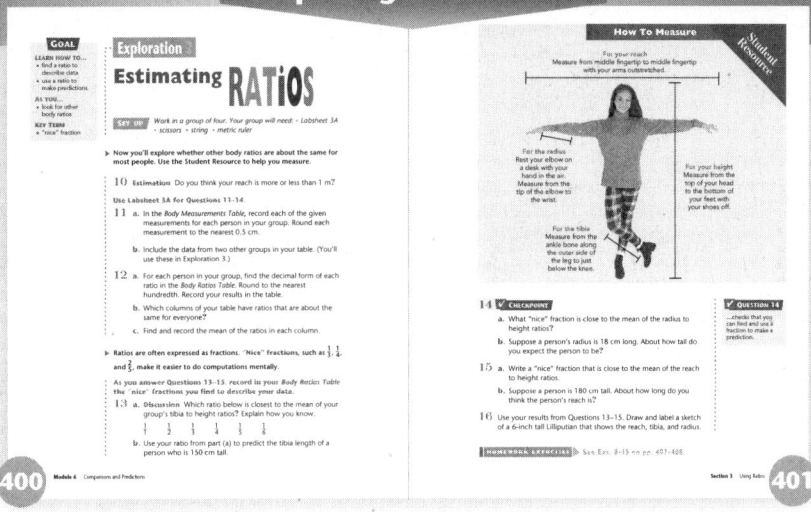

Exploration 2

PLAN

Classroom Management
Exploration 2 is best performed in groups of 4, with students working in partners to take the actual body measurements. In place of string, wide ribbon also works well for measuring. You may want to decide ahead of time which groups will share data and how that sharing will take place. Students will be rounding their measurements to the nearest 0.5 cm, so you may want to briefly review how to do this before beginning the exploration. Students will use the data from their completed Labsheet 3A later in Exploration 3 and then again in the Practice & Application section (*Exs. 13* and *17*).

GUIDE

Developing Math Concepts
Although proportions are not formally introduced until Section 4, students may instinctively use proportional thinking as they make predictions from ratios. Therefore, this exploration is important for building a conceptual framework for students' later work with proportions. To help students understand the key term "nice" fraction, you may want to discuss why they think the fractions in *Question 13* are considered "nice" fractions when other fractions are not. For *Question 16*, you may want to point out to students that although the units are now inches, the ratios are the same as the ones they found in centimeters.

Managing Time For any student who is absent for this exploration, you may want to make a copy of a group member's Labsheet 3A for the student to use in Exploration 3.

Checkpoint In *Question 14*, students will probably choose one of the "nice" fractions shown in *Question 13* to represent their data. All students in the group should understand and be able to explain why that particular fraction was chosen.

HOMEWORK EXERCISES

See the Suggested Assignment for Day 2 on page 6-23. For Exercise Notes, see page 6-23.

Customizing Instruction

Alternative Approach 1 Students who finish with extra time may wish to try a variation of *Question 16* on page 401. After visiting the Lilliputians, Gulliver went to a place called Brobdingnag, whose inhabitants are giants. There he meets a nine-year-old girl who stands forty feet high. In addition to their sketch of the Lilliputian, students could also draw and label a sketch that shows the reach, tibia, and radius of a Brobdingnag inhabitant.

Second Language Learners You will want to explain to students that the *tibia* is the larger of the two lower leg bones between the knee and the ankle, and the *radius* is the shorter of the two forearm bones between the elbow and the wrist. Be sure students do not confuse the radius bone with the term radius as it applies to the measurement of a circle.

Visual Learners Some students may appreciate a simple sketch on the board or overhead of a person showing the location of the three measures *reach*, *radius*, and *tibia*.

6-21

Teacher Support for Pupil Pages 402–403

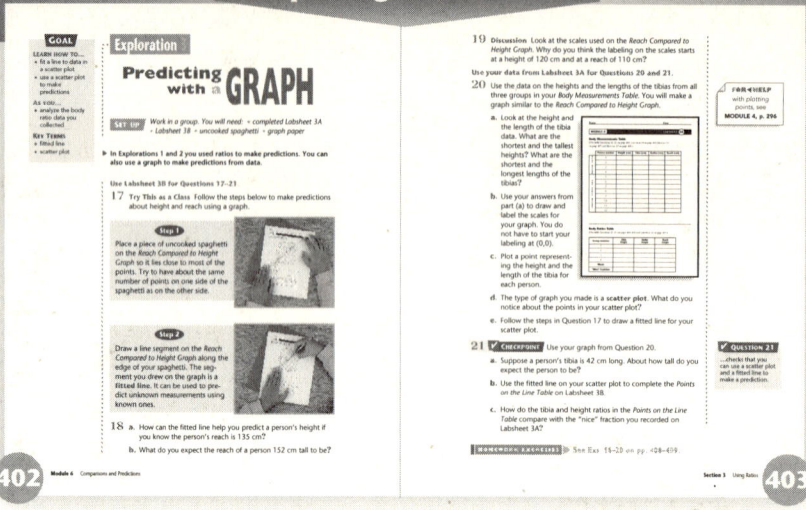

Exploration 3

PLAN

Classroom Management
Exploration 3 is best performed in groups of 2 to 4. When drawing the line segment on the graph along the edge of the spaghetti, it may be helpful for students to work in pairs so one student can hold the ends of the spaghetti steady while the other draws the segment. A clear plastic ruler can be used as an alternative to using a piece of uncooked spaghetti. You may want to prepare an overhead transparency of Labsheet 3B to use for *Question 17*. (See the Try This as a Class note on this page.) Teacher guidance is recommended for *Question 20(b)* as students determine the scales for their graph. (See the Developing Math Concepts notes on the next page.) Students will need Labsheet 3B for *Questions 17–21* and Labsheet 3A for *Questions 20* and *21*. Students will also need Labsheet 3A for *Exs. 13* and *17* in the Practice & Application section.

GUIDE

Try This as a Class Before students draw their line in *Question 17*, you may want to ask them what they notice about the points on the graph. Students should notice that although the points "cluster" in the middle, they tend to fall along a line. You may want to model finding a fitted line by making an overhead transparency of Labsheet 3B and placing a piece of uncooked spaghetti or a clear ruler along the points on the graph. As you move the "line" to various places on the graph, students could tell you as a class where they think it best "fits" the data points. Students could then draw their own fitted line.

Discussion In *Question 19*, it is important that students understand how the scale on the graph relates to the data, as they will be choosing a scale for their own data in *Question 20(b)*. In addition to looking at 120 cm and 110 cm as starting points on the graph, you may also want to point out the two greatest values and ask students why they think the scale stops at these values. You may also want to discuss why a 10 cm interval is appropriate to represent this data.

Customizing Instruction

Alternative Approach Students who finish the exploration with extra time may wish to use the data on Labsheet 3A to create a scatter plot that shows the relationship between height and tibia length. After the scatter plot is complete, students could draw a fitted line and use it to make predictions from their graph.

Second Language Learners You may want to explain that the word *scatter* means to "distribute loosely as if by sprinkling or strewing." Thus, the points on a *scatter plot* can be thought of as being distributed loosely about the graph as opposed to all falling exactly on the same line.

Visual Learners When first learning to draw a fitted line, some students may find it helpful to be able to look at actual lines drawn on the graph. You could do this by making several copies of Labsheet 3B and drawing a line in a different place on each copy. From these examples, students could choose the one they think best "fits" the data. This would give students an unchanging (permanent) visual to use for comparison as opposed to the "line" they can no longer see when the piece of uncooked spaghetti is moved to a different place on the graph.

6-22

Teacher Support for Pupil Pages 404–405

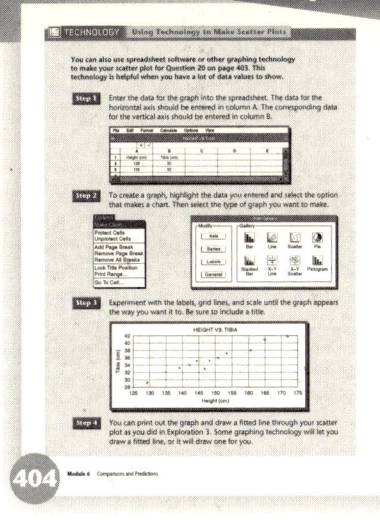

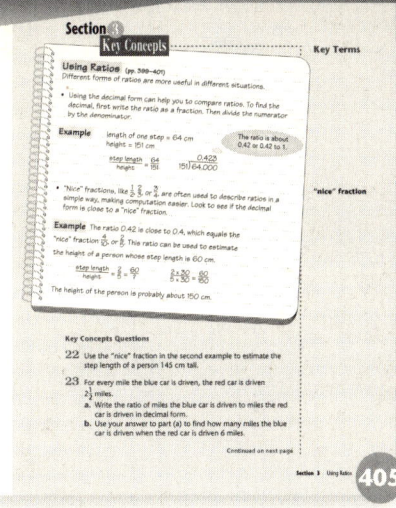

Exploration 3 continued

HOMEWORK EXERCISES

See the Suggested Assignment for Day 3 on page 6-23. For Exercise Notes, see page 6-23.

CLOSE

Closure Question Why do you think estimation is useful when comparing ratios and making predictions from graphs that involve experimental data?

Sample Response: Experimental data often do not fit into an exact pattern or do not produce values that can easily be calculated exactly. Using estimations, such as "nice" fractions or "nice" values, can often give a sufficient estimate for the problem.

SUGGESTED ASSIGNMENT

Core Course
Day 1: Exs. 1a, 2–7, 21–24
Day 2: Exs. 8–14
Day 3: Exs. 16–18, 20, 25–30

Extended Course
Day 1: Exs. 1–7, 21–24
Day 2: Exs. 8–14
Day 3: Exs. 16–18, 20, 25–30

Block Schedule
Day 2: Exs. 1a, 2, 4, 6, 9–12, 21–24
Day 3: Exs. 14, 16–20, 25–30; Sec. 4, Exs. 1–11, 19–24

EMBEDDED ASSESSMENT

These section objectives are tested by the exercises listed.

Use ratio as a tool for investigating measurements.
Exercises 1a, 8

Write the decimal form of a ratio to make comparisons.
Exercises 2, 4, 6

Find and use a "nice" fraction form of a ratio to describe data and make predictions.
Exercises 9–12, 14

Make a scatter plot.
Exercise 17a

Fit a line to data in a scatter plot and use it to make predictions
Exercises 16, 17b, 18

Customizing Instruction

Home Involvement Those helping students at home will find the Key Concepts on pages 405 and 406 a handy reference to the key ideas, terms, and skills of Section 3.

Absent Students For students who were absent for all or part of this section, the blackline Study Guide for Section 3 may be used to present the ideas, concepts, and skills of Section 3.

Extra Help For students who need additional practice, the blackline Practice and Applications for Section 3 provides additional exercises that may be used to confirm the skills of Section 3. The Extra Skill Practice on page 411 also provides additional exercises.

MODULE 6 ◆ SECTION 3

6-23

Teacher Support for Pupil Pages 406–407

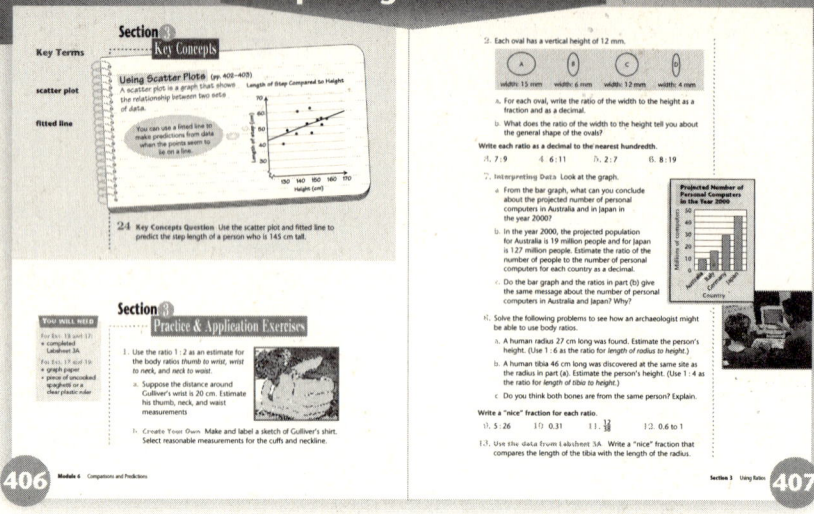

Practice & Application

EXERCISE NOTES

Developing Math Concepts
You may wish to extend *Ex. 2* by having students apply what they have learned about width to height ratios and their effect on the shape of the ovals, to the width to height ratios for squares and rectangles. Ask: "What width to height ratio does a square have? What would a rectangle with a width to height ratio of 0.5 look like? What are some possible dimensions for a rectangle with a width to height ratio of 0.25?" *Ex. 8(b)* is a good exercise for assessing whether students can use their reasoning skills to solve a problem. For *Exs. 9–13*, you may want to point out that students are not limited to just the "nice" fractions presented in the section.

Interpreting Data For *Ex. 7(c)*, students should realize that the bar graph and the ratios give a different impression. By finding the ratio in part (b), the number of people per computer for each country is determined, information that cannot be obtained from the bar graph alone. The ratio causes a person to think differently about the bar graph, especially when they realize that there are actually more computers per person in Australia than in Japan. In considering just the bar graph alone, a reader might mistakenly think that the reverse is true.

Background Information For *Ex. 8*, students may be interested to know that archaeologists actually use body ratios to make estimates and predictions, and to help them piece together information about past cultures. Forensic scientists also rely on body ratios to help them uncover clues and solve crimes.

Writing As students write their answers to *Ex. 8(b)*, encourage them to rely on the proportional reasoning skills they have developed in this section. You may want to have them think back to their work from Section 1 where they learned to compare the height of Mr. Short and Mr. Tall by using multiplication and division instead of by using addition and subtraction.

Teacher Support for Pupil Pages 408–409

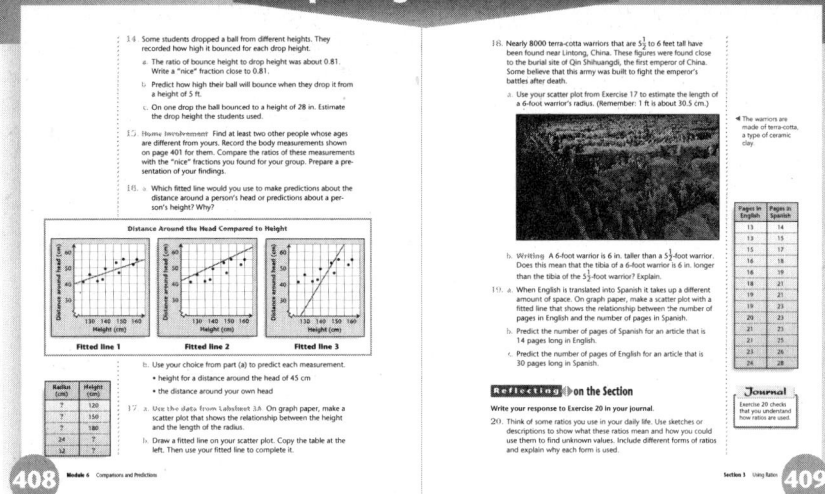

Practice & Application

Developing Math Concepts
Ex. 16 provides a good opportunity to check that all students understand the concepts of a fitted line. Students having difficulty with this concept should refer to page 402.

Ongoing Assessment You may wish to have students save their answer to *Ex. 20* for their portfolio to show their understanding of using ratios.

Research Students may wish to research the excavation of the terra-cotta army of Emperor Qin Shihuangdi presented in *Ex. 18*.

Writing For *Ex. 19*, you may wish to have any students proficient in Spanish translate this exercise into Spanish as an example of how the translation takes up a different amount of space.

Teacher Support for Pupil Pages 410–411

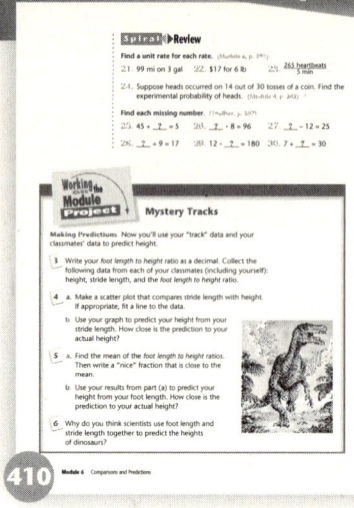

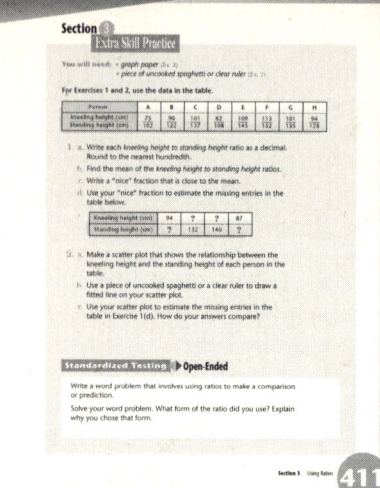

Working on the Module Project

You will want to provide an opportunity for students to collect the data from their classmates. To organize the information, you may want to have students create tables similar to the ones on Labsheet 3A. Remind students to choose their scale carefully when making their scatter plot. You will want to decide ahead of time whether you would like all students to use the same scale on the axes of their graphs. If you allow students to make their own choices, you may want to discuss as a class which scales and intervals are most appropriate for their data. If students use different intervals, it may also be interesting to have them share their scatter plots with the class for comparison.

As student think about their answer to **Question 6**, you may want to point out that the more data scientists have to base their predictions on, the more accurate their predictions will be.

Closing the Section

Students have learned to use different forms of ratios, and to use "nice" fractions to make their computations easier. Students have explored real-life applications of ratios as they used them to describe data and make predictions. In plotting data from their body measurements, students also learned to use scatter plots and a fitted line to make estimates and predictions. Students can reflect on their understanding of these concepts as they respond to the following questions: "How can "nice" fractions make your work with ratios easier? How can ratios be used to make estimates from data? How is a fitted line used to make predictions from a scatter plot?"

Quick Quiz on this Section

1. What is the ratio of the length of one side of a regular hexagon to its perimeter? If a regular hexagon has 12 in. sides, what is its perimeter?

2. Write each ratio as a decimal to the nearest hundredth.
   a. 8 : 11
   b. 5 : 9
   c. 13 : 20

3. Write a "nice" fraction for each ratio.
   a. 12 : 58
   b. 0.39
   c. 43 to 99

4. Make a scatter plot using the data in the table. Use the scatter plot to predict the missing numbers in the table.

1	2	3	4	5	6	8	11
2	5	8	12	?	18	?	?

For answers, see Quick Quiz blackline on p. 6-64.

Section 4 Proportions

Section Planner

DAYS FOR MODULE 6
1 2 3 4 5 **6 7** 8 9 10 11 12

SECTION 4

First Day
Setting the Stage, p. 413
Exploration 1, pp. 414–415

Second Day
Exploration 2, pp. 416–417
Key Concepts, p. 418

Block Schedule

Day 3 continued
Setting the Stage, Exploration 1

Day 4
Exploration 2, Key Concepts
(Day 4 continues in Sec. 5.)

RESOURCE ORGANIZER

Teaching Resources
- Practice and Applications, Sec. 4
- Study Guide, Sec. 4
- Warm-Up, Sec. 4
- Quick Quiz, Sec. 4

Section Overview

In Section 4, students will begin by reviewing equivalent ratios. In Section 1, they learned how to express equivalent ratios as equivalent fractions. In this section students will compare the cross products in a proportion to determine whether two ratios are equal. Using both pencil and paper and a calculator, they will also use cross products and division to find the missing term in a proportion. Having learned the cross product property of proportions, students will model real life problems with proportions, which they will then solve. Students will identify problem situations in which a proportion is not an appropriate way to solve some problems that involve ratios because a comparison between the two quantities cannot be made.

SECTION OBJECTIVES

Exploration 1
- use cross products to find the missing term in a proportion

Exploration 2
- write and use proportions to solve problems and make predictions
- explore when using a proportion is or is not appropriate

ASSESSMENT OPTIONS

Checkpoint Questions
- Question 7 on p. 415
- Question 10 on p. 415
- Question 15 on p. 417

Embedded Assessment
- For a list of embedded assessment exercises see p. 6-31.

Performance Task/Portfolio
- Exercise 18 on p. 421 (oral report)

Teacher Support for Pupil Pages 412–413

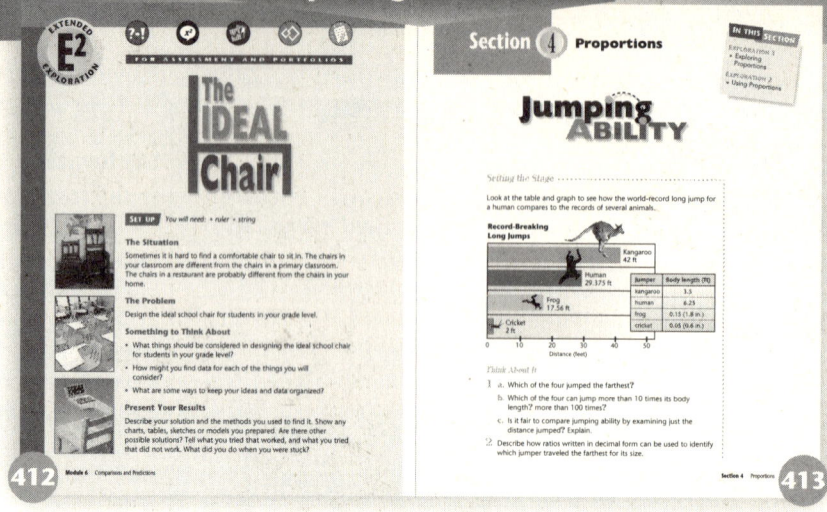

Setting the Stage

MOTIVATE

Students should study the table and graph on page 413 before answering *Questions 1* and *2*. You may want to tell students that a long jumper is striving for distance only and that his or her height during the jump is not measured. In the long jump, contestants run full speed down a runway to a takeoff board. The athlete may step on the board, but must not allow any portion of the foot to go beyond it. If time allows, you could have students from the class measure the distance they can long jump. If you do, you may want to work with a physical education teacher on this activity. Doing such an activity would provide students with an interesting point of reference as they think about the information shown in the table and on the graph.

Exploration 1

PLAN

Classroom Management
Students can work through Exploration 1 individually or in groups of 2 to 4. *Questions 3*, *6*, and *11(a)* are designated for whole class discussion so that all students have the same understanding of the underlying concepts. *Question 8* is highlighted for the class to work together so you can guide students to understand the steps in solving a proportion.

Customizing Instruction

Alternative Approach Students who finish the exploration with extra time may wish to research the jumping ability of other animals. They could then find the ratio of body length to long jump distance and compare these ratios with the ratios for the data on page 413.

Second Language Learners Since the phrase *cross products* is new to students, you may want to discuss how the two words work together to give the phrase its meaning. Some students may need to be reminded that a product is the result obtained by multiplying.

Visual Learners You may wish to post a copy of the proportion showing the circled numbers from the Example on page 414 to serve as a visual reminder of the meaning of cross products. Students could also create their own visuals using arrows or other symbols to illustrate the cross products of a proportion.

Teacher Support for Pupil Pages 414–415

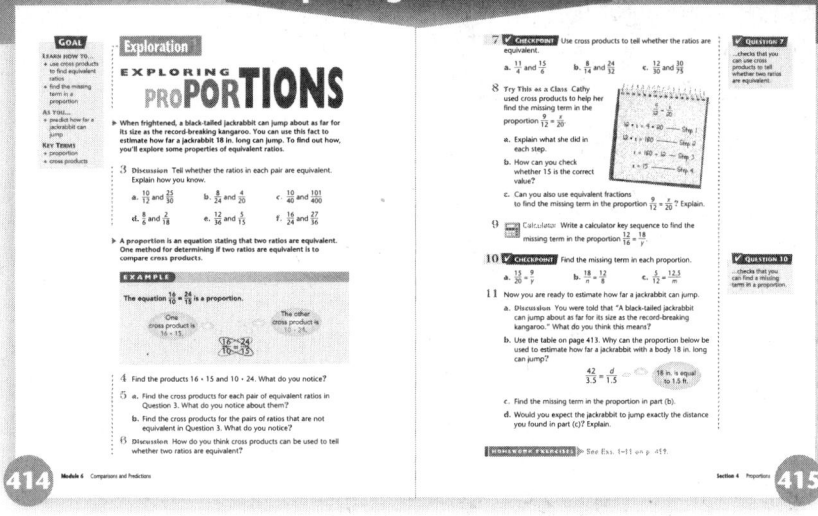

Exploration I continued

GUIDE

Developing Math Concepts
All students should understand that a fair comparison of jumping ability cannot be made by considering just the length of the jump. Both *Questions 1(c)* and *11(a)* indicate that a more meaningful comparison is made by using ratios to compare jumping distance to body length. At the end of the exploration, students use a proportion to estimate how far a jackrabbit can jump. Students will revisit this skill in Exploration 2 where they use a proportion to make a prediction. In *Question 8*, students will consider two methods of solving a proportion—finding cross products and finding an equivalent fraction. Be sure they understand that the value of x in the proportion $\frac{9}{12} = \frac{x}{20}$ is the number that makes the cross products $9 \cdot 20$ and $12 \cdot x$ equal. To solve the equation $12 \cdot x = 180$, students should think, "180 is 12 times what number?"

Discussion In *Question 3*, point out that students can use any number of approaches to determine if the ratios are equivalent, including fraction number sense, simplifying the fractions, multiplying or dividing both numerator and denominator by the same number, looking for numerator and denominator relationships, or writing the ratios as decimals.

Classroom Examples
Show that the equation $\frac{8}{14} = \frac{12}{21}$ is a proportion.

Answer:

Since $8 \cdot 21 = 168$ and $14 \cdot 12 = 168$, the cross products are equal. Therefore, the fractions are equivalent and the equation is a proportion.

Discussion In *Question 6*, students should realize that if the cross products are equal, then the ratios are equivalent. Since the definition of proportion was presented in the Example prior to *Question 6*, you may now want to ask students which pairs of ratios in *Question 3* could be written as proportions. (the ratios in parts (a) and (e))

Checkpoint In *Question 7*, you may want to point out that cross products can be found for any two ratios, especially when other comparison methods are difficult or inefficient.

Checkpoint Although students can use other methods to find each missing term in *Question 10*, encourage them to practice using the cross products method.

Discussion In *Question 11(a)*, some students may incorrectly think the jackrabbit is able to jump the same distance as the kangaroo. Emphasizing the phrase "as far for its size" will help students think about the comparison using proportional reasoning. To help students answer part (b), you can ask: "What does each ratio represent? How do you know the ratios are equivalent?"

HOMEWORK EXERCISES

See the Suggested Assignment for Day 1 on page 6-31. For Exercise Notes, see page 6-31.

Teacher Support for Pupil Pages 416–417

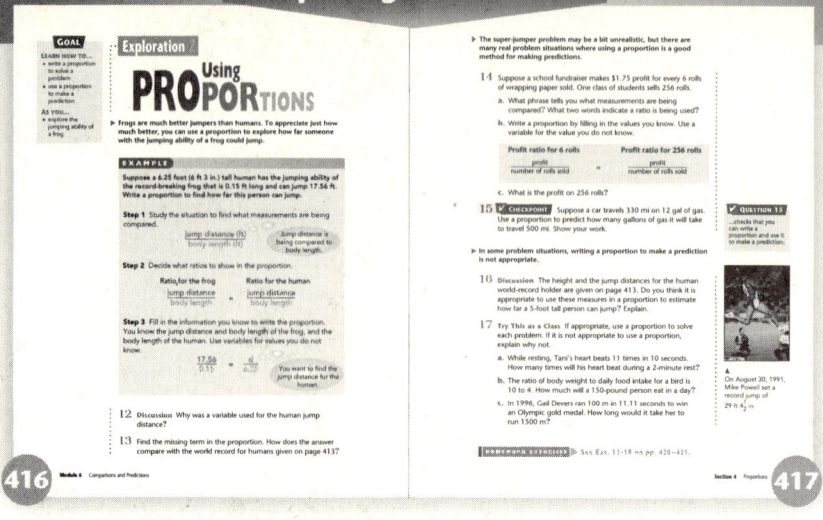

Exploration 2

PLAN

Classroom Management
Exploration 2 can be completed individually or in groups of 2 to 4. *Questions 12* and *16* are highlighted as appropriate for class discussion so you can guide students' conceptual understandings of setting up and using proportions. *Question 17* is designed to be completed as a class so students can benefit from their classmates' ideas on when it is appropriate to use a proportion.

GUIDE

Developing Math Concepts
In *Question 13*, be sure students understand what is represented by the value they find (the distance a 6.25 ft human with the jumping ability of a frog could jump). For *Question 17*, some students may need exposure to more examples before they can confidently tell whether it is appropriate to use a proportion to solve a problem.

Common Error Students may set up the proportions incorrectly by putting the units in the wrong place. Remind students that each ratio must compare the units in the same "order." Writing in the units as they write each ratio will help students avoid this error.

Classroom Examples
Suppose a 5.75 ft (5 ft 9 in.) tall human has the jumping ability of the record-breaking cricket that is 0.05 ft long and can jump 2 ft. Write a proportion to find how far this person can jump.

Answer: Fill in the information you know to write the proportion. Use variables for values you do not know. Solve the proportion.

$$\frac{2}{0.05} = \frac{d}{5.75}$$
$$0.05 \cdot d = 2 \cdot 5.75$$
$$0.05 \cdot d = 11.5$$
$$d = 11.5 \div 0.05$$
$$d = 230$$

The person could jump 230 ft.

Discussion In *Question 12*, you may want to point out that when writing a proportion to solve a problem, only one of the values will be represented by a variable. The remaining three values will be given in the problem.

Try This as a Class For *Question 17(c)*, students may think that since the problem is comparing one running time to another running time, it is appropriate to use a proportion. Be sure students understand why sprinting times are not appropriate for predicting the times for running longer distances.

HOMEWORK EXERCISES

See the Suggested Assignment for Day 2 on page 6-31. For Exercise Notes, see page 6-31.

CLOSE

Closure Question How can you tell if two ratios are equivalent?

Sample Response: Set up a proportion using the ratios. Find the cross products. If the cross products are equal, the two ratios are equivalent.

Teacher Support for Pupil Pages 418–419

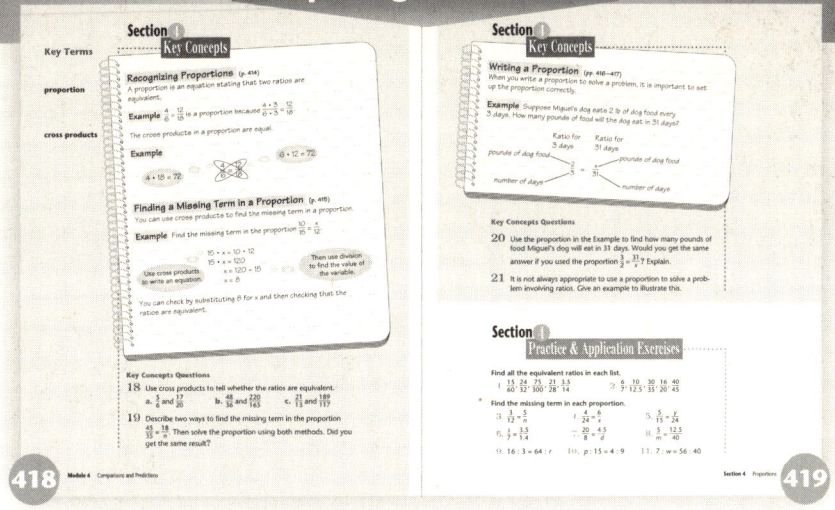

SUGGESTED ASSIGNMENT

Core Course
Day 1: Exs. 1–11, 19–24
Day 2: Exs. 12, 13, 15–18

Extended Course
Day 1: Exs. 1–11, 19–24
Day 2: Exs. 12–18

Block Schedule
Day 3: Sec. 3, Exs. 14, 16–20, 25–30; Exs. 1–11, 19–24
Day 4: Exs. 12, 13, 15–18; Sec. 5, Exs. 2–6, 8, 9, 31–33

EMBEDDED ASSESSMENT

These section objectives are tested by the exercises listed.

Use cross products to find the missing term in a proportion.
Exercises 3–5

Write and use proportions to solve problems and make predictions.
Exercises 12, 13, 15

Explore when using a proportion is or is not appropriate.
Exercises 16, 17

Practice & Application

EXERCISE NOTES

Developing Math Concepts
For *Ex. 1*, you may wish to discuss with students what they think is the best method for finding all the equivalent ratios. For *Exs. 9–11*, be sure students set up the proportions correctly before finding the missing term.

Customizing Instruction

Home Involvement Those helping students at home will find the Key Concepts on pages 418 and 419 a handy reference to the key ideas, terms, and skills of Section 4.

Absent Students For students who were absent for all or part of this section, the blackline Study Guide for Section 4 may be used to present the ideas, concepts, and skills of Section 4.

Extra Help For students who need additional practice, the blackline Practice and Applications for Section 4 provides additional exercises that may be used to confirm the skills of Section 4. The Extra Skill Practice on page 422 also provides additional exercises.

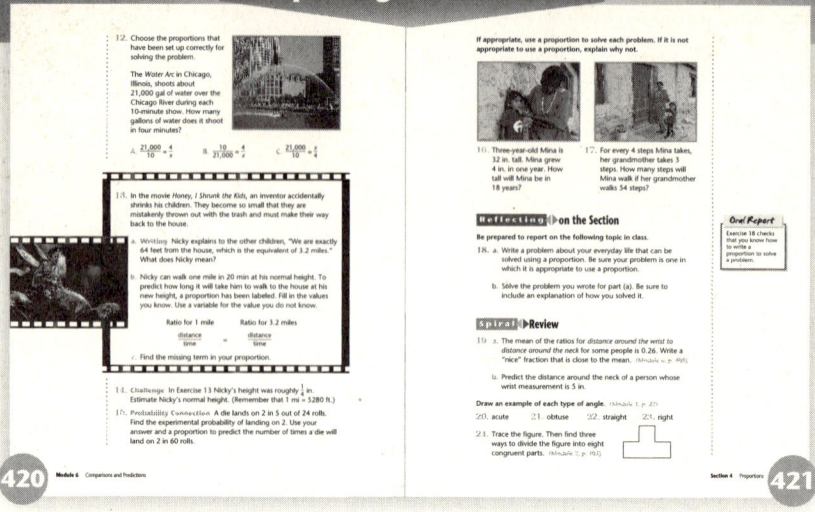

Practice & Application

Developing Math Concepts
Ex. 12 is a good problem for discussing the correct way to set up proportions. After completing the exercise, you might consider having students solve the proportions in choices B and C to show that although the two proportions are set up differently, they both result in the same value for the variable. Students could also solve the proportion in choice A to show that it results in a value that is unreasonable.

Writing As students plan their writing in *Ex. 13*, you may want to encourage them to think back to the poem *One Inch Tall* in Section 1 where the author says that for a 1 in. tall person "it would take about a month to get down to the store." Suggest to students that the measures of objects in the environment did not change when the children were shrunk, but their capacity to deal with these measures changed in proportion to their decreased height.

Ongoing Assessment You may wish to have students save their answers to *Ex. 18* for their portfolio to show their understanding of using proportions.

Closing the Section

In Section 4, students have learned to use proportions to compare ratios, to solve problems, and to make predictions as they explored the jumping ability of humans and animals. Students will be able to reflect on these understandings as they respond to the following questions: "How can you use proportions to make comparisons and predictions? Is it appropriate to always use a proportion to solve problems? Why or why not?"

QUICK QUIZ ON THIS SECTION

1. Use cross products to tell whether the ratios are equivalent.
   a. $\frac{12}{9}$ and $\frac{8}{6}$
   b. $\frac{14}{6}$ and $\frac{35}{15}$
   c. $\frac{10}{24}$ and $\frac{3}{8}$

2. Find the missing term in each proportion.
   a. $\frac{3}{25} = \frac{x}{175}$
   b. $\frac{7}{36} = \frac{21}{y}$
   c. $\frac{18}{48} = \frac{x}{40}$

3. If 16 notebooks cost $27.04, how much will 25 notebooks cost?

4. If two tractor trailers have 36 wheels, how many wheels are there on 5 tractor trailers?

5. Emily's nine hamsters eat 3 oz of food each day. How many ounces would 24 hamsters eat in a week?

For answers, see Quick Quiz blackline on p. 6-65.

Section 5: Geometry and Proportions

Section Planner

DAYS FOR MODULE 6

1 2 3 4 5 6 7 **8 9 10 11 12**

SECTION 5

First Day
Setting the Stage, p. 423
Exploration 1, pp. 424–426

Second Day
Exploration 2, pp. 427–428

Third Day
Exploration 3, pp. 429–430
Key Concepts, p. 430

Block Schedule

Day 4 continued
Setting the Stage, Exploration 1

Day 5
Exploration 2, Exploration 3, Key Concepts

RESOURCE ORGANIZER

Teaching Resources
- Practice and Applications, Sec. 5
- Study Guide, Sec. 5
- Warm-Up, Sec. 5
- Quick Quiz, Sec. 5

Section Overview

In Section 5, students will study similar figures, congruent figures, and scale drawings. They will also learn how to measure and draw angles. The terms *similar figures* and *corresponding parts* are defined. To provide visual representations of similar figures and their parts, students will use pattern blocks to build models of similar figures. They will use the models to explore relationships between corresponding sides and corresponding angles of similar figures. Students will investigate the similarities and differences between similar figures and *congruent figures*, which are also defined in this section. Using proportions, students will solve problems involving similar figures, including scale model problems.

The angle relationships in similar figures leads to an investigation of angle measures in Exploration 3. Students will learn to measure an angle with a protractor. Because acute, right, and obtuse angles are discussed in Exploration 3, students will have to be familiar with these terms. Students who will benefit from a review of angle classification should refer back to page 19 in Module 1.

SECTION OBJECTIVES

Exploration 1
- identify similar figures and their corresponding parts
- understand characteristics that make figures similar
- identify congruent figures

Exploration 2
- apply similarity to solving problems involving scale drawings, scale models, and map scales

Exploration 3
- measure and draw angles using a protractor

ASSESSMENT OPTIONS

Checkpoint Questions
- Question 9 on p. 426
- Question 13 on p. 428
- Question 15 on p. 428
- Question 20 on p. 430

Embedded Assessment
- For a list of embedded assessment exercises see p. 6-38.

Performance Task/Portfolio
- Exercise 24 on p. 434 (displaying data)
- Exercise 30 on p. 435 (research)
- Module Project on p. 436
- Standardized Testing on p. 437

SECTION 5 MATERIALS

Exploration 1
- Labsheet 5A
- pattern blocks
- metric ruler
- tracing paper

Exploration 2
- customary ruler

Exploration 3
- Labsheet 5B
- protractor

Module Project on page 436
- protractor
- ruler

Teacher Support for Pupil Pages 422–423

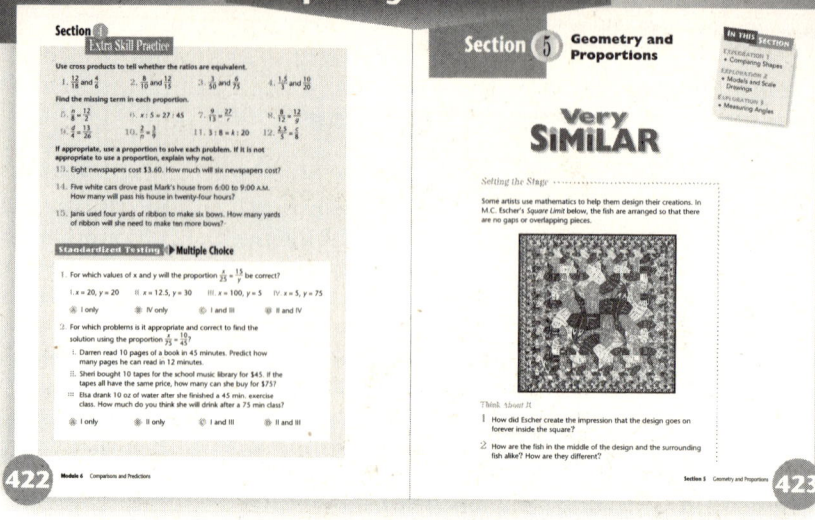

Setting the Stage

MOTIVATE

Students should study the design on page 423 before answering **Questions 1** and **2**. Students may enjoy looking at the designs and patterns in other works by M. C. Escher. If time allows, students may also enjoy emulating Escher's technique by sketching a simple design that can be repeated without leaving any gaps and without overlapping any parts of the design.

Exploration 1

PLAN

Classroom Management
Students should work with a partner to complete Exploration 1. Each pair of students will need a set of pattern blocks. **Questions 3** and **6** are designated as whole class discussion as students develop their understanding of corresponding sides and angles. **Questions 4** and **7** are Try This as a Class questions so that you can guide students as they learn to identify corresponding parts and similar figures.

6-34

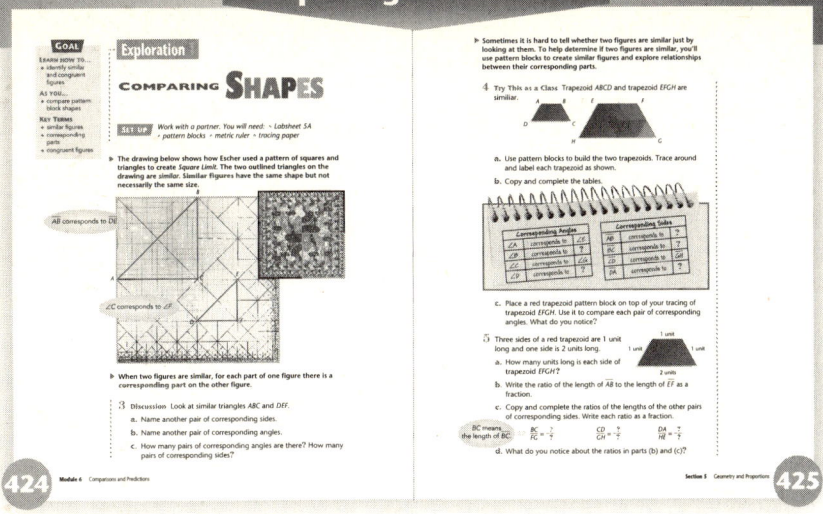

Exploration 1 continued

GUIDE

Developing Math Concepts
After discussing *Question 3*, you may want to check students' understanding by asking them why certain sides and angles do not correspond. For example, why does AB not correspond to DF? Point out that figures need not be similar in order to have corresponding parts. In *Question 5*, students should understand that the ratios of the lengths of corresponding sides are equivalent. For extra practice on this concept, students could measure the lengths of the sides of the triangles in the figure on page 424 and find the ratios of the lengths of the corresponding sides. When students have completed the exploration, you may want to have them look back at Escher's *Square Limit* design on page 423 and discuss it in relation to what they now understand about similar and congruent figures.

Discussion In *Question 3*, you may want to point out that since similar triangles ABC and DEF in the figure on page 424 are isosceles triangles, there are two possible ways to name the corresponding parts. To reinforce the definition of similar figures, you could ask students: "Are the triangles the same shape? Are the triangles the same size? If the triangles were the same size, would they still be similar triangles?"

Try This as a Class For *Question 4*, students should build the two trapezoids on a sheet of clean paper so they can trace around them and label the vertices. The two trapezoids ABCD and EFGH are isosceles, so there are two ways to match corresponding parts.

Common Error Students may have difficulty naming corresponding sides and angles when one figure is a reflection or rotation of the other. It may be helpful to have students trace one of the figures so they can manipulate its position to more clearly identify the corresponding sides and angles.

Customizing Instruction

Alternative Approach Students who finish the exploration with extra time may enjoy working in pairs and using pattern blocks to create congruent or similar figures. One student could build a design and challenge the other student to create either a congruent or a similar figure. Students could trace around their designs and display them in the classroom.

Second Language Learners Be sure students understand the meanings of the terms *similar*, *corresponding*, and *congruent*.

Visual and Tactile Learners Visual and tactile learners will find that using and sketching the pattern block figures in this exploration will be very helpful in building an understanding of similar and congruent figures. These students may need additional practice with the pattern blocks before working independently with just paper and pencil.

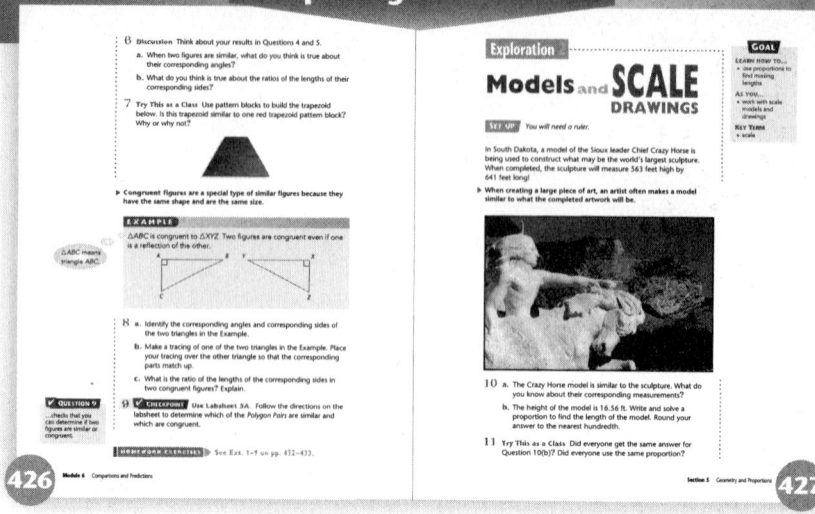

Exploration 1 continued

Try This as a Class To check their answers to *Question 7*, students could find the ratios of the lengths of the corresponding sides of the trapezoid they build and those of a red trapezoid pattern block. Students should then see that the ratios of the corresponding sides are not equivalent.

Classroom Examples
Is quadrilateral *DEFG* congruent to quadrilateral *KLMN*?

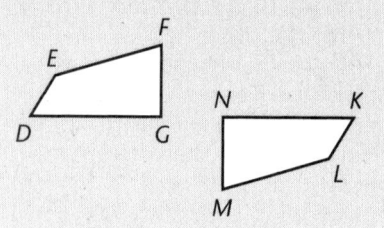

Answer: Yes; Two figures are congruent even if one is a rotation of the other.

Checkpoint Before completing Labsheet 5A in *Question 9*, you may want to have students predict which polygons they think will be similar and which polygons they think will be congruent.

HOMEWORK EXERCISES

See the Suggested Assignment for Day 1 on page 6-39. For Exercise Notes, see page 6-39.

Exploration 2

PLAN

Classroom Management
Students can work through Exploration 2 individually or in groups of 2 to 4. *Question 12* is designated for whole class discussion so you can point out the various ways a proportion can be set up to find a missing measure. *Questions 11* and *14* are Try This as a Class questions so you can guide students to correctly set up a proportion to find missing lengths in similar figures.

GUIDE

Developing Math Concepts
For *Question 10(b)*, have students work on their own so that you can compare and discuss their choices for proportions in *Question 11*. Students should be aware that there is more than one way to correctly set up a proportion for finding missing measures in similar figures. Following *Question 13* on page 428, students learn that the Crazy Horse model uses the scale 1 ft : 34 ft.

Common Error When a scale uses two different units, students may incorrectly write the wrong unit with their answer. Encourage students to read the problem carefully and to identify what unit the question is asking them to find before beginning their calculations. Instructing students to write in each unit when setting up the proportion will also help correct this error.

Try This as a Class For *Question 11*, ask several students to put their proportions from *Question 10(b)* on the board so that you can discuss and compare them. Use these examples to reemphasize the importance of writing the units in the correct places when setting up a proportion. Students can use the proportions $\frac{\text{height 1}}{\text{length 1}} = \frac{\text{height 2}}{\text{length 2}}$ and $\frac{\text{height 1}}{\text{height 2}} = \frac{\text{length 1}}{\text{length 2}}$, but should not use $\frac{\text{height 1}}{\text{height 2}} = \frac{\text{length 2}}{\text{length 1}}$.

Teacher Support for Pupil Pages 428–429

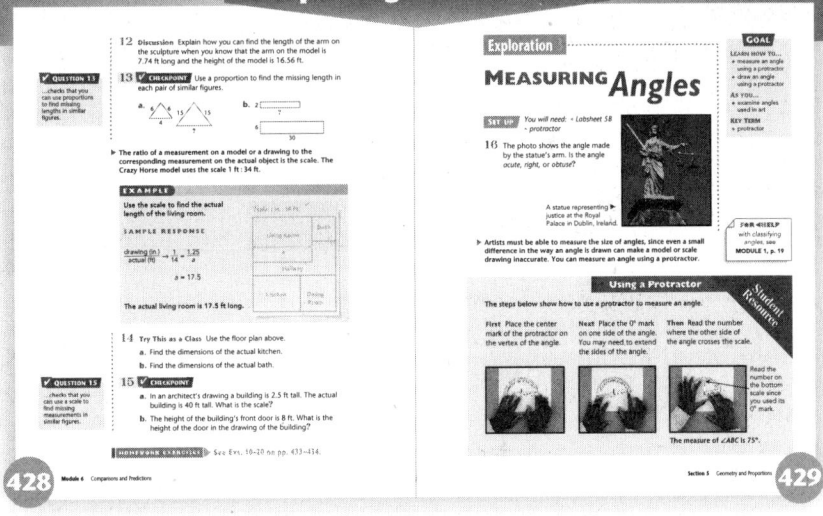

Exploration 2 continued

Discussion For *Question 12*, point out again that there is more than one correct way to set up the proportion. Students should be able to explain how they know their proportion is set up correctly.

Checkpoint In *Question 13*, you may want to ask students to share the proportions they used for finding each missing length. Encourage students to use number sense to check the reasonableness of their result. One of the incorrect proportions for part (a), $\frac{6}{4} = \frac{x}{15}$, will give a wrong answer of 22.5, while in part (b), $\frac{2}{x} = \frac{30}{6}$ will give an incorrect result of 0.4. Students should see that these incorrect answers do not make sense.

Classroom Examples
Refer to the Example on page 428. Use the scale to find the actual length of the hallway.

Answer:
$$\frac{\text{drawing (in.)}}{\text{actual (ft)}} \rightarrow \frac{1}{14} = \frac{1.75}{a}$$
$$1 \cdot a = 14 \cdot 1.75$$
$$a = 24.5$$

The actual hallway is 24.5 ft.

Checkpoint In *Question 15*, students will use their result from part (a) to answer part (b), so you will want to make sure students have answered part (a) correctly. Encourage students to use number sense to see if their answer for the height of the door in the drawing is reasonable.

HOMEWORK EXERCISES

See the Suggested Assignment for Day 2 on page 6-39. For Exercise Notes, see page 6-39.

Exploration 3

PLAN

Classroom Management
Students should complete Exploration 3 individually or in groups of 2 to 4. You may briefly want to review classifying angles before beginning the exploration.

Customizing Instruction

Alternative Approach 1 You may want to bring in pictures of other statues or works of art. You could have students look for angles in the picture, estimate their measure, then check their estimate by using a protractor.

Alternative Approach 2 Students who finish early may want to create their own drawings for more practice in measuring angles. Students could draw a picture of an object and have a classmate identify and measure the angles in the drawing.

Teacher Support for Pupil Pages 430–431

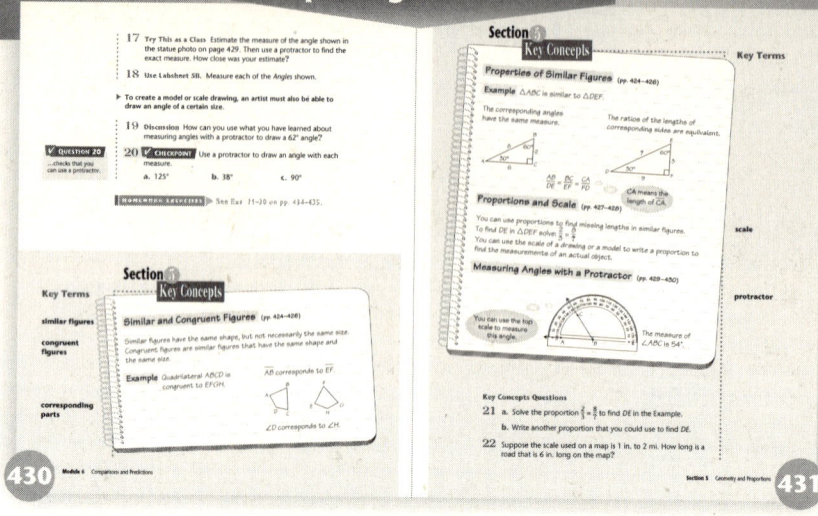

Exploration 3 continued

GUIDE

Developing Math Concepts Encourage students to use their number sense about measures to help them check that they have measured each angle correctly. For *Question 18*, you may wish to have students estimate the measure of each angle first before using their protractor.

Common Error Students who are not careful in placing the center mark of the protractor on the vertex of the angle will get an incorrect measure. Students must also be careful in placing the 0° mark on one side of the angle. Remind students to recheck the placement of the protractor before recording the measure of the angle.

Try This as a Class As students estimate the answer to *Question 17*, you may want to ask guiding questions, such as: "Is the measure of the angle greater than 90°?"

Discussion In *Question 19*, students should realize that the vertex is an important point of reference for drawing an angle, and that placing the 0° mark on one side of the angle applies to drawing an angle as well as measuring one.

HOMEWORK EXERCISES

See the Suggested Assignment for Day 3 on page 6-39. For Exercise Notes, see page 6-39.

CLOSE

Closure Question State the difference between similar figures and congruent figures.
Sample Response: Similar figures have the same shape. Congruent figures have the same shape and size.

Customizing Instruction

Home Involvement Those helping students at home will find the Key Concepts on pages 430 and 431 a handy reference to the key ideas, terms, and skills of Section 5.

Absent Students For students who were absent for all or part of this section, the blackline Study Guide for Section 5 may be used to present the ideas, concepts, and skills of Section 5.

Extra Help For students who need additional practice, the blackline Practice and Applications for Section 5 provides additional exercises that may be used to confirm the skills of Section 5. The Extra Skill Practice on page 437 also provides additional exercises.

Teacher Support for Pupil Pages 432–433

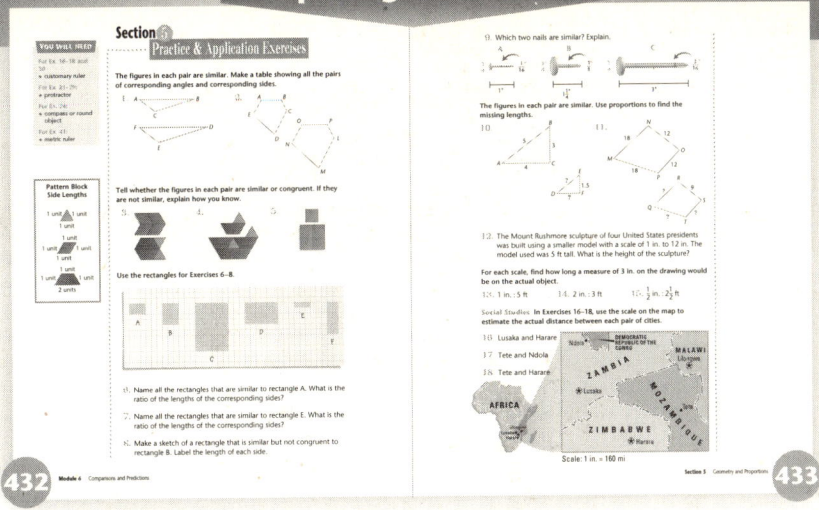

SUGGESTED ASSIGNMENT

Core Course
Day 1: Exs. 1–6, 8, 9, 31–33
Day 2: Exs. 10–18 even, 19, 34–36
Day 3: Exs. 22, 24–26, 28, 30, 37–40

Extended Course
Day 1: Exs. 1–6, 8, 9, 31–33
Day 2: Exs. 10–18 even, 19, 20, 34–36
Day 3: Exs. 22, 24–26, 28, 30, 37–40

Block Schedule
Day 4: Sec. 4, Exs. 12, 13, 15–18; Exs. 2–6, 8, 9, 31–33
Day 5: Exs. 10–18 even, 19, 22, 24–26, 28, 30, 34–40

EMBEDDED ASSESSMENT

These section objectives are tested by the exercises listed.

Identify similar figures and their corresponding parts.
Exercises 2, 4, 6, 9

Understand characteristics that make figures similar.
Exercises 3–6, 8

Identify congruent figures.
Exercises 3–5

Apply similarity to solving problems involving scale drawings, scale models, and map scales.
Exercises 10, 12, 14, 16, 19

Measure and draw angles using a protractor.
Exercises 25, 26, 28

Practice & Application

EXERCISE NOTES

Developing Math Concepts
For *Exs. 1* and *2*, suggest students create a table like those shown on page 425. If needed, students can use pattern blocks to build the figures in *Exs. 3–5*. For *Exs. 6–8*, students may want to make a table to record the dimensions of each rectangle for easy reference as they answer the question. Visual learners could make a quick sketch of each rectangle and record the dimensions on their sketch. Students who need extra manipulative practice with similarity and congruence could build each of the rectangles out of colored tiles or one-inch squares. For *Ex. 9*, remind students to consider all three measures when determining which two nails are similar.

Social Studies For *Exs. 16–18*, point out that using a map scale is an important skill in social studies courses, as well as in real life. You may want to bring some local or state maps to class to provide hands-on practice with this skill.

MODULE 6 ◆ SECTION 5

6-39

Teacher Support for Pupil Pages 434–435

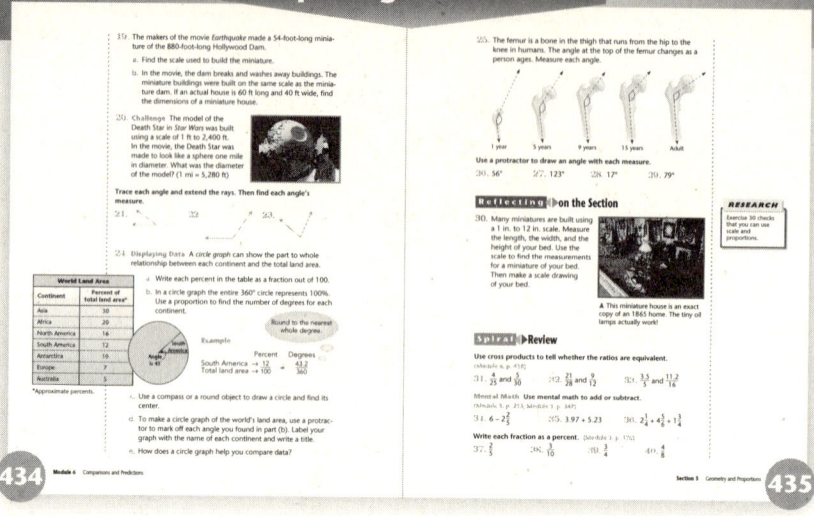

Practice & Application

Displaying Data In *Ex. 24*, students are shown how to apply two of the skills they have been working on (writing and solving proportions, and measuring angles) to make a circle graph. Although students have some familiarity with circle graphs (for example, see Ex. 15 on page 337), they probably have not made a circle graph before.

Managing Time You may wish to take time to develop the method in *Ex. 24* together in class. Students will think about circle graphs again later when they focus on choosing an appropriate graph in Section 5 of Module 8.

Measurement In *Ex. 25*, the rays of the angles do not extend far enough for students to read their measurements on the protractor. Have students trace the angles and extend the rays so they go beyond the outer edge of their protractors. As an alternative, after placing their protractors at the vertex of an angle with one 0° mark along one ray, students could place a ruler along the other ray to see where it crosses the protractor.

Career Information For *Ex. 25*, you may want to point out that the study of a person's bones can yield multiple clues about that person's existence. Archaeologists have discovered that flattened ribs and a fused breastbone resulted from the fashionable constraints of the 18th-century girdle called *stays*. Swollen and eroded joints signify the pain of rheumatoid arthritis. Jagged knee spurs formed on horsemen who spent too much time in the saddle. The thick cortex of a leg bone indicates a diet rich in high protein foods, while a narrower cortex suggests a protein-deficient diet. Bony bumps or calluses indicate bone breaks. And bone ravaged by osteoporosis appears more honeycombed than normal bone.

Ongoing Assessment You may wish to suggest that students save their answers to the Reflecting on the Section exercise (*Ex. 30*) for their portfolio to show their understanding of the concepts from this section.

Background Information For *Ex. 30*, students may be interested to know that the miniature house is from the Mott's Miniatures Museum in Des Moines, Iowa. It is an exact copy of the house built by Lamoine Mott during the Civil War period.

Teacher Support for Pupil Pages 436–437

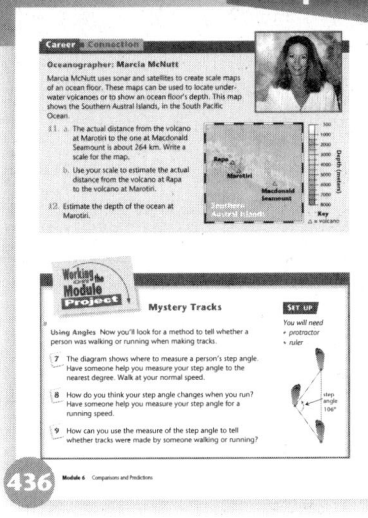

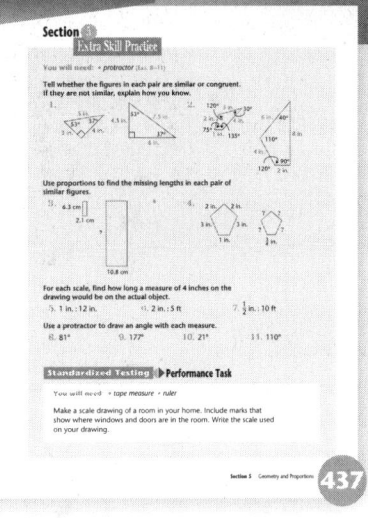

Working on the Module Project

You will need to clear enough floor space in the classroom so that students can take several normal walking steps. As an alternative, you could take the measurements in the hallway, gymnasium, or outdoors. If available, taking the measures on a tile floor may help students see how the step angle changes when running. Students may be able to see that the footprints land on (or near) one row of tiles when walking, and on a different row of tiles when running. Students could mark with chalk on the floor, or use markers on newspaper to record the steps. The "wet foot" method described in Section 1 may also work well. Encourage students not to increase or decrease their walking speed, but to walk at a normal rate.

Closing the Section

In Section 5, students have learned to identify similar and congruent figures, and to use proportions to find missing lengths. By examining scale models and drawings, students have seen how these skills can be applied to real life situations. Students also examined angles used in art as they learned to measure and draw angles using a protractor. Students will be able to reflect on these understandings as they respond to the following scenario: Pretend you are a sculptor or artist. Explain how you might apply the mathematics you learned in this section to your work with models, drawings, and art. Give specific examples of what skills and knowledge you might use, and how this knowledge is helpful to you as you create your art.

QUICK QUIZ ON THIS SECTION

1. The two triangles below are similar. Make a table showing the pairs of corresponding angles and sides. Then find the missing lengths.

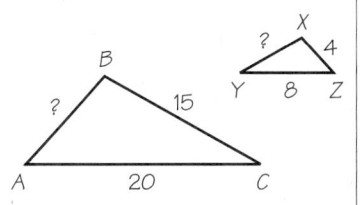

2. For each scale, find how long a measure of $1\frac{1}{2}$ in. on the drawing would be on the actual object.
   a. 1 in. : 18 ft
   b. 2 in. : 12 ft

3. Scientists estimate that the longest dinosaur was between 128 ft and 170 ft. To make a model of this dinosaur that would fit on your desk, what scale might you use?

4. On a map with a scale of 1 in. : 38 mi, it is $4\frac{1}{2}$ in. from town A to town B. What is the actual distance?

5. Use a protractor to draw an angle with each measure.
   a. 25°   b. 59°   c. 132°

For answers, see Quick Quiz blackline on p. 6-66.

6-41

Section 6 — Percents and Probability

Section Planner

DAYS FOR MODULE 6
1 2 3 4 5 6 7 8 9 10 **11 12**

SECTION 6

First Day
Setting the Stage, p. 438
Exploration 1, pp. 439–440

Second Day
Exploration 2, pp. 441–443
Key Concepts, p. 444

Block Schedule

Day 6
Setting the Stage, Exploration 1,
Exploration 2, Key Concepts

RESOURCE ORGANIZER

Teaching Resources
- Practice and Applications, Sec. 6
- Study Guide, Sec. 6
- Module Tests Forms A and B
- Standardized Assessment
- Module Performance Assessment
- Cumulative Test Modules 5–6
- Warm-Up, Sec. 6
- Quick Quiz, Sec. 6

Section Overview

Students will begin Section 6 by writing percents as fractions, a topic they studied in Module 3. Students who need to review this topic can do so on page 176, since they will use fractions to find a percent of a number. Students will also use "nice" fractions, which was discussed in Section 4, to estimate a percent or a percent of a number. The percent forms for the fractions $\frac{1}{3}$ and $\frac{2}{3}$ will be explored in this section as well. In Exploration 2, students will act out a probability experiment involving a game in which a numbered spinner is used. They will learn the meaning of a *fair game* and will draw probability *tree diagrams* to list the possible outcomes of a game. Students will learn how to use a tree diagram to calculate the probability of each outcome in order to determine if a game is fair. They will also convert probabilities to percents.

SECTION OBJECTIVES

Exploration 1
- use a "nice" fraction and mental math to find the percent of a number
- use a "nice" fraction to estimate a percent or percent of a number
- apply the percent equivalents for thirds

Exploration 2
- construct a tree diagram to list all the outcomes of an experiment
- use a tree diagram to determine and compare probabilities

ASSESSMENT OPTIONS

Checkpoint Questions
- Question 7 on p. 439
- Question 10 on p. 440
- Question 19 on p. 443

Embedded Assessment
- For a list of embedded assessment exercises see p. 6-46.

Performance Task/Portfolio
- Exercise 27 on p. 447
- ★Exercise 28 on p. 447 (visual thinking)
- ★Module Project on p. 449
- ★ = a problem solving task that can be assessed using the Assessment Scales

SECTION 6 MATERIALS

Exploration 1
- ◆ Labsheet 6A

Exploration 2
- ◆ Labsheets 6B and 6C
- ◆ paper clip

Teacher Support for Pupil Pages 438–439

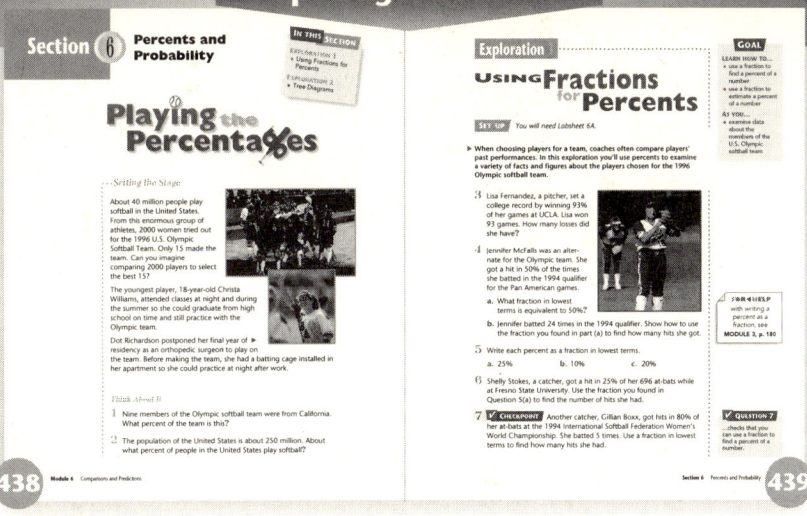

Setting the Stage

MOTIVATE

Students should read the material on page 438, either individually or in groups, before answering *Questions 1* and *2*. Students may be interested to know that all players who tried out for the Olympic team were required to pass several physical fitness tests, including running a mile in 8.5 min or less, doing 65 "crunches" in 60 s, and running around the bases in less than 12.5 s. Students may enjoy discussing their own experiences when trying out for a team. You may also want to ask students to discuss what they think the section title *Playing the Percentages* means.

Exploration 1

PLAN

Classroom Management
Exploration 1 can be completed individually or in groups of 2 to 4. You may want to review writing a percent as a fraction and finding a fraction of a whole number since this exploration builds on that previous knowledge. *Question 12* is designated as a whole class discussion so students can share their ideas on how to use a fraction to find a percent.

GUIDE

Developing Math Concepts
For *Question 3*, remind students that percent is the number out of 100. You may want to discuss why the percent and the number of wins is the same for *Question 3*. Throughout the exploration, you will want to make the connection between finding a fraction of a number and finding a percent of a number so students will understand how the two skills are related.

Checkpoint For *Question 7*, have students check their answers by finding 80% of 5.

Customizing Instruction

Alternative Approach 1 Students who finish the exploration with extra time may wish to try the Challenge problem (*Ex. 19*) on page 446. These students may also be interested in researching other statistics from the U.S. Olympic Softball Team, or from another team of their choice. They could present their findings to the class, and if applicable, use fractions to determine which player had the greatest and least percent of hits.

Alternative Approach 2 Students could create their own table similar to the one on page 440, but include a fourth column labeled *Percent of hits*. Students could also vary which column they leave blank so that classmates would have to find either the number of hits, the number of at-bats, or the percent of hits.

Teacher Support for Pupil Pages 440–441

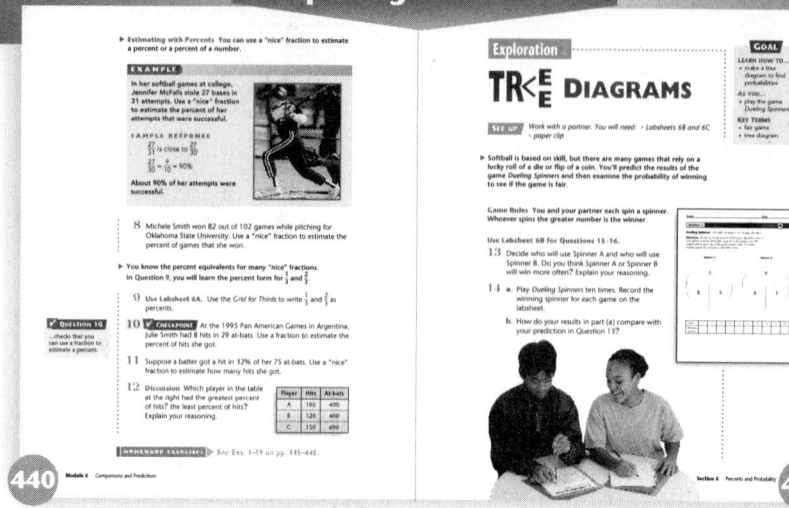

Exploration 1 continued

Classroom Examples
Suppose a player stole 11 bases in 16 attempts. Use a "nice" fraction to estimate the percent of her attempts that were successful.

Answer:
$\frac{11}{16}$ is close to $\frac{12}{16}$. → $\frac{12}{16} = \frac{3}{4} = 75\%$
About 75% of her attempts were successful.

HOMEWORK EXERCISES

See the Suggested Assignment for Day 1 on page 6-46. For Exercise Notes, see page 6-46.

Exploration 2

PLAN

Classroom Management
Students should work with a partner to complete Exploration 2. Suggest that both partners spin the same spinner from Labsheet 6B, with the student spinning the higher number getting to choose the spinner they would like to use. A large paper clip works best for making the spins. The game is easy to play and should not take longer than 5–8 min to complete. Students will need to save the results of their game for use in **Questions 13–16** on pages 441 and 442. **Questions 16** and **21** are designated as class discussion problems so you can be sure all students understand equally likely outcomes and using the percent form of probabilities.

GUIDE

Developing Math Concepts
Students who win *Dueling Spinners* may think the game is fair, while students who lose may think it is unfair. Encourage students to think about whether the outcomes of the two spinners were equally likely and whether the two players had an equal chance of winning.

Common Error Students may incorrectly think that if a game involves equally likely outcomes, then it is a fair game. Use *Dueling Spinners* to demonstrate why this is not always true. Although the outcomes are equally likely, the probability of Spinner B winning is greater than the probability of Spinner A winning.

Customizing Instruction

Alternative Approach 1 Students who finish the exploration with extra time may enjoy drawing other spinners for the game *Dueling Spinners*. You might want to give them specific criteria for their spinners, such as: draw a new Spinner A so that the probability of beating Spinner B is $\frac{6}{9}$ or $\frac{2}{3}$. (One possible answer is: spinner A outcomes of 4, 5, 8; spinner B outcomes of 2, 3, 9) You could also have students sketch various spinners, exchange them, and then draw tree diagrams to find the probability of one spinner beating the other.

Alternative Approach 2 To further reinforce the concepts from this exploration, you could have students bring in games from home which could be analyzed to decide whether they are fair games with equally likely outcomes. You may wish to have students respond to questions such as: "What are all the possible outcomes for the game? Are the outcomes equally likely? Does each player have an equal chance of winning? Is the game fair?"

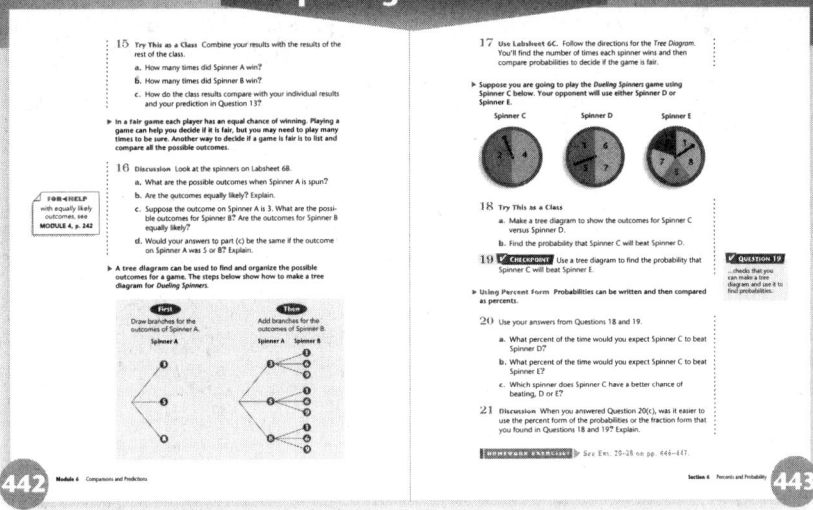

Exploration 2 continued

Try This as a Class To combine results in *Question 15*, one student from each pair could call out the results while classmates record the information. You may also want to record the information on the board or overhead to be sure all students have the correct information. An alternative is to put a table on the board and have students fill in their results as they complete the game. Students could then copy the table when all the results have been recorded.

Classroom Examples
Draw a tree diagram that shows the outcomes of flipping a coin and rolling a six-sided number cube.

First Draw branches for the outcomes of flipping a coin.

Second Add branches for the outcomes of rolling a six-sided number cube.

Then Write the outcomes.

Coin	Number cube	Outcome
H	1	H1
	2	H2
	3	H3
	4	H4
	5	H5
	6	H6
T	1	T1
	2	T2
	3	T3
	4	T4
	5	T5
	6	T6

Try This as a Class You may want to put the tree diagram on the board or overhead as students work through *Question 18*. If students have difficulty, they can use Labsheet 6C as a model for organizing their work. Remind students to write their answer to part (b) as a fraction. You may want to have them write the fraction in lowest terms since students will be writing this fraction as a percent in *Question 20*. After answering part (b), you may want to ask: "What is the probability that Spinner D will beat Spinner C?"

Checkpoint In *Question 19*, check students' tree diagrams to be sure they have drawn and labeled the branches correctly. You may want to call on a student to draw his or her diagram on the board.

▸ **HOMEWORK EXERCISES**

See the Suggested Assignment for Day 2 on page 6-46. For Exercise Notes, see page 6-46.

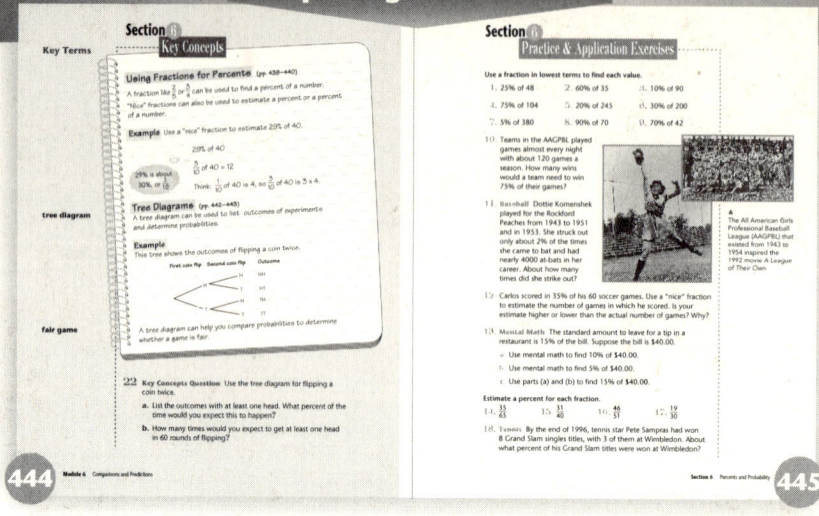

Exploration 2 continued

CLOSE

Closure Question Explain how tree diagrams can be used to find probabilities.

Sample Response: Tree diagrams make an organized list of all the possibilities for a game or problem. The final column of a tree diagram can be used to find and write probabilities for specific outcomes.

SUGGESTED ASSIGNMENT

Core Course
Day 1: Exs. 2–16 even, 17, 18, 29–32
Day 2: Exs. 20–25, 27, 28

Extended Course
Day 1: Exs. 2–16 even, 17–19, 29–32
Day 2: Exs. 20–28

Block Schedule
Day 6: Exs. 2–18 even, 20–25, 27–32

EMBEDDED ASSESSMENT

These section objectives are tested by the exercises listed.

Use a "nice" fraction and mental math to find the percent of a number.
Exercises 2, 4, 6, 10

Use a "nice" fraction to estimate a percent or percent of a number.
Exercises 12, 14, 16,

Apply the percent equivalents for thirds.
Exercises 12, 17, 18

Construct a tree diagram to list all the outcomes of an experiment.
Exercises 20a, 22a, 27a

Use a tree diagram to determine and compare probabilities.
Exercises 20b, 22b, 27b

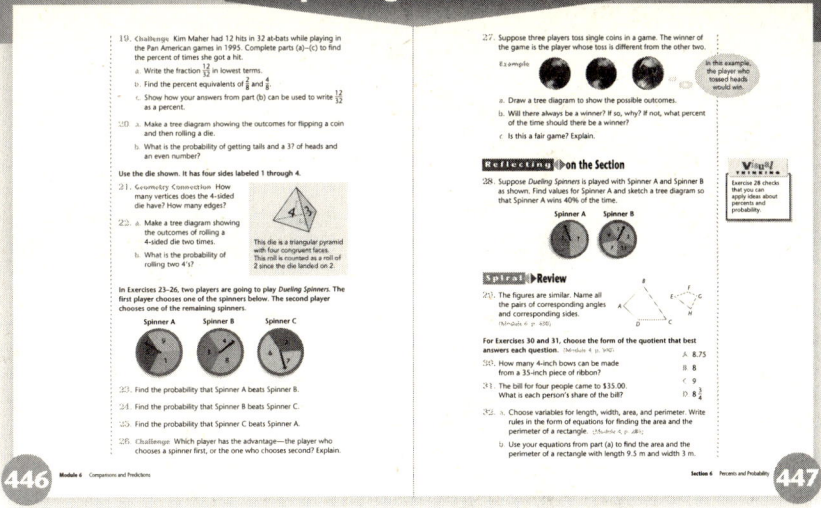

Practice & Application

Developing Math Concepts
For *Exs. 20–22* and *27*, you may want to explain what a fair coin and fair die are, and that the coins and dice discussed in these exercises are assumed to be fair.

Ongoing Assessment You may wish to have students save their answers to the Reflecting on the Section exercise (*Ex. 28*) for their portfolio to show they can apply the concepts of percent and probability.

Customizing Instruction

Home Involvement Those helping students at home will find the Key Concepts on page 444 a handy reference to the key ideas, terms, and skills of Section 6.

Absent Students For students who were absent for all or part of this section, the blackline Study Guide for Section 6 may be used to present the ideas, concepts, and skills of Section 6.

Extra Help For students who need additional practice, the blackline Practice and Applications for Section 6 provides additional exercises that may be used to confirm the skills of Section 6. The Extra Skill Practice on page 448 also provides additional exercises.

Teacher Support for Pupil Pages 448–449

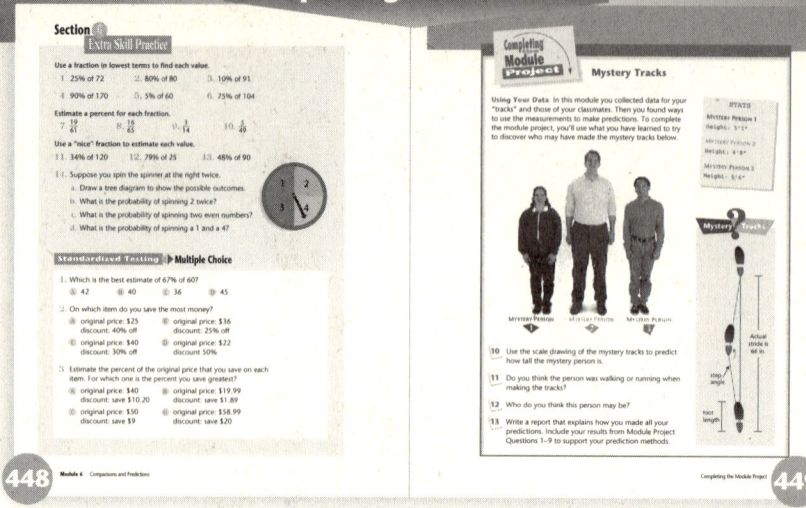

Closing the Section

Students have learned to use fractions to estimate a percent and to estimate a percent of a number. They have also explored tree diagrams to find probabilities and learned to write probabilities as percents. The concept of a fair game is just one of the real-world applications of these concepts. Students will be able to reflect on these understandings as they answer the Reflecting on the Section exercise (*Ex. 28*).

QUICK QUIZ ON THIS SECTION

1. Estimate a percent for each fraction.
   a. $\dfrac{39}{59}$ b. $\dfrac{18}{51}$ c. $\dfrac{181}{203}$

2. Lou Brock has the highest batting average in World Series play. He got a hit in 39% of his at-bats. If he had 82 at-bats, use a "nice" fraction to estimate how many hits he got.

3. A pitcher won 15 games out of 21. Use a "nice" fraction to estimate the percent of the games that she won.

4. Make a tree diagram showing the possible outcomes when one player spins Spinner A and the other player spins Spinner B.

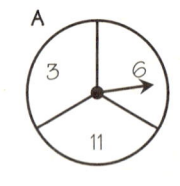

For answers, see Quick Quiz blackline on p. 6-67.

Completing the Module Project

You may want to allow students to share their ideas about the mystery person with a partner or in a small group. Emphasize to students that the report should explain how the predictions were made and should present evidence to support their choice of persons. If time allows, you may want to have students present their reports to the class. Students could debate the validity of each others' predictions and try to "sway" classmates to change their mind about the identity of the mystery person.

Name _____   Date _____

MODULE 6 **LABSHEET 2A**

Sandbag Brigade Data   (Use with Exercise 18 on page 394.)

Directions Use your class's data to complete the table. Then plot the time and distance data on the grid below. Draw segments to connect the points in order from left to right.

Number of students	Length of the brigade (feet)	Time to pass the sandbag from end to end (seconds)
10		
20		
30		
40		

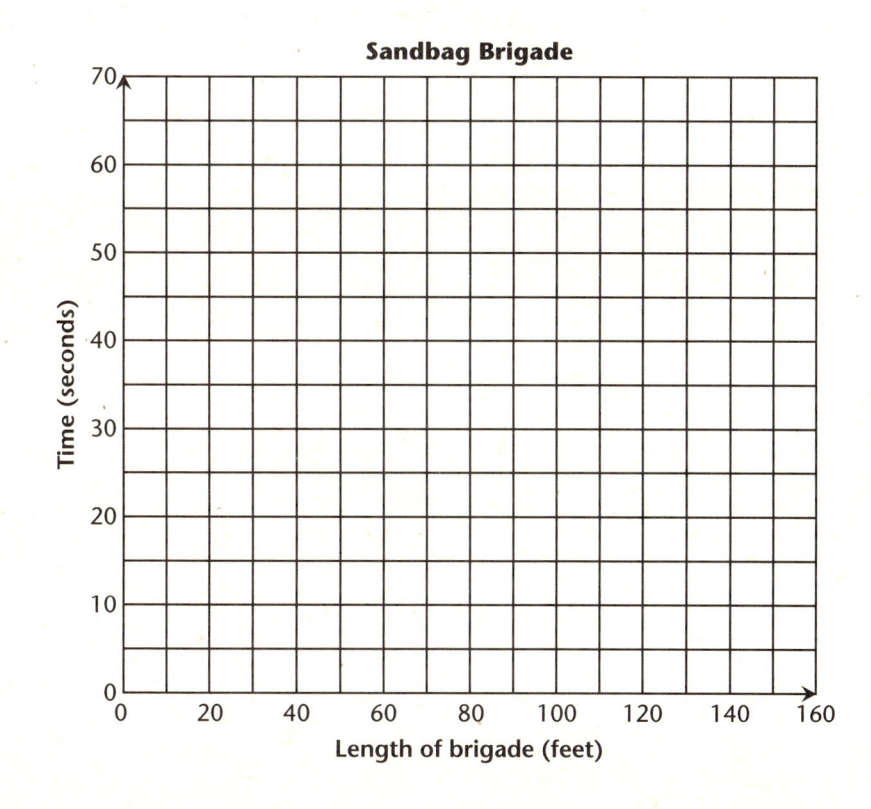

Sandbag Brigade

(grid: Time (seconds) 0–70 vs. Length of brigade (feet) 0–160)

Name _____ Date _____

MODULE 6 **LABSHEET 3A**

Body Measurements Table

(Use with Questions 11–12 on page 400, Question 20 on page 403, Exercise 13 on page 407, and Exercise 17 on page 408.)

	Person number	Height (cm)	Tibia (cm)	Radius (cm)	Reach (cm)
Your group	1				
	2				
	3				
	4				
Two other groups	5				
	6				
	7				
	8				
	9				
	10				
	11				
	12				

Body Ratios Table

(Use with Questions 12–15 on pages 400–401 and Question 21 on page 403.)

Group member	$\dfrac{\text{Tibia}}{\text{Height}}$	$\dfrac{\text{Radius}}{\text{Height}}$	$\dfrac{\text{Reach}}{\text{Height}}$
1			
2			
3			
4			
Mean			
"Nice" fraction			

6-50 Math Thematics, Book 1   Copyright © by McDougal Littell Inc. All rights reserved.

Name   Date

MODULE 6   **LABSHEET 3B**

Reach Compared to Height Graph

(Use with Questions 17–20 on pages 402–403.)

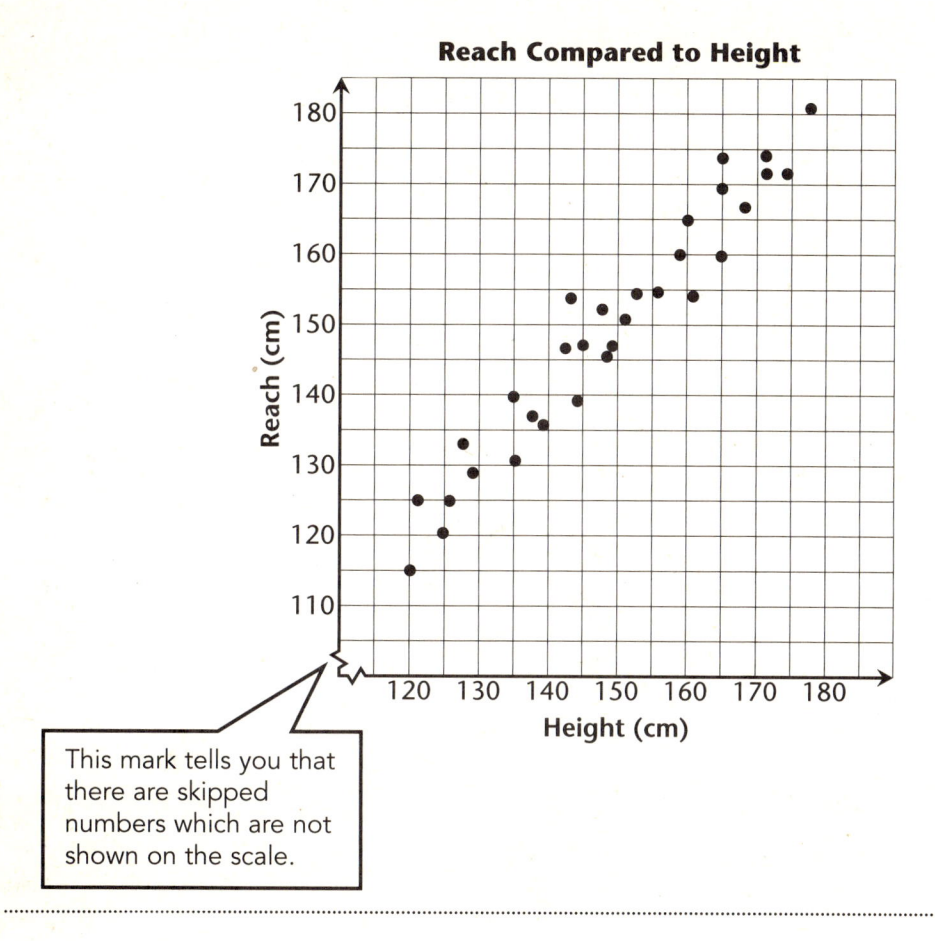

Reach Compared to Height

[Scatter plot with Height (cm) on x-axis from 120 to 180, and Reach (cm) on y-axis from 110 to 180.]

This mark tells you that there are skipped numbers which are not shown on the scale.

....

Points on the Line Table

(Use with Question 21 page 403.)

Directions Use the fitted line on your scatter plot to complete the table.

Tibia (cm)				40	45
Height (cm)	130	140	150		
Tibia / Height					

Copyright © by McDougal Littell Inc. All rights reserved.   Math Thematics, Book 1 **6-51**

Name _____ Date _____

| MODULE 6 | LABSHEET 5A |

Polygon Pairs (Use with Question 9 on page 426.)

Directions For each pair of polygons:

- Measure and record all of the side lengths in centimeters.

- Make a tracing of one of the polygons. Then place the tracing over the other polygon to check the measures of corresponding angles.

- Tell whether the polygons are similar, congruent, or neither. Explain how you know.

a.

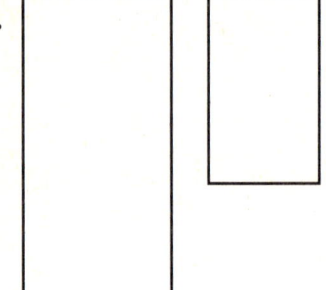

b.

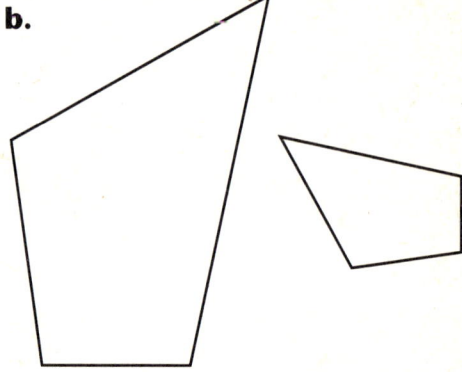

c.

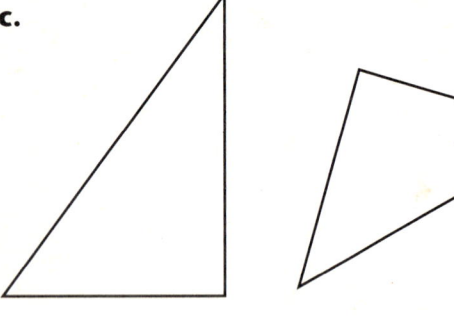

d.

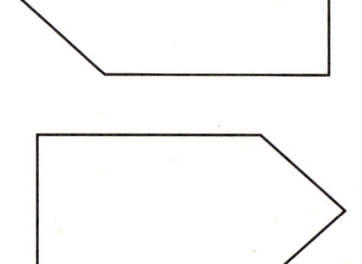

Name   Date

MODULE 6   **LABSHEET 5B**

Angles (Use with Question 18 on page 430.)

Directions Use a protractor to find the measure of each angle.

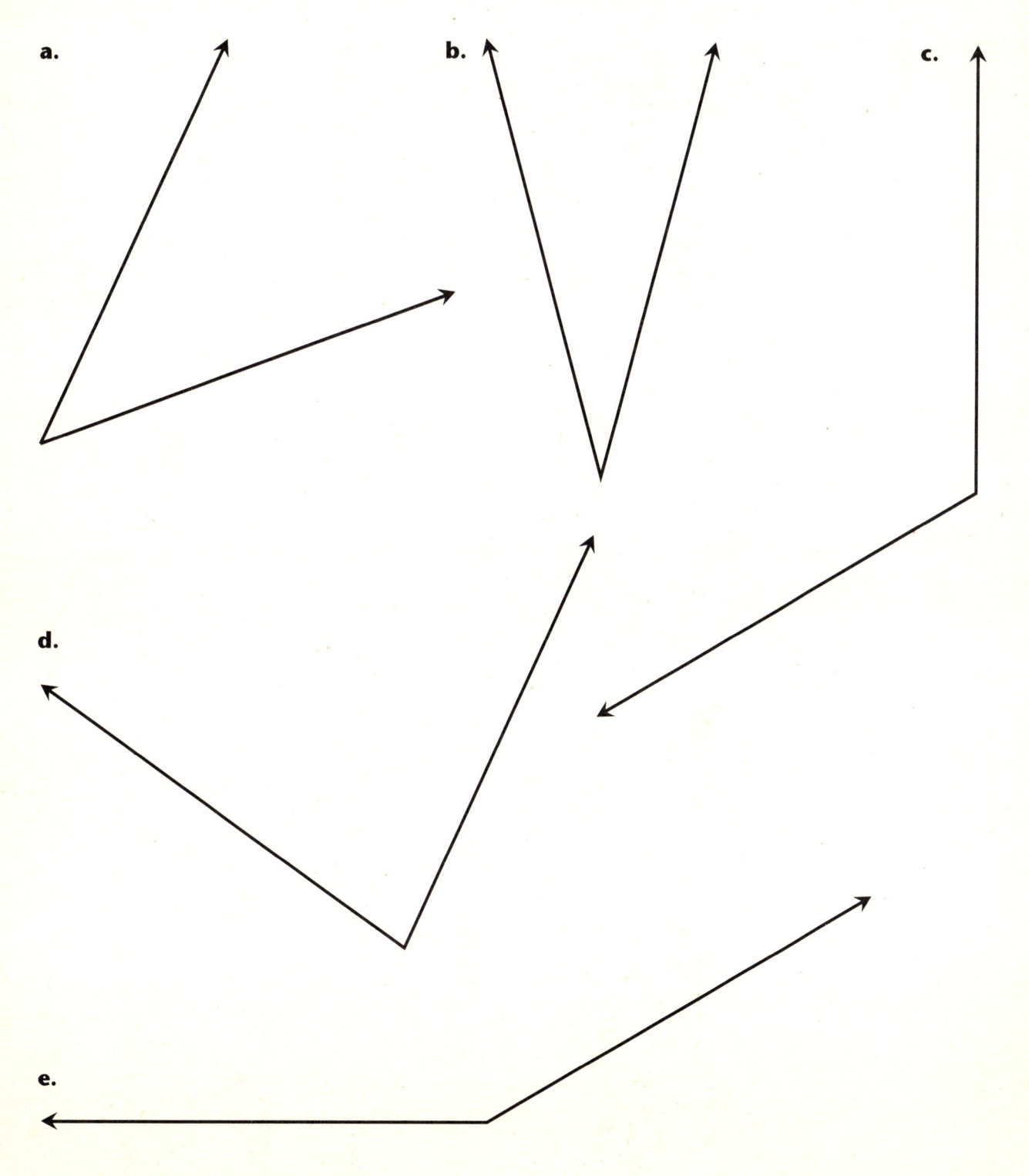

a.

b.

c.

d.

e.

| MODULE 6 | LABSHEET 6A |

Grid for Thirds (Use with Question 9 on page 440.)

Directions Complete parts (a)–(e) to write $\frac{1}{3}$ and $\frac{2}{3}$ as percents.

a. Divide the 100 squares into 3 groups with the same number of squares in each group. How many squares are in each group? How many squares are left over?

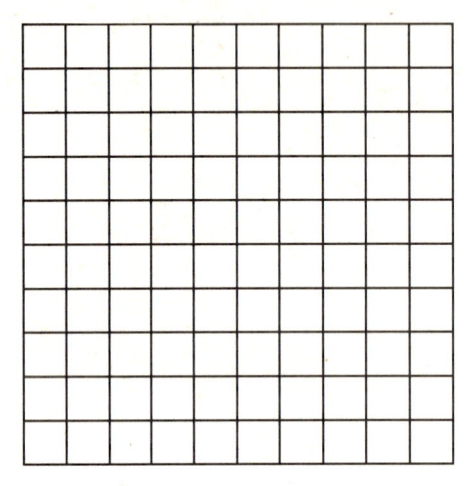

b. Shade one of the groups from part (a).

c. Divide the left-over square or squares from part (a) into 3 parts. Shade one of the parts.

d. How many squares in all did you shade on the grid? How many hundredths of the grid did you shade? Write a percent for $\frac{1}{3}$.

e. Use your answer to part (d) to write a percent for $\frac{2}{3}$. Explain how you found your answer.

Name _____ Date _____

| MODULE 6 | LABSHEET **6B** |

Dueling Spinners (Use with Questions 13–16 on pages 441–442.)

Directions Use the tip of your pencil to hold a paper clip at the center of your spinner. Each player spins his or her spinner once. The spinner with its paper clip on the greater number wins. Record the winning spinner for each game in the table below.

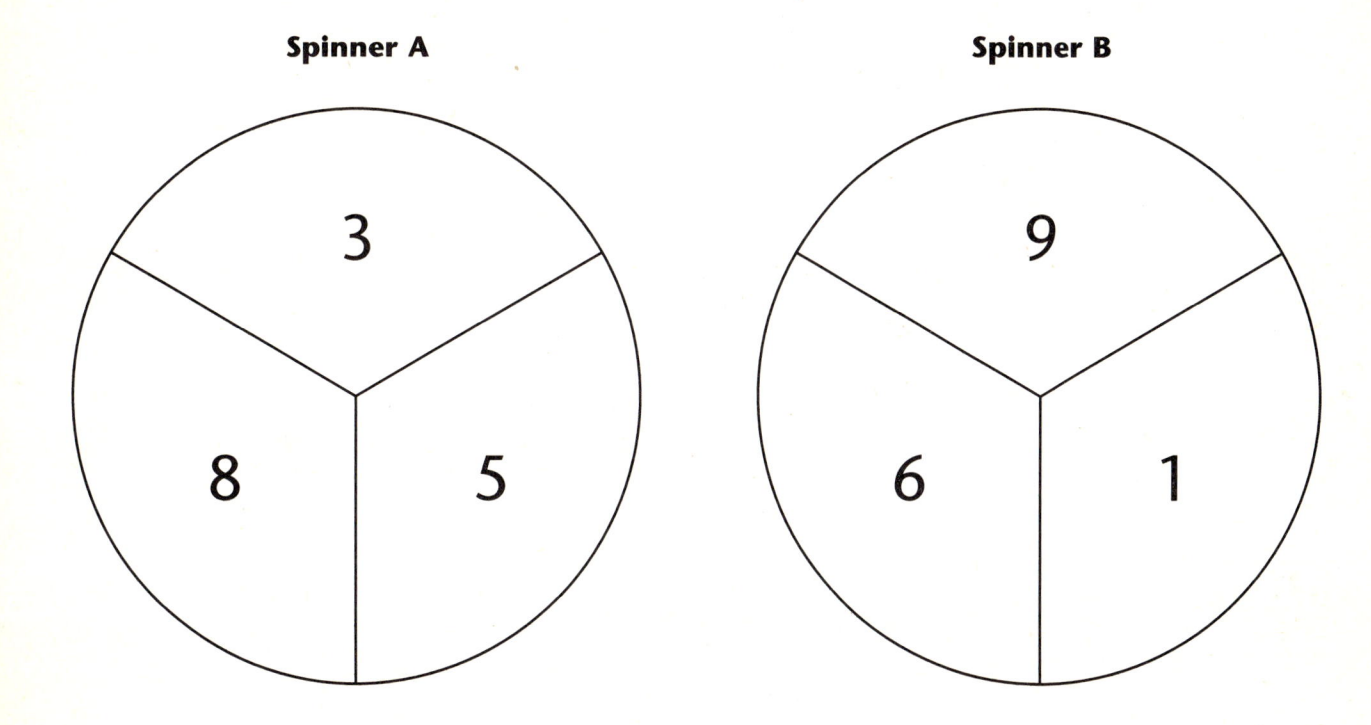

Spinner A

3, 8, 5

Spinner B

9, 6, 1

Game	1	2	3	4	5	6	7	8	9	10
Winning Spinner										

Copyright © by McDougal Littell Inc. All rights reserved.

Math Thematics, Book 1 **6-55**

Name _____ Date _____

MODULE 6 **LABSHEET 6C**

Tree Diagram (Use with Question 17 on page 443.)

Directions Use the tree diagram below to complete parts (a)–(g).

a. Trace along the branches of the tree diagram and list the possible outcomes. One entry has been done for you.

b. For each outcome, decide which spinner wins and list the letter beside the outcome.

c. Count the winning outcomes for Spinner A.

d. Write a ratio in fraction form that compares the total number of winning outcomes for Spinner A to the total number of outcomes. This is the probability that Spinner A wins.

e. Find the probability that Spinner B wins.

f. How is the probability that Spinner A wins related to the probability that Spinner B wins?

g. Is *Dueling Spinners* a fair game? Explain.

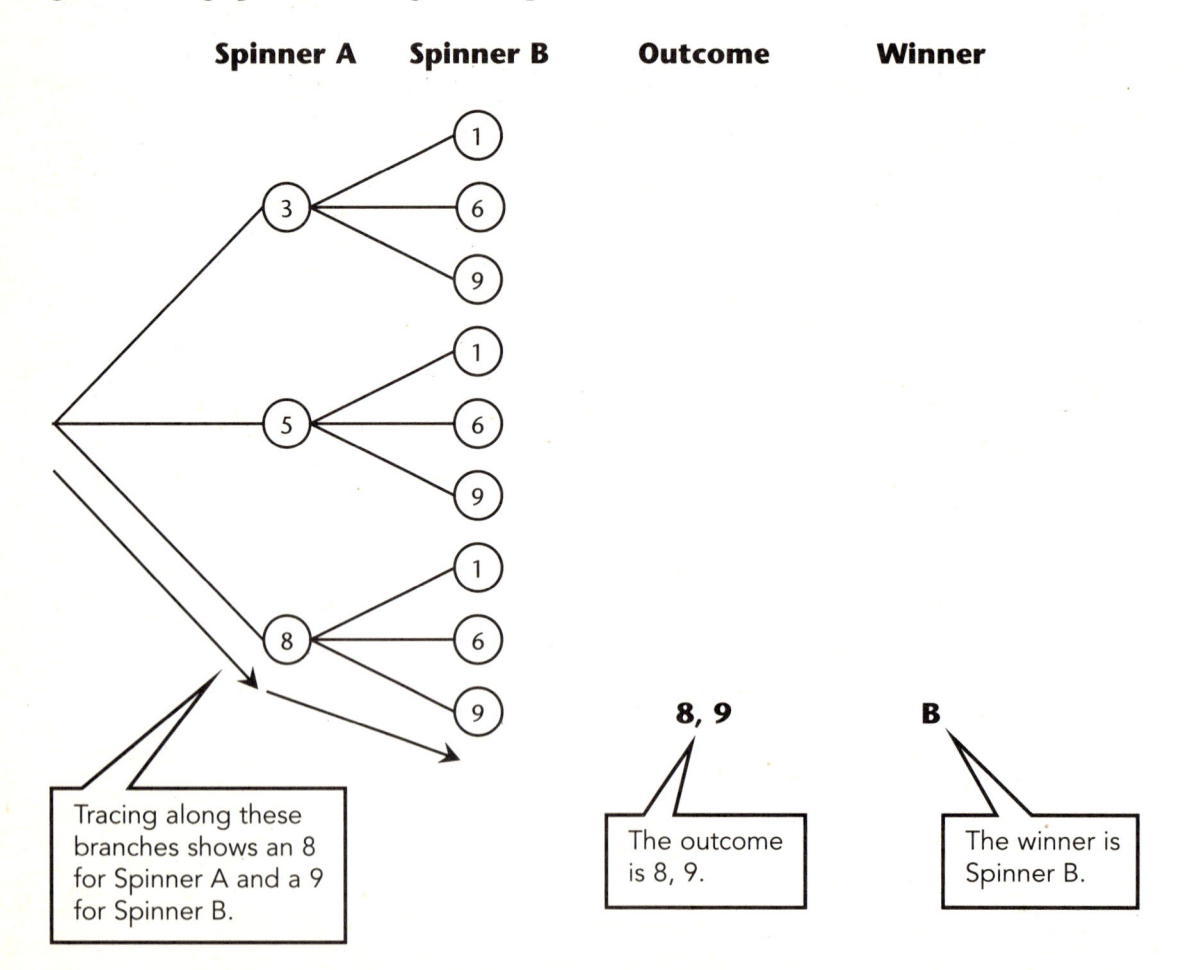

Spinner A   **Spinner B**   **Outcome**   **Winner**

Tracing along these branches shows an 8 for Spinner A and a 9 for Spinner B.

8, 9
The outcome is 8, 9.

B
The winner is Spinner B.

6-56 Math Thematics, Book 1   Copyright © by McDougal Littell Inc. All rights reserved.

Name _____   Problem _____

TEACHER   ASSESSMENT SCALES

☆ *The star indicates that you excelled in some way.*

❓→❗ Problem Solving

```
|——①——②——③——④——⑤——☆→
```

① You did not understand the problem well enough to get started or you did not show any work.

③ You understood the problem well enough to make a plan and to work toward a solution.

⑤ You made a plan, you used it to solve the problem, and you verified your solution.

x^2 Mathematical Language

```
|——①——②——③——④——⑤——☆→
```

① You did not use any mathematical vocabulary or symbols, or you did not use them correctly, or your use was not appropriate.

③ You used appropriate mathematical language, but the way it was used was not always correct or other terms and symbols were needed.

⑤ You used mathematical language that was correct and appropriate to make your meaning clear.

Representations

```
|——①——②——③——④——⑤——☆→
```

① You did not use any representations such as equations, tables, graphs, or diagrams to help solve the problem or explain your solution.

③ You made appropriate representations to help solve the problem or help you explain your solution, but they were not always correct or other representations were needed.

⑤ You used appropriate and correct representations to solve the problem or explain your solution.

Connections

```
|——①——②——③——④——⑤——☆→
```

① You attempted or solved the problem and then stopped.

③ You found patterns and used them to extend the solution to other cases, or you recognized that this problem relates to other problems, mathematical ideas, or applications.

⑤ You extended the ideas in the solution to the general case, or you showed how this problem relates to other problems, mathematical ideas, or applications.

Presentation

```
|——①——②——③——④——⑤——☆→
```

① The presentation of your solution and reasoning is unclear to others.

③ The presentation of your solution and reasoning is clear in most places, but others may have trouble understanding parts of it.

⑤ The presentation of your solution and reasoning is clear and can be understood by others.

Content Used: _____   **Computational Errors:**   Yes ☐   No ☐

Notes on Errors: _____

Copyright © by McDougal Littell Inc. All rights reserved.   Math Thematics, Book 1 **6-57**

Name _____   Problem _____

STUDENT SELF-ASSESSMENT SCALES

▬ *If your score is in the shaded area, explain why on the back of this sheet and stop.*

☆ *The star indicates that you excelled in some way.*

Problem Solving

① — **②** — **③** — **④** — **⑤** — ☆→

① I did not understand the problem well enough to get started or I did not show any work.

③ I understood the problem well enough to make a plan and to work toward a solution.

⑤ I made a plan, I used it to solve the problem, and I verified my solution.

Mathematical Language (x^2)

① — **②** — **③** — **④** — **⑤** — ☆→

① I did not use any mathematical vocabulary or symbols, or I did not use them correctly, or my use was not appropriate.

③ I used appropriate mathematical language, but the way it was used was not always correct or other terms and symbols were needed.

⑤ I used mathematical language that was correct and appropriate to make my meaning clear.

Representations

① — **②** — **③** — **④** — **⑤** — ☆→

① I did not use any representations such as equations, tables, graphs, or diagrams to help solve the problem or explain my solution.

③ I made appropriate representations to help solve the problem or help me explain my solution, but they were not always correct or other representations were needed.

⑤ I used appropriate and correct representations to solve the problem or explain my solution.

Connections

① — **②** — **③** — **④** — **⑤** — ☆→

① I attempted or solved the problem and then stopped.

③ I found patterns and used them to extend the solution to other cases, or I recognized that this problem relates to other problems, mathematical ideas, or applications.

⑤ I extended the ideas in the solution to the general case, or I showed how this problem relates to other problems, mathematical ideas, or applications.

Presentation

① — **②** — **③** — **④** — **⑤** — ☆→

① The presentation of my solution and reasoning is unclear to others.

③ The presentation of my solution and reasoning is clear in most places, but others may have trouble understanding parts of it.

⑤ The presentation of my solution and reasoning is clear and can be understood by others.

MODULE 6

SOLUTION GUIDE TEXTBOOK E²

The Ideal Chair (E² on textbook page 412)

This open-ended problem can be approached in a number of ways. Because of the limited experience and resources of students, we would expect few students to find tables of anthropometry data. The most likely methods include measuring and surveying. The most applicable Assessment Scales to use are Problem Solving, Representations, and Presentation. You may want to consider using the Mathematical Language Scale for some student work.

One way to introduce this problem to your students is to display a chair used in a primary classroom and one used in their class. Students should think about why the chair used in a primary classroom is inappropriate for their classroom. It is important for students to think about what an "ideal" chair is in this context. Students should focus on the height of the chair, length and width of the seat, and the height of the back rest.

In the partial solution below, the dimensions used are appropriate for at least 95% of 11 year olds.

Partial Solution
Height of the chair
I decided to survey 20 students at my grade level to find out what is the best height for a chair. I borrowed Mrs. Hendrick's chair since it can be adjusted for height. During lunch I asked students to sit in the chair and adjust it until they got the height that felt best. Then I measured the height of the chair from the floor to the bottom of the seat. I determined the mean of the heights (41.7 cm) and used this as the height of my ideal chair.

Width and length of the seat
The width and length of the chair seat is also important for comfort. To get the best fit, I asked the same 20 students to sit with their legs outstretched on a large sheet of paper and trace around their upper legs and bottom. I also had them mark where their knees were on the paper. I measured across the widest part of their bottoms and found the mean of all the widths (33.8 cm). I then added 6 cm because I thought most people would want a little extra room. This gave me a seat width of 39.8 cm. I then measured the length from the knee to the back of the bottom for all 20 students. I used the mean of these lengths as the length of my ideal chair. The mean length was 50.5 cm.

Height of the back rest
The back rest of chairs seems to be most comfortable if the top of the back rest reaches a person's shoulder blades. I asked the same 20 students to sit upright in a chair and measured the length from their bottoms to the midsection of their shoulder blades. The mean length was 45.6 cm. This seemed like a reasonable height for the back rest.

Other Considerations
- **Problem Solving** Since the problem does not state the criteria of an ideal chair, a student must determine that the dimensions of the chair are the most important factors. Students may come up with other attributes of the chair that are important to him or her, but these factors should be considered an extension of the problem. If students do not address the real concern of the E², they should score below a 3 on the Problem Solving Scale. The solutions to this problem will vary.
- **Presentations** Students should include the data they collected in their final report, along with any drawings or photos of their ideal chair.

MODULE 6

ALTERNATE E²

Squeeze Across America

The Situation

You will need a map of the United States.

On May 25, 1986, an organization called USA for Africa sponsored Hands Across America. This fund-raising event was designed to join 6 million people in a human chain across the United States.

Suppose you are one of the organizers of an event called *Squeeze Across America* in which students at your grade level pass a hand squeeze from Los Angeles to New York City. The students line up holding hands with their arms outstretched. The first person in Los Angeles squeezes the hand of the second person who immediately squeezes the hand of the third person and so on until the squeeze reaches the last person holding hands in New York City.

The Problem

How long would it take to pass the squeeze along a route of your choice from Los Angeles to New York City?

Something to Think About

- Are there enough students at your grade level in the United States to pass a hand squeeze from Los Angeles to New York City? How would you determine this?
- Which cities would your route pass through? Think about any difficulties you might encounter.

Present Your Results

Describe the route you would use. How long would it take to pass the squeeze across the United States? Include any tables, graphs, or diagrams that would help explain your plan.

MODULE 6 — SOLUTION GUIDE ALTERNATE E²

Squeeze Across America

Expect a variety of answers to this open-ended E². The best Assessment Scales to use are Problem Solving, Mathematical Language, Representations, and Presentation. Students will need access to an almanac for data on population and mileage. Students will need to do their own surveying or experimenting to find the arm span of the average student and the amount of time it takes to pass along a squeeze.

Partial Solution

I picked a route going through Denver, Omaha, Chicago and Cleveland. This seemed like the quickest way to get from Los Angeles to New York City. The total mileage is 3084 miles. I found this information in the 1996 *Information Please Almanac*.

Los Angeles to Denver	1174 miles
Denver to Omaha	559 miles
Omaha to Chicago	493 miles
Chicago to Cleveland	344 miles
Cleveland to New York City	514 miles
Total from Los Angeles to New York City	3084 miles

I then measured the arm span of 10 students in my class. The mean arm span was 5.25 ft. Since 3084 mi = 16,283,520 ft, I would need 16,283,520/5.25 = 3,101,622.857 kids, or about 3.1 million students.

According to the almanac, there are 15,281,000 students aged 10 to 13 years old in the United States. So I knew there were enough students in the total U.S., but I didn't know where they all were. Were enough of them in the states my route would travel through? The almanac also lists the population by state. I used this information to approximate the percent of the U.S. population for the states my route would travel through.

I assumed there is the same distribution of students in these states. 45% of 15,281,000 is 6,876,450 students aged 10 to 13 years. This is greater than my estimated need of 3.1 million students. Because many states, like California, are large many of the students would not be able to participate in the event. Since there are over twice the number of students needed however, we should be able to get 3.1 million students aged 10 to 13 years to participate.

State	Percent of total US population
California	12.0
Arizona	1.5
Utah	0.7
Colorado	1.3
Nebraska	0.6
Iowa	1.1
Illinois	4.6
Michigan	3.7
Ohio	4.4
Pennsylvania	4.8
New Jersey	3.1
New York	7.2
Total	45.0

I asked 10 of my friends to line up and pass a hand squeeze so I could figure out how much time it would take. They were able to do it in 7 seconds. I used a proportion to find the total time for 3.1 million people.

$$\frac{x \text{ seconds}}{3.1 \text{ million people}} = \frac{7 \text{ seconds}}{10 \text{ people}}$$

$x = 2,170,000$ seconds $\approx 36,167$ minutes ≈ 602.8 hours ≈ 25.12 days

It would take about 25 days to pass the squeeze across the United States!

Other Considerations

- **Problem Solving** Students will need to state their assumption about how long it takes a squeeze to travel. They will also need to consider the impact of deserts, mountain ranges, lakes, rivers, and the time of year on the event.

MODULE 6 SECTION 1 — WARM-UPS

Write each fraction in lowest terms.

1. $\dfrac{4}{14}$
2. $\dfrac{8}{36}$
3. $\dfrac{9}{36}$
4. $\dfrac{6}{11}$
5. $\dfrac{57}{152}$
6. $\dfrac{10}{10}$

MODULE 6 SECTION 1 — QUICK QUIZ

1. A certain trail mix contains 12 peanuts for every 20 raisins. Write the ratio of raisins to peanuts in each of three ways.

2. Which pair of ratios is equivalent?

    A. 2 : 7 and 6 : 14

    B. $\dfrac{4}{11}$ and $\dfrac{12}{33}$

    C. 2 to 3 and 4 to 9

3. What is the ratio of vowels to consonants in the word MATHEMATICS?

4. An animal shelter has 12 dogs, 20 cats, and 4 other animals. What is the ratio of dogs to all of the animals at the shelter?

5. What is the ratio of the number of vertices of a polygon to its number of sides?

ANSWERS

Warm-Ups: 1. $\dfrac{2}{7}$ 2. $\dfrac{2}{9}$ 3. $\dfrac{1}{4}$ 4. $\dfrac{6}{11}$ 5. $\dfrac{3}{8}$ 6. $\dfrac{1}{1}$ or 1

Quick-Quiz: 1. 3 to 5; 3 : 5; $\dfrac{3}{5}$ 2. B 3. 4 to 7 4. 12 to 36, or 1 to 3 5. 1 to 1

| MODULE 6 SECTION 2 | WARM-UPS |

Name at least three different units of measurement for each category.

1. distance   2. time   3. volume   4. weight

| MODULE 6 SECTION 2 | QUICK QUIZ |

1. Are the rates equivalent ratios?
    a. 120 mi in 2 h, 210 mi in 3 h
    b. $10 for 50 lb, $25 for 125 lb

2. Find a unit rate for each rate.
    a. 1000 m in 5 min   b. $120 for 15 h

3. Which is the better buy, 5 lb of flour for $1.69 or 12 lb of flour for $4.25?

4. If Eric can read 130 pages in 2 h, how long will it take him to read a 325 page novel?

5. It takes $\frac{1}{3}$ c of sugar to make 12 muffins. Complete the table.

Cups of sugar	Number of muffins
$\frac{2}{3}$	
1	
2	
3	

ANSWERS

Warm-Ups: Sample responses are given. **1.** feet, centimeters, inches **2.** seconds, minutes, hours **3.** gallons, milliliters, cups **4.** pounds, grams, ounces

Quick-Quiz: 1. a. No **b.** Yes **2. a.** 200 m/min **b.** $8/h **3.** 5 lb for $1.69 **4.** 5 h **5.** 24, 36, 72, 108

MODULE 6 SECTION 3 — WARM-UPS

Compare the numbers. Use >, <, or =.

1. $\dfrac{1}{2}$ ___?___ $\dfrac{1}{3}$

2. $\dfrac{4}{5}$ ___?___ $\dfrac{5}{6}$

3. $\dfrac{9}{12}$ ___?___ $\dfrac{3}{4}$

4. $\dfrac{10}{15}$ ___?___ $\dfrac{14}{21}$

5. $\dfrac{8}{9}$ ___?___ $\dfrac{9}{8}$

6. $\dfrac{4}{3}$ ___?___ 1

MODULE 6 SECTION 3 — QUICK QUIZ

1. What is the ratio of the length of one side of a regular hexagon to its perimeter? If a regular hexagon has 12 in. sides, what is its perimeter?

2. Write each ratio as a decimal to the nearest hundredth.

   a. 8 : 11   b. 5 : 9   c. 13 : 20

3. Write a "nice" fraction for each ratio.

   a. 12 : 58   b. 0.39   c. 43 to 99

4. Make a scatter plot using the data in the table. Use the scatter plot to predict the missing numbers in the table.

1	2	3	4	5	6	8	11
2	5	8	12	?	18	?	?

ANSWERS

Warm-Ups: 1. >   2. <   3. =   4. =   5. <   6. >

Quick-Quiz: 1. 1 : 6; 72 in.   2. a. 0.73 b. 0.56 c. 0.65   3. a. $\dfrac{1}{5}$ b. $\dfrac{2}{5}$ c. $\dfrac{4}{9}$
4. Sample Response: 15, 24, 33

6-64   Math Thematics, Book 1

| **MODULE 6 SECTION 4** | **WARM-UPS** |

Use mental math to solve.

1. $\dfrac{1}{3} = \dfrac{x}{6}$

2. $\dfrac{y}{21} = \dfrac{2}{7}$

3. $\dfrac{40}{m} = \dfrac{10}{12}$

4. $\dfrac{100}{10} = \dfrac{10}{n}$

5. $\dfrac{a}{13} = \dfrac{12}{13}$

6. $\dfrac{5}{b} = \dfrac{2}{4}$

| **MODULE 6 SECTION 4** | **QUICK QUIZ** |

1. Use cross products to tell whether the ratios are equivalent.

   a. $\dfrac{12}{9}$ and $\dfrac{8}{6}$
   b. $\dfrac{14}{6}$ and $\dfrac{35}{15}$
   c. $\dfrac{10}{24}$ and $\dfrac{3}{8}$

2. Find the missing term in each proportion.

   a. $\dfrac{3}{25} = \dfrac{x}{175}$
   b. $\dfrac{7}{36} = \dfrac{21}{y}$
   c. $\dfrac{18}{48} = \dfrac{x}{40}$

3. If 16 notebooks cost $27.04, how much will 25 notebooks cost?

4. If two tractor trailers have 36 wheels, how many wheels are there on 5 tractor trailers?

5. Emily's nine hamsters eat 3 oz of food each day. How many ounces would 24 hamsters eat in a week?

ANSWERS

Warm-Ups: 1. $x = 2$ 2. $y = 6$ 3. $m = 48$ 4. $n = 1$ 5. $a = 12$ 6. $b = 10$

Quick-Quiz: 1. a. Yes b. Yes c. No 2. a. 21 b. 108 c. 15 3. $42.25 4. 90 wheels
5. 56 oz

| MODULE 6 SECTION 5 | WARM-UPS |

Draw two triangles that have the given characteristics. If it is not possible to draw the triangles, write *not possible*.

1. same size, same shape
2. different size, same shape
3. different size, different shape

| MODULE 6 SECTION 5 | QUICK QUIZ |

1. The two triangles shown are similar. Make a table showing all the pairs of corresponding angles and corresponding sides. Then find the missing lengths.

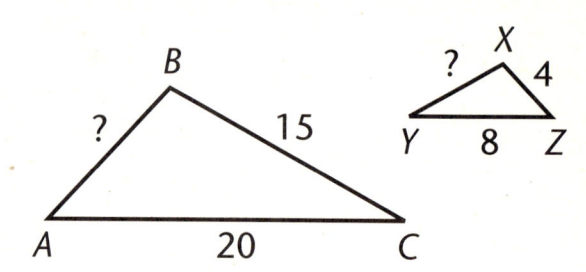

2. For each scale, find how long a measure of $1\frac{1}{2}$ in. on the drawing would be on the actual object.

   a. 1 in. : 18 ft
   b. 2 in. : 12 ft

3. Scientists estimate that the longest dinosaur was between 128 ft and 170 ft long. To make a model of this dinosaur that would fit on your desk, what scale might you use?

4. On a map with a scale of 1 in. : 38 mi, it is $4\frac{1}{2}$ in. from town A to town B. What is the actual distance?

5. Use a protractor to draw an angle with each measure.

   a. 25°
   b. 59°
   c. 132°

ANSWERS

Warm-Ups: Sample drawings. 1. 2. 3.

Quick-Quiz: 1. ∠A corresponds to ∠Z, ∠B corresponds to ∠X, ∠C corresponds to ∠Y, $\overline{AB}$ corresponds to $\overline{XZ}$, $\overline{BC}$ corresponds to $\overline{XY}$, $\overline{AC}$ corresponds to $\overline{YZ}$, AB = 10, XY = 6
2. a. 27 ft b. 9 ft 3. Sample Response: 1 in. to 10 ft 4. 171 mi

5. a.   b.   c.

MODULE 6 SECTION 6 — WARM-UPS

Write each percent as a decimal.

1. 67%
2. 100%
3. 9%

Write each percent as a fraction.

4. 89%
5. 7%
6. 43%

MODULE 6 SECTION 6 — QUICK QUIZ

1. Estimate a percent for each fraction.

   a. $\dfrac{39}{59}$ b. $\dfrac{18}{51}$ c. $\dfrac{181}{203}$

2. Lou Brock holds the record for the highest batting average in World Series play. He got a hit in 39% of his at-bats. If he had 82 at-bats, use a "nice" fraction to estimate how many hits he got.

3. Suppose a pitcher won 15 games out of the 21 she pitched. Use a "nice" fraction to estimate the percent of the games she pitched that she won.

4. Make a tree diagram showing the possible outcomes in a game of Dueling Spinners in which one player spins Spinner A and the other player spins Spinner B.

   Spinner A (sections: 3, 6, 11)   Spinner B (sections: 1, 4, 7, 15)

ANSWERS

Warm-Ups: 1. 0.67   2. 1.00   3. 0.09   4. $\dfrac{89}{100}$ 5. $\dfrac{7}{100}$ 6. $\dfrac{43}{100}$

Quick-Quiz: 1. a. about $66\tfrac{2}{3}$%   b. about 40%   c. about 90%   2. about 32   3. about 75%

4.

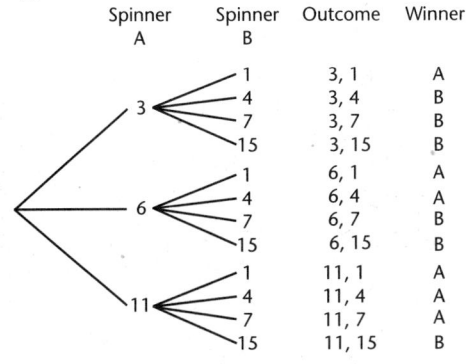

Spinner A	Spinner B	Outcome	Winner
3	1	3, 1	A
3	4	3, 4	B
3	7	3, 7	B
3	15	3, 15	B
6	1	6, 1	A
6	4	6, 4	A
6	7	6, 7	B
6	15	6, 15	B
11	1	11, 1	A
11	4	11, 4	A
11	7	11, 7	A
11	15	11, 15	B

MODULE 6 SECTION 1 PRACTICE AND APPLICATIONS

For use with Exploration 1

1. Write each ratio in three ways.

Fruit Supply Warehouse	
Fruit	Number of Cases
apples	248
oranges	160
pears	38
bananas	90
grapes	52

   a. cases of apples to cases of oranges

   b. cases of pears to cases of grapes

   c. cases of bananas to cases of apples

   d. cases of grapes to cases of oranges

   e. cases of apples to cases of pears

   f. cases of oranges to cases of bananas

2. Draw a picture to show each ratio.

   a. Number of circles to number of squares is four to seven.

   b. Number of stars to number of diamonds is 3 : 8.

   c. Number of cups to number of glasses is $\frac{5}{2}$.

   d. Number of bananas to number of apples is two to three.

   e. Number of triangles to number of rectangles is 6 : 1.

3. Tell whether the ratios are equivalent.

   a. 8 : 3 and 24 : 9   **b.** 5 : 8 and 30 : 40   **c.** 15 : 9 and 9 : 15

   d. $\frac{12}{15}$ and $\frac{4}{5}$ **e.** $\frac{45}{6}$ and $\frac{90}{12}$ **f.** $\frac{6}{9}$ and $\frac{10}{15}$

   g. 7 to 9 and 35 to 45   **h.** 3 to 8 and 13 to 8   **i.** 5 to 12 and 120 to 50

4. There are 8 pencils for every 5 students.

   a. Write the ratio of pencils to students in three ways.

   b. Write the ratio of students to pencils in three ways.

Name _____ Date _____

MODULE 6 SECTION 2 | PRACTICE AND APPLICATIONS

For use with Exploration 1

1. Tell whether each ratio is a rate.

   a. 60 words in 2 min

   b. 6 ft in 1 sec

   c. 5 min for every 30 min

   d. 8 ft to 80 ft

   e. 95 m in 4 sec

   f. 12 pages in 3 min

   g. 7 km for every 15 km

   h. 8 gal per minute

   i. 3 baskets in 5 free throws

2. Tell whether the rates are equivalent ratios.

   a. $\frac{9 \text{ pages}}{5 \text{ min}}, \frac{90 \text{ pages}}{45 \text{ min}}$

   b. $\frac{120 \text{ words}}{4 \text{ min}}, \frac{480 \text{ words}}{16 \text{ min}}$

   c. $6 for 8 lb, $36 for 48 lb

   d. 65 mi on 12 gal, 6.5 mi on 6 gal

3. Find a unit rate for each rate.

   a. 15 pages in 5 min

   b. 3000 km in 4 days

   c. 92 mi on 4 gal

   d. 300 ft in 125 steps

   e. $50 for 8 books

   f. 20 ft in 3 min

4. Tell which is a better buy.

   a. $1.62 for 9 lb of onions or $2.25 for 15 lb of onions

   b. $12.70 for 9 lb of peanuts or $10.90 for 8 lb of peanuts

   c. $2.88 for 24 oz of grape juice or $11.52 for 64 oz of grape juice

   d. $2.10 for 6 apples or $5.25 for 15 apples

5. Copy and complete the table.

Number of miles	5	10	15	20	?
Time (minutes)	6	?	?	?	30

6. Kevin runs about 9 ft in one second.

   a. At this rate, how far does he run in 1 minute? In 10 minutes?

   b. Does it take Kevin more or less than 10 minutes to run one mile? Explain.

Copyright © by McDougal Littell Inc. All rights reserved.

Math Thematics, Book 1 **6-69**

MODULE 6 SECTION 3 **PRACTICE AND APPLICATIONS**

For use with Exploration 1

1. Use the ratio 1 : 3 as an estimate for the body ratios thumb length to hand length, hand length to shoulder width, and shoulder width to body length. Suppose the length of Mark's hand is 12 cm.

   a. Estimate his thumb length.

   b. Estimate his shoulder width.

   c. Estimate his body length.

2. Write each ratio as a decimal to the nearest hundredth.

   a. 5 : 7   b. 4 : 9   c. 2 : 11
   d. 8 : 15   e. 7 : 12   f. 3 : 16

For use with Exploration 2

3. Write a "nice" fraction for each ratio.

   a. 4 : 23   b. 0.69   c. $\frac{11}{45}$
   d. 0.8 to 1   e. 6 : 50   f. $\frac{9}{44}$

For Exercise 4, use the data in the table.

Child	A	B	C	D	E
Seated height (cm) / Standing height (cm)	$\frac{62}{98}$	$\frac{72}{115}$	$\frac{69}{112}$	$\frac{74}{114}$	$\frac{81}{128}$

4. a. Find the mean of the *seated height* to *standing height* ratios.

   b. Write a simple fraction that is close to the mean.

   c. Use your simple fraction to estimate the missing entries in the table.

Seated height (cm)	68	?	?	75
Standing height (cm)	?	120	124	?

(continued)

MODULE 6 SECTION 3
PRACTICE AND APPLICATIONS

For use with Exploration 3

For Exercise 5, use the data in the table, which shows the seated height and standing height of five children.

Seated height (cm)	62	72	69	74	81
Standing height (cm)	98	115	112	114	128

5. a. Make a scatterplot that shows the relationship between the seated height and the standing height of each child in the table.

   b. Use a piece of uncooked spaghetti or a clear ruler to draw a fitted line on your scatterplot.

   c. Use your scatterplot to estimate the missing entries in the table.

Seated height (cm)	68	?	?	75
Standing height (cm)	?	120	124	?

6. a. Which fitted line would you use to make predictions about the shoulder width of a child or predictions about a child's height? Why?

Height Compared to Shoulder Width

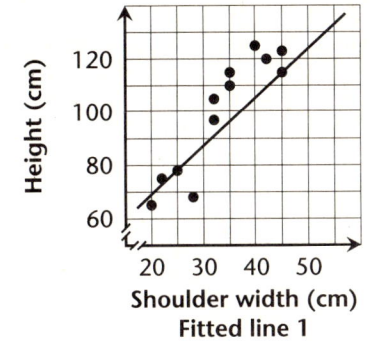

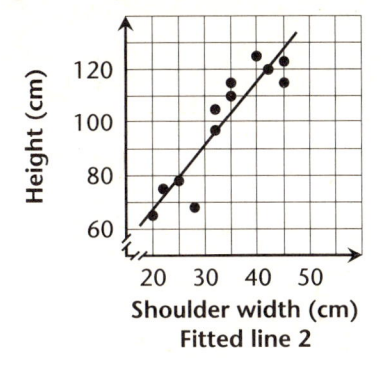

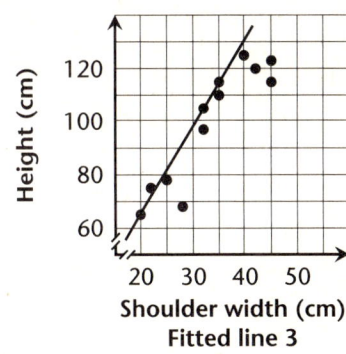

Fitted line 1

Fitted line 2

Fitted line 3

   b. Use your choice from part (a) to predict the height of a child with a shoulder width of 35 cm.

MODULE 6 SECTION 4 — **PRACTICE AND APPLICATIONS**

For use with Exploration 1

1. Use cross products to tell whether the ratios are equivalent.

   a. $\dfrac{36}{45}$ and $\dfrac{12}{15}$ b. $\dfrac{17}{24}$ and $\dfrac{51}{72}$ c. $\dfrac{8}{9}$ and $\dfrac{36}{40}$

   d. $\dfrac{3}{8}$ and $\dfrac{15}{24}$ e. $\dfrac{16}{30}$ and $\dfrac{56}{105}$ f. $\dfrac{26}{15}$ and $\dfrac{65}{38}$

2. Find all the equivalent ratios in each list.

   a. $\dfrac{12}{30}, \dfrac{27}{72}, \dfrac{4.5}{12}, \dfrac{60}{150}, \dfrac{18}{48}$ b. $\dfrac{5}{9}, \dfrac{14}{8.5}, \dfrac{40}{72}, \dfrac{7}{12}, \dfrac{56}{34}$

3. Find the missing term in each proportion.

   a. $\dfrac{4}{18} = \dfrac{10}{x}$ b. $\dfrac{8}{14} = \dfrac{12}{n}$ c. $\dfrac{9}{15} = \dfrac{b}{75}$

   d. $\dfrac{m}{8} = \dfrac{4.2}{2.4}$ e. $\dfrac{24}{18} = \dfrac{38.4}{s}$ f. $\dfrac{6}{y} = \dfrac{21}{52.5}$

   g. $14 : 5 = 70 : c$ h. $a : 20 = 24 : 96$ i. $9 : p = 45 : 18$

For use with Exploration 2

4. If appropriate, use a proportion to solve each problem. If it is not appropriate to use a proportion, explain why not.

   a. Six pairs of shorts cost $27. How much will nine pairs of shorts cost?

   b. Carmen used 5 ft of string to make 4 mobiles. How much string will she need to make 18 mobiles?

   c. Five art magazines cost $14.25. How much will eight sports magazines cost?

   d. Four baseball caps cost $25. How many baseball caps can you buy with $43.75?

   e. Two helicopters were used for rescue missions from 8 A.M. to 11 A.M. How many helicopters will be used for rescue missions in a twelve hour period?

Name _____ Date _____

MODULE 6 SECTION 5 — PRACTICE AND APPLICATIONS

For use with Exploration 1

1. The figures in each pair are similar. List all the pairs of corresponding angles and corresponding sides.

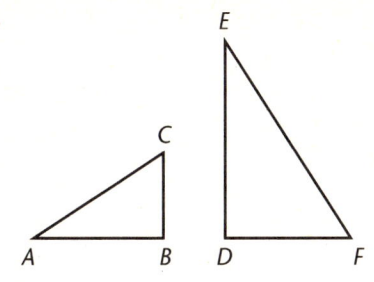

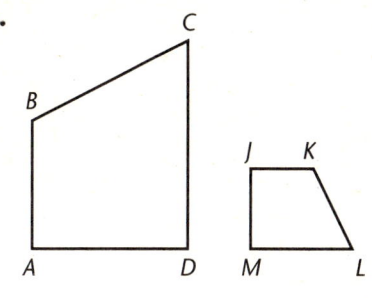

   a. [Triangles ACB and EDF]

   b. [Quadrilaterals ABCD and MJKL]

2. Tell whether the figures in each pair are similar or congruent. If they are not similar, explain how you know.

   a. [Two triangles]

   b. [Two rectangles]

3. The figures in each pair are similar. Use proportions to find the missing lengths.

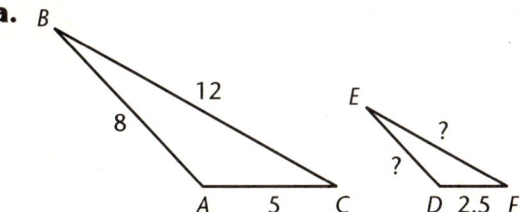

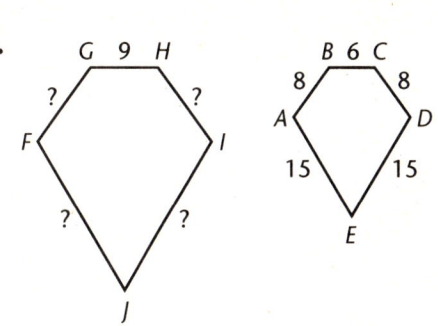

   a. [Triangle BAC with BA = 8, BC = 12, AC = 5; Triangle EDF with DF = 2.5, ED = ?, EF = ?]

   b. [Pentagon FGHIJ with GH = 9, and ? marks; Pentagon ABCDE with BC = 6, AB = 8, CD = 8, AE = 15, DE = 15]

4. A rectangular tablecloth is similar to a rectangular table. The table is 8 ft long by 6 ft wide. How wide is the tablecloth if it is 10 ft long?

(continued)

Copyright © by McDougal Littell Inc. All rights reserved.   Math Thematics, Book 1 6-73

| MODULE 6 SECTION 5 | PRACTICE AND APPLICATIONS |

For use with Exploration 2

5. For each scale, find how long a measure of 4 in. on the drawing would be on the actual object.

   a. 1 in. : 8 ft   **b.** 2 in. : 5 ft   **c.** $\frac{1}{2}$ in. : $3\frac{1}{2}$ in.

6. a. In a floor plan drawing of a home, the living room is 3.4 in. wide. The actual living room is 51 ft wide. What is the scale?

   b. The length of the master bedroom is 37.5 ft. What is the length of the bedroom in the drawing?

   c. The width of the hallway in the drawing is 0.5 in. How wide is the actual hallway?

   d. In the drawing, the length of the house is 8 in. and the width is 5 in. What is the perimeter of the actual house?

For use with Exploration 3

7. Trace each angle and extend the rays. Then find each angle's measure.

   a.    **b.** 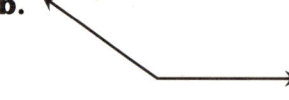   **c.**

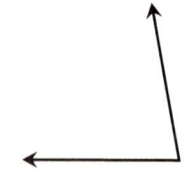

8. Use a protractor to draw an angle with each measure.

   a. 24°   **b.** 136°   **c.** 82°
   d. 47°   **e.** 169°   **f.** 64°

Name _____ Date _____

MODULE 6 SECTION 6 — PRACTICE AND APPLICATIONS

For use with Exploration 1

1. Use a fraction in lowest terms to find each value.

   a. 20% of 65   **b.** 10% of 70   **c.** 25% of 56

   d. 30% of 400   **e.** 75% of 112   **f.** 5% of 500

   g. 70% of 30   **h.** 80% of 60   **i.** 90% of 40

   j. 25% of 120   **k.** 60% of 90   **l.** 40% of 40

   m. 4% of 75   **n.** 70% of 140   **o.** 75% of 280

2. A jacket is discounted 25%. The original cost of the jacket is $50.

   a. Use mental math to find 10% of $50.

   b. Use mental math to find 20% of $50.

   c. Use mental math to find 5% of $50.

   d. Use parts (a)-(c) to find 25% of $50.

   e. Use mental math to find 50% of $50.

   f. Use mental math to find $\frac{1}{2}$ of 50% or 25% of $25. Which method do you think is easier for finding 25% of $50?

3. Estimate a percent for each fraction.

   a. $\frac{45}{85}$ **b.** $\frac{21}{80}$ **c.** $\frac{22}{52}$

   d. $\frac{11}{30}$ **e.** $\frac{63}{81}$ **f.** $\frac{48}{99}$

4. Lindsay scored in about 76% of the basketball games in which she played. She played in 21 games. Use a "nice" fraction to estimate the number of games in which she scored. Is your estimate higher or lower than the actual number of games? Why?

(continued)

Name	Date

MODULE 6 SECTION 6 — PRACTICE AND APPLICATIONS

For use with Exploration 2

5. This tree shows the outcomes of flipping a coin and spinning the spinner.

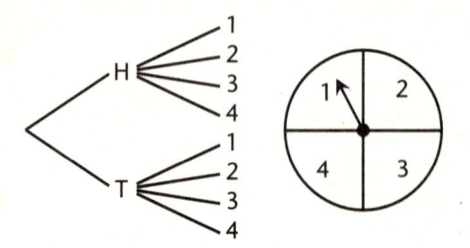

    a. List the outcomes.

    b. List the outcomes with an even number.

    c. What percent of the time would you expect an outcome to contain an even number?

    d. How many times would you expect to get an even number in 40 trials?

    e. What percent of the time would you expect to get a head and a 1 or a tail and a 3?

    f. How many times would you expect this to happen in 60 trials?

6. Suppose you spin the spinner at the right twice.

    a. Draw a tree diagram to show the possible outcomes.

    b. What is the probability of spinning 3 twice?

    c. What is the probability of spinning doubles (both 1s, both 2s, or both 3s)?

    d. What is the probability of spinning a 2 and a 3?

7. Nick flips a coin and draws a card at random (without looking) from five number cards numbered 1, 2, 3, 4, and 5.

    a. What is the probability of a head and a 1?

    b. What is the probability of a tail and an even number?

    c. What is the probability of a head and a number less than 5?

MODULE 6 SECTIONS 1–6 — PRACTICE AND APPLICATIONS

For use with Section 1

1. Write each ratio three ways.

  a. Number of circles to number of squares.

  b. Number of diamonds to number of triangles.

  ○ ○ ○ □ □ □ □ □   ◇ ◇ ◇ ◇ ◇ ◇ △ △

2. Tell whether the ratios are equivalent.

  a. 7 : 5 and 49 : 35   **b.** $\frac{26}{32}$ and $\frac{65}{80}$ **c.** 15 to 18 and 5 to 9

3. There are 3 soccer balls for every 4 players on the soccer team. What is the ratio of players to balls? Write the ratio three ways.

For use with Section 2

4. Find a unit rate for each rate.

  a. 1125 mi in 5 days   **b.** $144 for 6 art books   **c.** 128 km on 4 gal

5. Tell which is a better buy.

  a. $1.40 for 5 oranges or $1.84 for 8 oranges

  b. $2.40 for 16 oz of cherry juice or $3.84 for 24 oz of cherry juice

6. Cindy can read 48 pages in 24 minutes. At this rate, how many pages can Cindy read in one half hour? In two hours?

For use with Section 3

7. Write each ratio as a decimal to the nearest hundredth.

  a. 3 : 7   **b.** 2 : 9   **c.** 7 : 11

  d. 16 : 19   **e.** 4 : 15   **f.** 5 : 12

8. Write a "nice" fraction for each ratio.

  a. 24 : 31   **b.** 0.29   **c.** $\frac{12}{52}$

(continued)

Name _____ Date _____

MODULE 6 SECTIONS 1–6 — PRACTICE AND APPLICATIONS

For use with Section 4

9. Find the missing term in each proportion.

   a. $\dfrac{8}{15} = \dfrac{28}{x}$ **b.** $\dfrac{7}{n} = \dfrac{112}{384}$ **c.** $\dfrac{12}{76} = \dfrac{b}{171}$

For use with Section 5

10. The figures in each pair are similar. Use proportions to find the missing lengths.

   a.

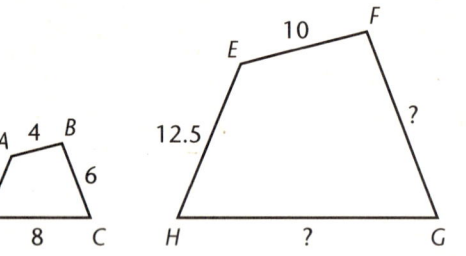

   b.

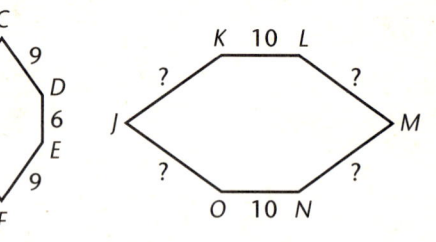

11. For each scale, find how long a measure of 3 in. on the drawing would be on the actual object.

   a. 1 in. : 15 ft   **b.** 2 in. : 7 ft   **c.** $\dfrac{1}{2}$ in. : $5\dfrac{1}{2}$ yd

12. Use a protractor to draw an angle with each measure.

   a. 38°   **b.** 160°   **c.** 73°

For use with Section 6

13. Use a fraction in lowest terms to find each value.

   a. 75% of 80   **b.** 40% of 55   **c.** 60% of 90

14. Estimate a percent for each fraction.

   a. $\dfrac{38}{79}$ **b.** $\dfrac{1}{9}$ **c.** $\dfrac{41}{52}$

15. Suppose you spin the spinner at the right twice.

   a. What is the probability of spinning an even number?

   b. What is the probability of spinning 3 twice?

Name _____ Date _____

MODULE 6 SECTION 1   STUDY GUIDE

Mr. Short and Mr. Tall   Exploring Ratios

GOAL   **LEARN HOW TO:** • make comparisons using ratios
• recognize and write equivalent ratios
AS YOU: • compare numbers and measures

Exploration 1: Comparing Measures

Ratios

A **ratio** is a special type of comparison of two numbers or measures. A ratio can be written in three ways: (1) using the word *to*, (2) using a colon, and (3) as a fraction.

> **Example**
>
> The ratio comparing 6 to 12 can be written in these three ways:
>
> | using the word *to* | using a colon | as a fraction |
> |---|---|---|
> | 6 to 12 | 6 : 12 | $\frac{6}{12}$ |
>
> The order of the numbers in a ratio is important. 6 : 12 is not the same as 12 : 6.

Equivalent Ratios

Sometimes a ratio of two measures can be shown another way by separating the two measures into the same number of groups.

> **Example**
>
> In the 3rd period study hall, there are 20 boys and 12 girls. You can compare the number of boys to the number of girls by using the ratio 20 to 12,
>
> or by using 2 groups of each kind   or by using 4 groups of each kind.
>
> | BBBBB | ↔ | GGG |
> | BBBBB | ↔ | GGG |
>
> | BBBBBBBBBB | ↔ | GGGGGG | | BBBBB | ↔ | GGG |
> | BBBBBBBBBB | ↔ | GGGGGG | | BBBBB | ↔ | GGG |
>
> 10 boys   to   6 girls   5 boys   to   3 girls
>
> So, to compare the number of boys to the number of girls in the study hall, you can use the ratio 20 : 12, or the ratio 10 : 6, or the ratio 5 : 3.

Name _____ Date _____

MODULE 6 SECTION 1 — STUDY GUIDE

Ratios that can be written as equivalent fractions are called **equivalent ratios**. The table shows that the ratio 20 : 12 is equivalent to the ratio 10 : 6.

Ratio	Fraction	Equivalent Fraction
20 : 12	$\frac{20}{12}$	$\frac{5}{3}$
10 : 6	$\frac{10}{6}$	$\frac{5}{3}$

MODULE 6 SECTION 1 — PRACTICE & APPLICATION EXERCISES

Exploration 1

1. **a.** In one study hall, there are 16 boys and 12 girls. In another study hall, there are 20 boys and 15 girls. What is the ratio of boys to girls in each study hall?

   b. Are the ratios you found in part (a) equivalent? Explain.

2. **Physics** An *inclined plane*, such as a *ramp*, is a simple machine that is designed to move a mass. When a man rolls a heavy barrel up a ramp of length l to a height of h, the man does not have to exert as much force as he would need to in order to lift the barrel straight up from the ground to the same height h. An inclined plane provides a mechanical advantage equal to the *ratio of the length of the plane to its height*.

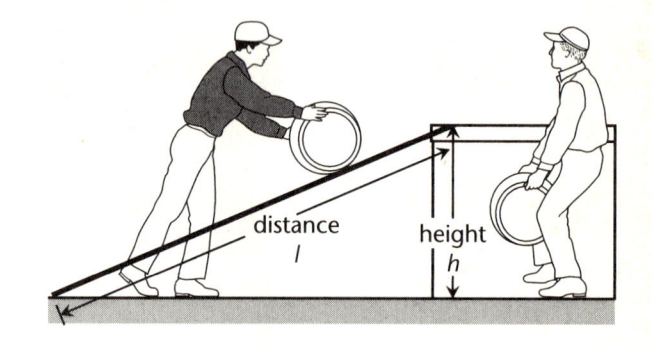

   a. Suppose a man is rolling a barrel a distance of 5 ft along a ramp in order to raise the barrel to a height of 3 ft. Write the mechanical advantage of this inclined plane as a ratio in three different ways.

   b. Suppose the barrel was rolled 10 ft along a ramp to raise it to a height of 6 ft. Write this mechanical advantage as a ratio in three different ways.

   c. Are the ratios you wrote in parts (a) and (b) equivalent? Explain.

For Exercises 3–6, tell whether the ratios are equivalent.

3. $\frac{2}{3}$ and $\frac{4}{9}$ 4. $\frac{4}{7}$ and $\frac{16}{28}$ 5. 1 : 5 and 15 : 3   6. 2 : 9 and 8 : 36

7. **Probability** When a coin is tossed, there are two possible outcomes, *heads* or *tails*. These outcomes are equally likely. Write the ratio that expresses the theoretical probability of getting *heads* in one toss of the coin.

MODULE 6 SECTION 1 | PRACTICE & APPLICATION EXERCISES | STUDY GUIDE

8. **Writing** The triangles represent the inclines for two hills. Which hill do you think is harder to climb? Explain.

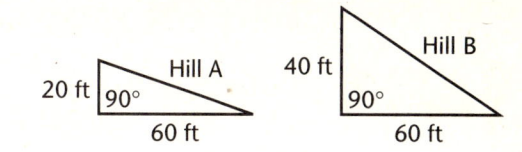

9. **a.** Write the coordinates of points *A*, *B*, and *C*.

   b. What is the difference in the vertical coordinates of points *A* and *B*? What is the difference in the horizontal coordinates? Write the ratio of these differences.

   c. What is the difference in the vertical coordinates of points *B* and *C*? What is the difference in the horizontal coordinates? Write the ratio of these differences.

   d. Make an observation about the ratios you wrote in parts (b) and (c).

   e. Make an observation about the way in which the points *A*, *B*, and *C* fall on the grid.

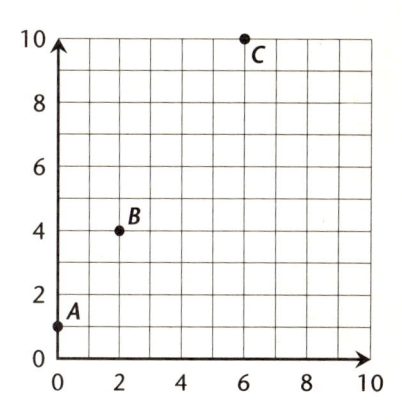

Spiral Review

10. On Thanksgiving Day of 1997, despite the blustery winds, 17 giant character balloons tried to fly in the 71st Macy's Parade in New York City. Most of the balloons made it through the entire parade route. The table at the right lists the balloons in their intended order of appearance and shows their lengths (or height if the balloon travels upright).

    a. Find the range of the lengths.
    (Module 3, pp. 184)

    b. Find the mean, the median, and the mode of the lengths. (Module 3, pp. 196–198)

    c. Make a stem-and-leaf plot of the lengths.
    (Module 3, pp. 219–220)

Lengths of the Character Balloons in 1997 Macy's Thanksgiving Day Parade

Balloon Character	Length (ft)
Arthur	68
Big Bird	67
Garfield	61
Peter Rabbit	60
Flying Fish	30
Pink Panther	100
Barney	58
The Cat in the Hat	59
Cloe the Holiday Clown	30
Rugrats	60
Bumpé	55
Sonic the Hedgehog	64
Spider Man	78
Harold the Fireman	32
Quik Bunny	68
Ms. Petula Pig	36
Eben Bear	62

Name _____ Date _____

MODULE 6 SECTION 2 **STUDY GUIDE**

The Sandbag Brigade   Rates

GOAL **LEARN HOW TO:** • find unit rates
• use rates to make predictions
AS YOU: • analyze data

Exploration 1: Using Rates and Unit Rates

Rates

A **rate** is a ratio that compares two quantities measured in different units. For instance, taking 20 min to read 2 pages is a rate. Rates may also be expressed as equivalent ratios.

> **Example**
>
> The pairs of numbers in this table form equivalent ratios.
>
> $\dfrac{20 \text{ min}}{2 \text{ pages}} = \dfrac{30 \text{ min}}{3 \text{ pages}} = \cdots$
>
> | Time (min) | Pages read |
> |---|---|
> | 20 | 2 |
> | 30 | 3 |
> | 40 | 4 |
> | 50 | 5 |

Unit Rates

A rate that gives an amount per one unit is called a **unit rate.**

> **Example**
>
> To find a unit rate for the situation discussed in the previous example, you need to find an equivalent ratio with a denominator of 1 page.
>
> First write the given rate as a ratio. $\dfrac{20 \text{ min}}{2 \text{ pages}}$
>
> Then set up a rate for the number of minutes per one page. Use the variable x to represent the number of minutes. $\dfrac{20 \text{ min}}{2 \text{ pages}} = \dfrac{x \text{ min}}{1 \text{ page}}$
>
> To find the value of x, compare the denominators.
>
> Since you must divide 2 pages by 2 to obtain 1 page, divide the numerator, 20 min, by 2 also: $20 \div 2 = 10$.
>
> So, $x = 10$.
>
> The unit rate for the situation is $\dfrac{10 \text{ min}}{1 \text{ page}}$, or 10 min/page (read "10 minutes per page").

Name _____ Date _____

MODULE 6 SECTION 2 — STUDY GUIDE

Using Unit Rates to Make Predictions

When you know a unit rate, you can use that value to make predictions.

Example

Use the unit rate $\frac{10 \text{ min}}{1 \text{ page}}$ to predict how long it will take a person reading at this rate to read 15 pages.

Sample Response

Set up equivalent ratios. Use the variable y to represent the number of minutes.

$$\frac{10 \text{ min}}{1 \text{ page}} = \frac{y \text{ min}}{15 \text{ pages}}$$

To find the value of y, compare the denominators.

Since you must multiply 1 page by 15 to obtain 15 pages, multiply the numerator, 10 min, by 15: $10 \cdot 15 = 150$.

So, $y = 150$.

So, at a rate of 10 min/page, it would take 150 min (or 2 h 30 min) to read 15 pages.

MODULE 6 SECTION 2 — PRACTICE & APPLICATION EXERCISES

Exploration 1

Tell whether the rates are equivalent ratios.

1. $\frac{2 \text{ nurses}}{5 \text{ patients}}, \frac{6 \text{ nurses}}{15 \text{ patients}}$

2. $\frac{275 \text{ students}}{11 \text{ teachers}}, \frac{50 \text{ students}}{2 \text{ teachers}}$

3. $\frac{86 \text{ baskets}}{100 \text{ attempts}}, \frac{40 \text{ baskets}}{50 \text{ attempts}}$

4. $2.80 for 14 pens, $5.60 for 30 pens

5. 450 words in 10 min, 135 words in 3 min

For Exercises 6–8, find a unit rate for each rate.

6. 234 km in 6 h

7. $48.60 for 12 h

8. 208 mi on 16 gal

9. Mr. Foy, a certified public accountant, can complete 54 basic tax forms in 18 h.

   a. Find a unit rate in forms per hour.

   b. Working at this rate, how long would it take Mr. Foy to complete 144 such forms?

MODULE 6 SECTION 2 | PRACTICE & APPLICATION EXERCISES | STUDY GUIDE

10. The length of runway recommended for a commercial passenger plane to land safely is related to its airspeed (in knots) when it touches down. A 727 jet touching down at 168 knots requires a 6000 ft runway.

   a. Find a unit rate.

   b. If, during a peak traffic period, an air traffic controller must direct a 727 jet to a 5000 ft runway, what is the maximum permissible touchdown speed its pilot can use?

11. As a salesperson, Nat earns a *commission*, an amount of money based on the dollar amount of his sales. The table shows Nat's commissions for the last 4 weeks.

Commission ($)	Sales ($)
100	1000
125	1250
75	750
150	1500

   a. Graph the data in the table. Draw segments connecting the points you graphed, in order from left to right.

   b. Use your graph to predict the amount of commission Nat would earn if his sales were $900.

   c. Use a ruler to extend the line of your graph to predict Nat's commission for sales of $2000.

   d. Find a unit rate for the data in dollars of commission per dollars of sales. Use the unit rate to make the predictions asked for in parts (b) and (c). Compare the predictions you made using a unit rate with those you made using the graph.

Spiral Review

Use the double bar graph. (Module 3, pp. 183–184)

12. Into how many regions has the world been divided for this data?

13. What was the approximate population of Asia in 1950? in 1997?

14. For which two regions was the population about the same in 1997?

15. Which region showed the least amount of population growth from 1950 to 1997?

16. What was the approximate world population in 1950? in 1997?

17. About what percent of the world's population lived in North America in 1950? in 1997?

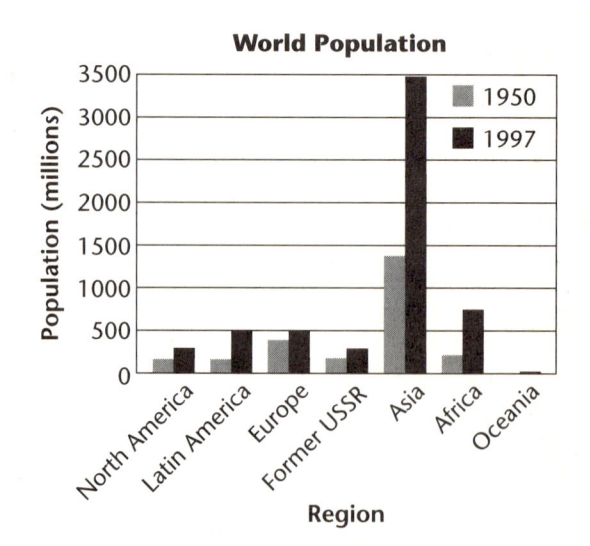

Name _____ Date _____

MODULE 6 SECTION 3　　　　　　　　　　　　　　STUDY GUIDE

Body Ratios　Using Ratios

GOAL　**LEARN HOW TO:** • use measurements to decide whether a ratio is reasonable
　　　　　　　　　• write a ratio as a decimal
　　　　　　　　　• find a ratio to describe data
　　　　　　　　　• use the ratio to make predictions

　　　　AS YOU: • analyze body ratio data

Exploration 1: Comparing Ratios

The decimal form of a ratio can help you to compare ratios. To find its decimal form, first write the ratio as a fraction.

Example

Hildie, who is 5 ft 4 in. tall, found that the distance from the middle of her abdomen to the floor is 39 in. Write the ratio *total height* : *distance from mid-abdomen to floor* as a decimal, rounded to the nearest hundredth.

■ Sample Response ■

First, write the ratio as a fraction. Convert 5 ft 4 in. to 64 in.

$$\frac{\text{total height}}{\text{distance from mid-abdomen to floor}} = \frac{64 \text{ in.}}{39 \text{ in.}}$$

Then divide the numerator by the denominator.

$39 \overline{)64.000}^{1.641}$ ← Carry to 3 decimal places in order to round to the nearest hundredth.

So, for Hildie, the ratio to the nearest hundredth is 1.64.

Exploration 2: Estimating Ratios

"Nice" fractions, such as $\frac{1}{2}$, $\frac{2}{3}$, and $\frac{3}{4}$ are often used to describe ratios in a simple way, making further computation easier.

Example

Use Hildie's ratio to predict Rick's total height if the distance from his mid-abdomen to the floor is 35 in.

■ Sample Response ■

Hildie's ratio of 1.64 is close to 1.6, which equals a mixed number with a "nice" fraction.

$$1.64 \approx 1\frac{6}{10} = 1\frac{3}{5}, \text{ or } \frac{8}{5}$$

Predict Rick's total height.

$$\frac{8}{5} = \frac{?}{35} \quad \text{Observe: } \frac{8 \times 7}{5 \times 7} = \frac{56}{35}$$

So, Rick's total height is about 56 in. or 4 ft 8 in.

Name _____   Date _____

MODULE 6 SECTION 3 — STUDY GUIDE

Exploration 3: Predicting with a Graph

To display a relationship between two sets of data, you can use a graph called a **scatter plot**.

Example

The data for Hildie and nine other people are shown in this table. Construct a scatter plot of the data.

Mid-abdomen to floor (in.)	39	35	40	38	36	37	38	39	37	35
Total height (in.)	64	56	63	62	57	60	60	60	57	55

Sample Response

To construct a scatter plot, prepare a coordinate grid with appropriate axes and scales.

If necessary, show a "break" in the axes to indicate that part of the graph is not shown. (This may only be done if the omitted part of the graph does not distort the appearance of the graphed data.) Different scales may be used on the two axes. Each scale must include the entire range of values for the portion of the data represented along its axis.

Use a clear ruler to draw a line on the graph that lies close to most of the points. Try to have about the same number of points on each side of the line. The line may pass through some of the points. This line, drawn to fit the data, is called a **fitted line**.

Total Height Compared to Distance from Mid-abdomen to Floor

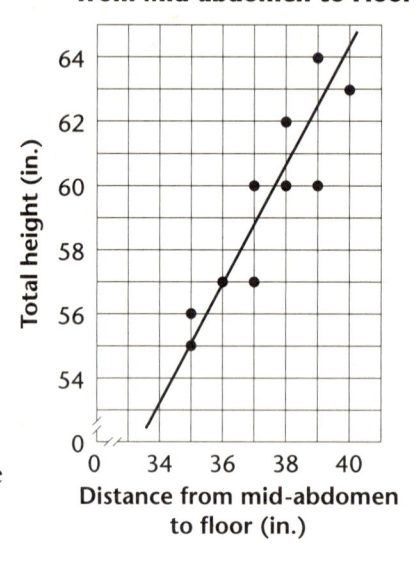

You can use the fitted line on a scatter plot to make predictions.

Example

The fitted line on the graph above shows that:

• for a mid-abdomen-to-floor distance of 38.5 in., the corresponding total height is about 61.5 in.

• for a total height of 58 in., the corresponding mid-abdomen-to-floor distance is about 36.5 in.

You can extend a fitted line to make predictions for values that are outside the range of the graphed data. When extended, the fitted line above would show that for a mid-abdomen-to-floor distance of 41 in., the corresponding total height is about 66 in.

Name _____ Date _____

| MODULE 6 SECTION 3 | PRACTICE & APPLICATION EXERCISES | STUDY GUIDE |

Exploration 1

For Exercises 1–4, write each ratio as a decimal to the nearest hundredth.

1. 5 : 9   **2.** 7 : 11   **3.** 3 : 7   **4.** 6 : 13

5. Each of these rectangles has a height of 9 m.

12 m   18 m   9 m   4.5 m

   a. For each rectangle, write the ratio *width to height* as a fraction and as a decimal.

   b. What do the ratios in part (a) tell you about the general shape of the rectangles?

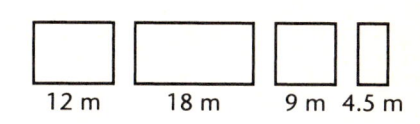

Exploration 2

Write a "nice" fraction for each ratio.

6. 4 : 19   **7.** 15 : 42   **8.** 0.42   **9.** 0.7 to 1

Use the ratio 1.6 as an estimate for the body ratio *shoulder to fingertip* : *elbow to fingertip*.

10. If Al's shoulder-to-fingertip distance is 28 in., estimate his elbow-to-fingertip distance.

11. If Bo's elbow-to-fingertip distance is 14 in., estimate her shoulder-to-fingertip distance.

Exploration 3

Use the scatter plot for Exercises 12–15.

12. Do you think the fitted line shown is a good fit? Explain.

13. How much did the seedling grow that received 1 cm of rainfall?

14. How much rainfall was received by the seedling that grew the most?

15. Use the fitted line to estimate the growth of a seedling during a week when it received 3.5 cm of rain.

Comparison of Tree Seedling Growth to Weekly Rainfall

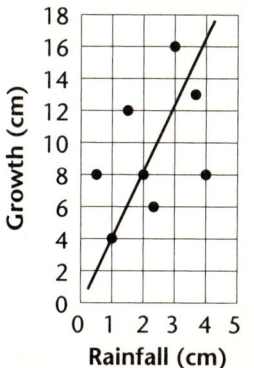

Spiral Review

16. Evaluate $30 + 7 \cdot x$ when $x = 5$. **(Module 5, p. 286)**

17. Name a quadrilateral that has exactly two lines of symmetry. **(Module 2, pp. 84–86)**

Name _____ Date _____

MODULE 6 SECTION 4   **STUDY GUIDE**

Jumping Ability   Proportions

GOAL **LEARN HOW TO:** • use cross products to find equivalent ratios
• find the missing term in a proportion
• write a proportion to solve a problem
• use a proportion to make a prediction

AS YOU: • make predictions

Exploration 1: Exploring Proportions

Recognizing Proportions

A proportion is an equation stating that two ratios are equivalent. The **cross products** in a proportion are equal.

$\frac{5}{10} = \frac{1}{2}$ is a proportion.

$10 \times 1 = 5 \times 2$

One method for determining if two ratios are equivalent is to compare cross products.

> **Example**
>
> To tell whether $\frac{10}{15}$ and $\frac{32}{48}$ are equivalent ratios, compare the cross products.
>
> $15 \times 32 = 480$ and $10 \times 48 = 480$
>
> Since the cross products are equal, the ratios are equivalent.

Finding a Missing Term in a Proportion

You can use cross products to find the missing term in a proportion.

> **Example**
>
> Find the missing term in the proportion $\frac{18}{72} = \frac{x}{144}$.
>
> **Sample Response**
>
> Use cross products to write an equation. $72 \cdot x = 18 \cdot 144$
> $72 \cdot x = 2592$
> Then use division to find the value of the variable. $x = 2592 \div 72$
> $x = 36$
>
> Check by substituting 36 for x to verify that the ratios are equivalent.
>
> $\frac{18}{72} \stackrel{?}{=} \frac{36}{144}$
> $\frac{1}{4} = \frac{1}{4}$ ✔   So, since the ratios are equivalent when $x = 36$, the missing term of the proportion is 36.

6-88 Math Thematics, Book 1

Name _____ Date _____

| MODULE 6 SECTION 4 | STUDY GUIDE |

Exploration 2: Using Proportions

Writing a Proportion

When you write a proportion to solve a problem, it is important to use the correct order.

Example

The North American jumping mouse has very long hind legs and is able to leap 9–15 ft. Suppose that leaping distance is related to body length for these mice. If a 6 in. jumping mouse can leap 9 ft, predict how far an 8 in. jumping mouse can leap.

Sample Response

Determine what measurements are being compared and what units are being used.

$$\frac{\text{leap distance (ft)}}{\text{body length (in.)}}$$

Decide what ratios to show in the proportion. Let x represent the missing term, which in this problem is the leaping distance of the bigger mouse.

$$\frac{\text{Ratio for}}{\text{smaller mouse}} = \frac{\text{Ratio for}}{\text{bigger mouse}}$$

$$\frac{9 \text{ ft}}{6 \text{ in.}} = \frac{x \text{ ft}}{8 \text{ in.}}$$

Use the cross products.

$6 \cdot x = 9 \cdot 8$
$6 \cdot x = 72$

Divide.

$x = 72 \div 6$
$x = 12$

Check by substituting 12 for x to verify that the ratios are equivalent.

$\frac{9}{6} \stackrel{?}{=} \frac{12}{8}$

$\frac{3}{2} = \frac{3}{2}$ ✔   So, an 8 in. jumping mouse should leap about 12 ft.

| MODULE 6 SECTION 4 | PRACTICE & APPLICATION EXERCISES |

Exploration 1

Find all the equivalent ratios in each list.

1. $\frac{24}{36}, \frac{8}{24}, \frac{30}{45}, \frac{25}{15}, \frac{30}{90}$

2. $\frac{250}{1000}, \frac{8}{2}, \frac{67.6}{16.9}, \frac{7.2}{28.8}, \frac{3.5}{14}$

Use the given numbers to form a proportion.

3. 1, 3, 30, 10
4. 15, 40, 8, 3
5. 28, 6, 24, 7

Use cross products to tell whether the ratios are equivalent.

6. $\frac{2}{3}$ and $\frac{12}{18}$
7. $\frac{5.2}{13}$ and $\frac{7.6}{19}$
8. $\frac{5}{11}$ and $\frac{11}{23}$

MODULE 6 SECTION 4 — PRACTICE & APPLICATION EXERCISES — STUDY GUIDE

Find the missing term in each proportion.

9. $\dfrac{3}{5} = \dfrac{18}{n}$

10. $4 : 6 = z : 42$

11. $\dfrac{x}{9} = \dfrac{35}{63}$

12. $16 : y = 12 : 9$

Exploration 2

13. Choose the two proportions that have been set up correctly for solving the problem.

    At Old Faithful in Yellowstone National Park, the best-known geyser in the United States, an eruption that rises to 115 ft discharges about 10,000 gal of water. About how many gallons of water are discharged by an eruption that rises to 165 ft?

    A. $\dfrac{10{,}000}{115} = \dfrac{x}{165}$
    B. $\dfrac{115}{10{,}000} = \dfrac{165}{x}$
    C. $\dfrac{115}{10{,}000} = \dfrac{x}{165}$

14. Choose the proportion that is *not* correctly set up for solving the problem.

    If 48 oz of a certain juice cost $1.89, what will 72 oz of the juice cost?

    A. $\dfrac{48}{1.89} = \dfrac{72}{x}$
    B. $\dfrac{48}{72} = \dfrac{1.89}{x}$
    C. $\dfrac{1.89}{72} = \dfrac{x}{48}$
    D. $\dfrac{1.89}{48} = \dfrac{x}{72}$

15. Because of large-scale commercial seal hunting operations, certain species of fur seals were brought close to extinction. In 1972, the United States prohibited the hunting of seals in its waters. The National Marine Fisheries Service monitors the fur seal population. Suppose that to estimate the number of fur seal pups in a rookery during one summer breeding season, workers tagged 2734 of the pups. Several weeks later, 600 pups in the same rookery were inspected and 163 of these were found to have already been tagged. Use a proportion to estimate the number of fur seals in the rookery.

Spiral Review

For Exercises 16 and 17, solve each problem. Tell the strategies you used. (Module 1, pp. 30–34)

16. Three lines are drawn across a sheet of paper. Into how many separate regions can the lines divide the paper?

17. A restaurant offers a lunch special consisting of an appetizer, a main dish, and a dessert. There are 2 choices for the appetizer, 3 choices for the main dish, and 3 choices for the dessert. How many different meals are possible?

18. Find the GCF of 135 and 180. (Module 4, p. 250)

Name _____ Date _____

MODULE 6 SECTION 5 **STUDY GUIDE**

Very Similar   Geometry and Proportions

GOAL **LEARN HOW TO:** • identify similar and congruent figures
• use proportions to find missing lengths in scale models
• use a protractor to measure and draw angles

AS YOU: • compare shapes
• work with scale models and drawings
• examine angles used in art

Exploration 1: Comparing Shapes

Similar and Congruent Figures

Similar figures have the same shape but not necessarily the same size.

The symbol ~ means "is similar to."

When two figures are similar, for each part of one figure there is a corresponding part on the other figure.

In similar figures, the corresponding angles have the same measure and the ratios of the lengths of the corresponding sides are equivalent. AB means the length of $\overline{AB}$.

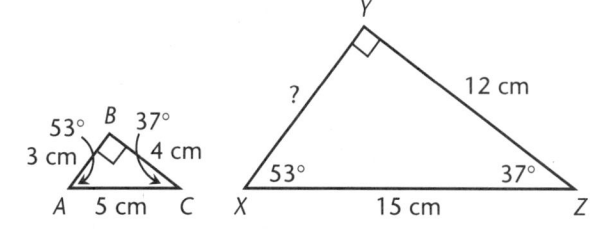

In the similar triangles above, $\angle A$ corresponds to $\angle X$ and $\overline{BC}$ corresponds to $\overline{YZ}$.

The measures of $\angle A$ and $\angle X$ are both 53°.

$$\frac{AB}{XY} = \frac{BC}{YZ} = \frac{AC}{XZ}$$

Congruent figures are a special type of similar figures that are the same shape and *the same size.*

Exploration 2: Models and Scale Drawings

You can use proportions to find missing lengths in similar figures.

Example

Find XY in the similar triangles above by writing a proportion.

■ **Sample Response** ■

$\frac{AB}{XY} = \frac{AC}{XZ}$ → $\frac{3}{XY} = \frac{5}{15}$

$5 \cdot XY = 3 \cdot 15$ ← The cross products are equal.

$XY = 45 \div 5$ ← Divide both sides by 5.

$XY = 9$ cm

Name   Date

MODULE 6 SECTION 5   **STUDY GUIDE**

Proportions and Scale

The ratio of a measurement on a drawing (or model) to the corresponding measurement on the actual object is called the **scale** of the drawing. You can use the scale of a drawing to write a proportion to find the measurements of an actual object.

Example

Suppose a drawing of a computer chip uses a scale of 1 in. : 0.5 mm.

In the drawing, the width of the chip is 1.5 in. To find the width of the actual chip, use a proportion.

$$\frac{\text{drawing measure}}{\text{actual measure}} = \frac{\text{drawing measure}}{\text{actual measure}}$$

$$\frac{1 \text{ in.}}{0.5 \text{ mm}} = \frac{1.5 \text{ in.}}{x \text{ mm}} \leftarrow \text{Let } x \text{ represent the unknown dimension.}$$

$$1 \cdot x = 1.5 \cdot 0.5$$

$$x = 0.75$$

So, the width of the actual chip is 0.75 mm.

Exploration 3: Measuring Angles

Measuring Angles with a Protractor

A **protractor** is an instrument used to measure an angle.

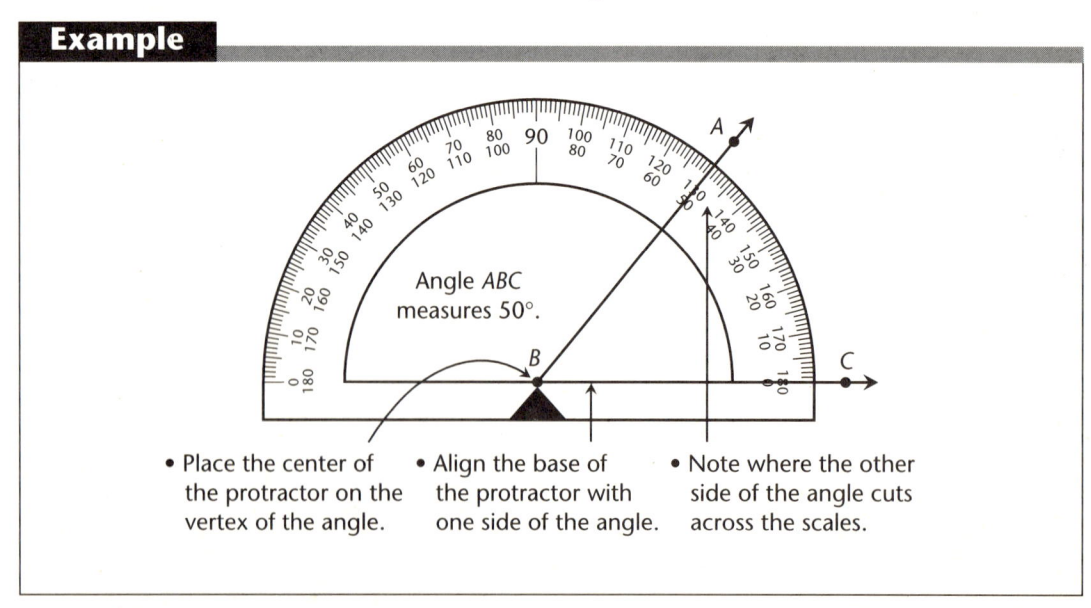

Example

Angle ABC measures 50°.

- Place the center of the protractor on the vertex of the angle.
- Align the base of the protractor with one side of the angle.
- Note where the other side of the angle cuts across the scales.

6-92   Math Thematics, Book 1   Copyright © by McDougal Littell Inc. All rights reserved.

Name _____ Date _____

MODULE 6 SECTION 5 | PRACTICE & APPLICATION EXERCISES | STUDY GUIDE

Exploration 1

For Exercises 1 and 2, the figures in each pair are similar. Make a table showing all the pairs of corresponding angles and corresponding sides.

1.

2.

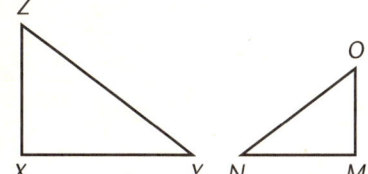

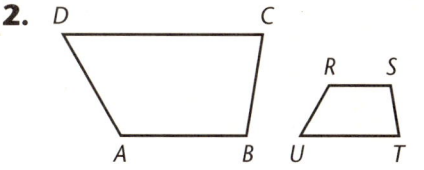

3. Of figures A, B, and C, which two triangles are similar? Explain.

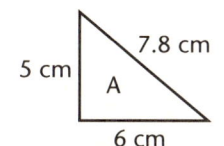

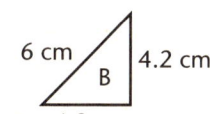

Exploration 2

4. The two quadrilaterals are similar. Find the missing lengths.

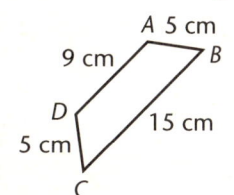

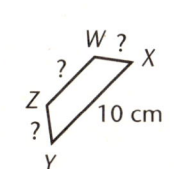

5. One of the four basic sizes of model railroads uses the HO scale, $\frac{1}{8}$ in. : 1 ft. Using this scale, what would be the actual length of a freight car if the length of its model is 5 in.?

Exploration 3

6. **Displaying Data** The table at the right shows the various ways in which the employees of an electronics company commute to work.

   a. In a circle graph, the entire 360° represents 100%. Use a proportion to find the number of degrees for each method of commuting, rounding to the nearest degree.

   b. Draw a circle graph of the data.

Commuting

Method	Percent
Bus	30
Car	20
Train	36
Walk	14

Spiral Review

7. One letter is chosen at random from the vowels *a*, *e*, *i*, *o*, and *u*. What is the theoretical probability that the letter will be alphabetically before the letter *h*? (Module 4, p. 240)

Evaluate each expression when *x* = 6. (Module 4, pp. 254–256)

8. $3 \cdot x^2$ 9. $(3 \cdot x)^2$ 10. $(3 + x)^2$ 11. $3 + x^2$

Name _____ Date _____

| MODULE 6 SECTION 6 | **STUDY GUIDE** |

Playing the Percentages Percents and Probability

GOAL **LEARN HOW TO:** • use a fraction to find a percent of a number
• use a fraction to estimate a percent of a number
• make a tree diagram to find probabilities

AS YOU: • examine data

Exploration 1: Using Fractions for Percents

When percents are equivalent to "nice" fractions, it is convenient to use the fractional form.

Find 40% of 175.

40% is equivalent to $\frac{40}{100}$ or $\frac{2}{5}$.

Then $\frac{2}{\cancel{5}} \cdot \cancel{175}^{35} = 70$
            $_1$

So, 40% of 175 is 70.

"Nice" fractions can also be used to estimate a percent of a number.

Use a "nice" fraction to estimate 73% of 120.

Note that 73% is close to 75%, which is equivalent to $\frac{75}{100}$ or $\frac{3}{4}$.

Since $\frac{1}{4}$ of 120 is 30, $\frac{3}{4}$ of 120 is 90.

So, 73% of 120 is about 90.

Exploration 2: Tree Diagrams

A diagram used to organize possible outcomes is called a **tree diagram**.

Example

Suppose you have two round plastic chips. Chip 1 has the letter A on one side and the letter B on the other, and chip 2 has B on one side and C on the other.

A tree diagram can be used to show that there are 4 possible outcomes when both chips are flipped.

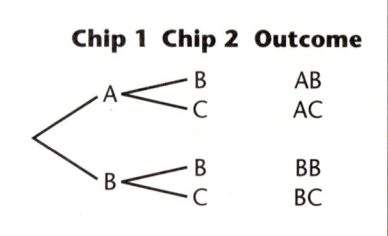

Chip 1 Chip 2 Outcome

A — B   AB
  — C   AC
B — B   BB
  — C   BC

A **fair game** is one in which each player has the same chance of winning.

Example

Lena and Chris will play a game flipping the two chips described above. Lena wins if the chips land so that there is exactly one B. Chris wins if both chips show B. To determine if the game is fair, use the tree diagram to find each person's probability of success.

Lena's chance to win = $\frac{2}{4}$.   Chris's chance to win = $\frac{1}{4}$.   So the game is not fair.

Name _____ Date _____

MODULE 6 SECTION 6 | PRACTICE & APPLICATION EXERCISES | STUDY GUIDE

Exploration 1

For Exercises 1–4, use a fraction in lowest terms to find each value.

1. 50% of 359
2. 20% of 295
3. 60% of 1000
4. 5% of 460

5. The tuition for the first year at the college that Adelle Simpson is planning to attend is $12,000. The college is offering 25% of the tuition in financial aid. What is the remaining amount of the tuition that the Simpson family must pay?

6. Jorge had a total of 25 math tests for the year. He achieved an honors grade in 76% of them. Use a "nice" fraction to estimate the number of math tests in which Jorge achieved an honors grade. Is your estimate higher or lower than the actual number of tests? Explain.

Estimate a percent for each fraction.

7. $\frac{23}{49}$
8. $\frac{61}{80}$
9. $\frac{32}{91}$
10. $\frac{15}{74}$

Exploration 2

11. **a.** Marta has 2 sweaters and 3 skirts that coordinate. One sweater is red and the other is white. One skirt is red, a second is white, and the third is blue. Make a tree diagram showing the outcomes of pairing a sweater and a skirt.

    b. If Marta chose a sweater and a skirt at random, what is the probability that they will both be the same color?

12. **a.** Make a tree diagram showing the outcomes of spinning this spinner two times.

    b. What is the probability of getting two A's? at least one B?

    c. Paul and Robyn are playing a game. The spinner is spun two times. Paul wins if there are two A's. Robyn wins if there is at least one B. Is the game fair? Explain.

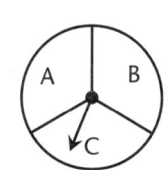

Spiral Review

13. On a coordinate grid, the point $A(5, 9)$ is translated 4 units to the right and 3 units down. What are the coordinates of the image point? (Module 2, p. 122)

14. Write the prime factorization of 240. (Module 4, pp. 251–253)

15. A bookcase 4 ft 8 in. tall is to stand on top of a cabinet that is 4 ft 6 in. tall. What will be the total height of the structure? (Module 5, p. 326)

Name _____ Date _____

| MODULE 6 | TECHNOLOGY |

For Use with Section 3

In this activity, a graphing calculator is used to solve the problems on page 411.

First enter the data. Enter the kneeling height in the first list, list L1. Enter the standing heights in the second list, list L2.

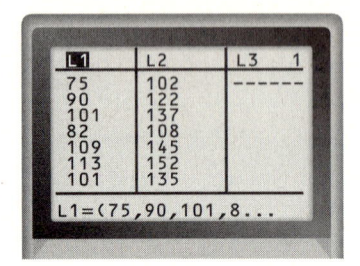

Next, use the LINREG (ax+b) command to find an equation for the line of best fit. Using the VARS menu, the equation for the line of best fit (REGEQ) can be pasted in Y1. To plot the points for the scatter plot, first activate the plot in the STAT PLOT menu. Graph the line by pressing GRAPH.

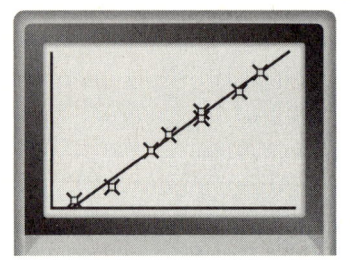

If you trace along the line of best fit using TRACE, you can answer Exercise 1(d). For a kneeling height of about 94 cm, the standing height will be about 126 cm.

6-96 Math Thematics, Book 1   Copyright © by McDougal Littell Inc. All rights reserved.

Name _____ Date _____

MODULE 6   TECHNOLOGY

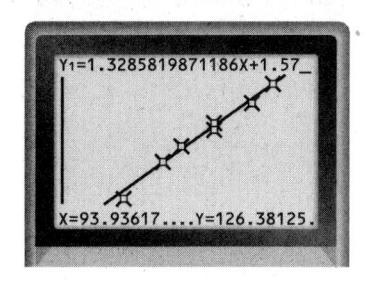

```
Y₁=1.3285819871186X+1.57
X=93.93617....Y=126.38125.
```

1. By tracing on the line of best fit, tell what kneeling height corresponds to a standing height of 132 cm? _____

2. What standing height corresponds to a kneeling height of 87 cm? _____

To find a ratio for the kneeling height to the standing height, find the value of $\frac{1}{a}$, where a is the ratio of standing height to kneeling height. This was calculated from the line of best fit. In this example, $a \approx 1.328581987$, so $\frac{1}{a} \approx 0.75$.

3. What is a "nice" fraction for 0.75? _____

4. Use the ratio 0.75 to find the kneeling height of someone whose standing height is 115cm. _____

Name _____ Date _____

MODULE 6 QUIZ — MID-MODULE

For Exercises 1–3, refer to the flag design at the right. Write each ratio in three ways.

1. the ratio of the blue area in the flag to the white area

2. the ratio of the red area to the blue area

3. the ratio of the white area to the red area

Tell whether or not the ratios are equivalent.

4. $\frac{16}{40}$ and $\frac{26}{65}$ 5. $6:14$ and $18:32$ 6. $9:21$ and $19:50$ 7. $\frac{40}{72}$ and $\frac{15}{27}$

8. If you need 3 c of pineapple juice to make 2 gallons of punch, how many quarts of pineapple juice are needed for 10 gallons of punch?

9. Find the ratio of consonants to vowels in your first name, in your last name, and in your first and last names together.

Find a unit rate for each rate.

10. 160 mi in $3\frac{1}{4}$ h   11. $82 per dozen   12. 1450 lb in 8 cases

13. Which is a better buy: 18 oz of jelly for $1.69 or 64 oz for $5.99?

14. For a holiday party you figure you will need 8 cookies per person. The cookies are sold by the dozen.

   a. Copy and complete the table.

Number of guests	3	6	9	12	15	18	21
Number of cookies (in dozens)	?	?	?	?	?	?	?

   b. How many dozen cookies would you need for 30 people?

   c. How many guests could you serve if you had 18 dozen cookies?

15. A trapezoid with the two nonparallel sides of equal length is an isosceles trapezoid. Sketch isosceles trapezoids with bottom base to top base ratios of $5:4$, $10:1$, and $1:12$. What do the ratios tell you about the shape of the trapezoids?

Write each ratio as a decimal to the nearest hundredth.

16. $8:25$ 17. $34:45$ 18. $8:9$ 19. $10:55$

20. Make a scatter plot using the data in the table. Use the scatter plot to estimate the missing entries in the table.

x	0	2	4	5	6	8	10
y	3	7	10	14	15	?	?

Name _____ Date _____

MODULE 6 TEST   FORM A

Write each ratio in three ways.

1. the ratio of the perimeter of square A to the perimeter of square B

2. the ratio of the area of square A to the area of square B

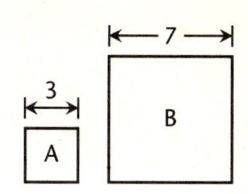

Tell whether or not the ratios are equivalent.

3. $\frac{7}{9}$ and $\frac{14}{16}$

4. $3:11$ and $15:55$

5. $\frac{2}{3}$ and $\frac{15}{45}$

6. Flo's Fripperies sells ribbon by the yard, and they charge the same amount per yard regardless of how much you buy. Suppose you buy 4 yards of her fanciest satin ribbon for $10.

   a. Copy and complete the table.

Length (yd)	1	2	3	4	5	6
Cost ($)	?	?	?	10	?	?

   b. How much does a 10 yd piece of ribbon cost?

   c. How long is a $32.50 piece of ribbon?

7. Consider a kite where the cross-pieces intersect about $\frac{1}{3}$ of the way down the vertical piece.

   a. Sketch three such kites where the cross-pieces have *height* to *width* ratios of $3:1$, $2:3$, and $9:2$. Draw the cross-pieces, and then connect the endpoints to make a kite shape.

   b. Write each *height* to *width* ratio as a decimal. Round to the nearest hundredth.

   c. What do the decimals you wrote for part (b) tell you about the general shape of the kites?

8. Use the scatter plot to estimate the missing entries in the table.

Hours studied	$\frac{1}{2}$	$\frac{3}{4}$	1	?	?
Grade on test	?	?	?	75	95

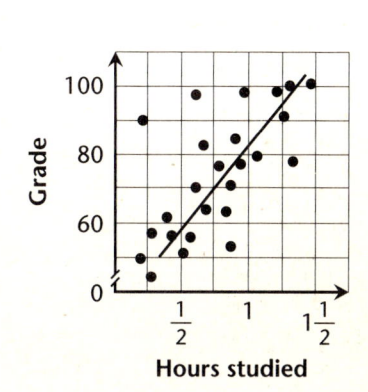

Copyright © by McDougal Littell Inc. All rights reserved.   Math Thematics, Book 1 **6-99**

Name _____ Date _____

MODULE 6 TEST   FORM A

Find the missing term in each proportion.

9. $\dfrac{3}{5} = \dfrac{x}{75}$ 10. $\dfrac{2}{5} = \dfrac{16}{y}$ 11. $8 : 11 = z : 88$

If appropriate, use a proportion to solve Exercises 12 and 13. If it is not appropriate, explain why not.

12. Tom can run a mile in 6 min 20 s. How long will it take him to run 25 miles?

13. In planning for a party, you figure that one bottle of soda will serve 4 people. How many bottles do you need to buy if you are expecting 60 guests?

14. The pentagons are similar. Use a proportion to find the missing lengths x and y.

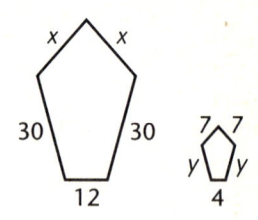

15. Use a protractor to measure $\angle XYZ$.

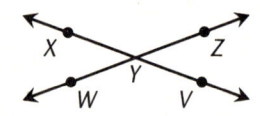

For Exercises 16–18, find each value.

16. 40% of 140   17. 75% of 320   18. 10% of 400

19. In a no-hitter, Ryan struck out 11 of the 34 batters he faced. Use a "nice" fraction to estimate what percent of the batters he struck out.

20. Manuel and Ronnie are going to play Dueling Spinners. The one who spins the lower number wins.

   a. Make a tree diagram showing the possible outcomes.

   b. Find the probability that Ronnie beats Manuel.

   c. What percent of the time do you expect Manuel to win?

6-100 Math Thematics, Book 1   Copyright © by McDougal Littell Inc. All rights reserved.

Name _____   Date _____

MODULE 6 TEST   FORM B

Write each ratio in three ways.

1. the ratio of the perimeter of triangle A to the perimeter of triangle B

2. the ratio of the area of triangle A to the area of triangle B

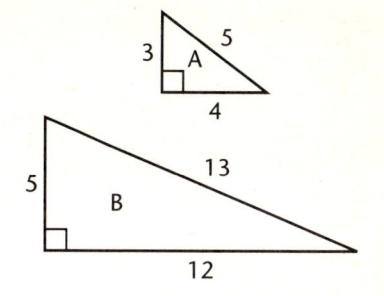

Tell whether or not the ratios are equivalent.

3. $\frac{4}{11}$ and $\frac{24}{66}$

4. 2 : 5 and 6 : 20

5. $\frac{8}{12}$ and $\frac{24}{36}$

6. Ye Olde Cheddar Shoppe sells cheese by the pound, and you are charged the same amount per pound regardless of how much you buy. You buy 6 lb of their fine sharp cheddar for $30.

   a. Copy and complete the table.

Cheese (lb)	2	4	6	8	10
Cost ($)	?	?	30	?	?

   b. How much does a 15 lb wheel of cheese cost?

   c. How heavy is a $17.50 wedge of cheese?

7. **a.** Sketch three right triangles with *base* to *height* ratios of 4 : 3, 2 : 5, and 10 : 1.

   b. Write each *base* to *height* ratio as a decimal. Round to the nearest hundredth.

   c. What do the decimals you wrote for part (b) tell you about the general shape of the triangles?

8. Use the scatter plot to estimate the missing entries in the table.

Height (in.)	?	?	54	58	65
Shoe size	3	4	?	?	?

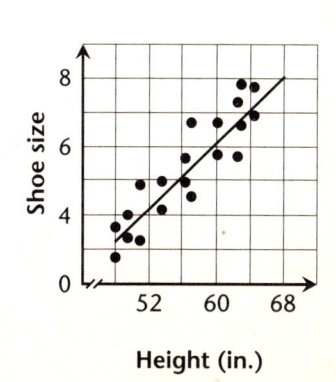

Name _____   Date _____

MODULE 6 TEST   FORM B

Find the missing term in each proportion.

9. $\frac{4}{7} = \frac{x}{42}$ **10.** $\frac{2}{9} = \frac{y}{36}$ **11.** $5 : 13 = 45 : z$

If appropriate, use a proportion to solve Exercises 12 and 13. If it is not appropriate, explain why not.

12. On a scale model for a formal garden 3 in. represents 16 ft. To the nearest foot, how many feet are represented by 8 in. on the model?

13. After 10 minutes of exercise your heart rate increases from 75 to 115 beats per minute. How fast would you expect your heart to beat after 25 min of exercise?

14. The hexagons are similar. Use a proportion to find the missing lengths.

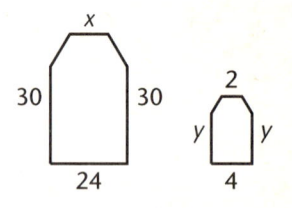

15. Use a protractor to measure ∠XYZ.

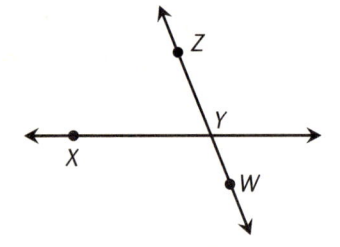

For Exercises 16–18, find each value.

16. 60% of 160   **17.** 25% of 340   **18.** 50% of 500

19. Michael scored in about 65% of the hockey games he played in. If he played in 24 games this winter, use a "nice" fraction to estimate how many games he scored in.

20. Angelique and Rhoda are going to play Dueling Spinners. The one who spins the higher number wins.

  a. Make a tree diagram showing the possible outcomes.

  b. Find the probability that Angelique beats Rhoda.

  c. What percent of the time do you expect Rhoda to win?

MODULE 6 — STANDARDIZED ASSESSMENT

1. What is the ratio of the number of months whose names start with vowels to the number of months whose names start with consonants?
 a. 1 : 4 **b.** 1 : 3
 c. 2 : 3 **d.** 3 : 12

2. Which of the following pairs of ratios are not equivalent?
 a. $\frac{3}{8}$ and $\frac{12}{32}$ **b.** $\frac{4}{10}$ and $\frac{14}{35}$
 c. 1 : 5 and 4 : 20 **d.** 3 : 2 and 9 : 4

3. The temperature dropped 42° F in 6.2 h. What is the unit rate for the drop, to the nearest tenth?
 a. 6.6° /h **b.** 6.7° /h
 c. 6.8° /h **d.** 6.9° /h

4. If Mr. Brown can milk 42 cows in 50 min, how long would it take him to milk 150 cows (to the nearest 5 min)?
 a. 2 h 15 min **b.** 2 h 30 min
 c. 2 h 50 min **d.** 3 h

5. There are 12 girls in a class of 21. Write the ratio of girls to boys in the class as a decimal rounded to the nearest hundredth.
 a. $\frac{12}{21}$ **b.** 0.57
 c. 1.33 **d.** 1.67

6. If the two triangles are similar, find the missing length.
 a. 6 **b.** 8
 c. 12 **d.** 18

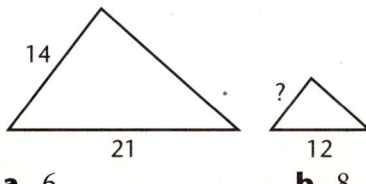

7. Find the missing term in the proportion $\frac{8}{28} = \frac{18}{x}$.
 a. 38 **b.** 43
 c. 58 **d.** 63

8. Bobbi earns $25.80 for 6 h work. How much will she earn if she works 10 h?
 a. $43.00 **b.** $45.50
 c. $47.00 **d.** $48.50

9. What is the unit rate for 203 mi in $3\frac{1}{2}$ h?
 a. 56 mi/h **b.** 58 mi/h
 c. 60 mi/h **d.** 62 mi/h

10. You are building a model of the Eiffel Tower, which is 984 ft tall. If you use a scale of 1 in. = 24 ft, how tall will your model be?
 a. 38 in. **b.** 41 in.
 c. 43 in. **d.** 45 in.

11. The Blue Jays won 89 out of 147 games. Use a "nice" fraction to estimate the percent of games they won.
 a. 45% **b.** 55%
 c. 60% **d.** 75%

12. Player 1 uses spinner A and player 2 uses spinner B in the game Dueling Spinners. The player who spins the greater number wins. Use a tree diagram to find the expected percent of time player 1 would win.
 a. 50% **b.** 67%
 c. 44% **d.** 56%

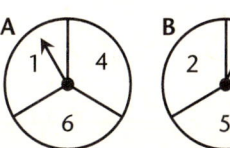

| MODULE 6 | MODULE PERFORMANCE ASSESSMENT |

Many years ago, there was a pirate named Phineas. Phineas wished people would call him Phineas the Fierce, but instead they called him Forgetful Phineas. Poor Phineas always forgot where he buried his treasure! To help him remember, he made a map, but he never marked the treasure's location on the map. Instead, he recorded a series of steps which, if properly followed, would lead him to it.

Now you have the map and the instructions left by Forgetful Phineas. Follow the instructions to find the location of the treasure! Use Forgetful Phineas's map on the next page.

Step 1: Find the trees which are southwest of Villain's Origin. Draw 4 lines to connect the trees, forming trapezoid *ABCD*.

Step 2: Draw a similar trapezoid with a scale factor of $\frac{1}{2}$. Label the corresponding points *W*, *X*, *Y*, and *Z*. Place point *Y* on point *O* at Villain's Origin with segment *ZY* on the *x*-axis to the west of point *O*.

Step 3: Draw a straight line connecting point *N*, at Skull Rock, with point *W*. Continue the line through the southeast quadrant of the map.

Step 4: Starting at point *R*, by Rascal's Cave, move three units north for every one unit east until you intersect the line *WN*. Mark the intersection as point *P*. How many units east did you go? east = __?__ How many units north did you go? north = __?__

Step 5: Find the ratio of *the distance east from Rascal's Cave to point P* to *the distance north from Rascal's Cave to point P*.

Step 6: The treasure is on the Northern Coast, east of Quicksand Beach. The ratio of *the distance of the treasure east of Quicksand Beach* to *the distance of the treasure north of Villain's Origin* will form a ratio equal to the ratio found in Step 5, as shown in the proportion below. Use this proportion comparing the two ratios to solve for the unknown distance from Quicksand Beach, point *Q*, to the treasure. Mark the location of the treasure as point *T*, and write the coordinates.

$$\frac{\text{treasure's distance east of } Q \text{ (unknown)}}{\text{treasure's distance north of } O} = \frac{\text{distance east from } R \text{ to } P}{\text{distance north from } R \text{ to } P}$$

MODULE 6

MODULE PERFORMANCE ASSESSMENT

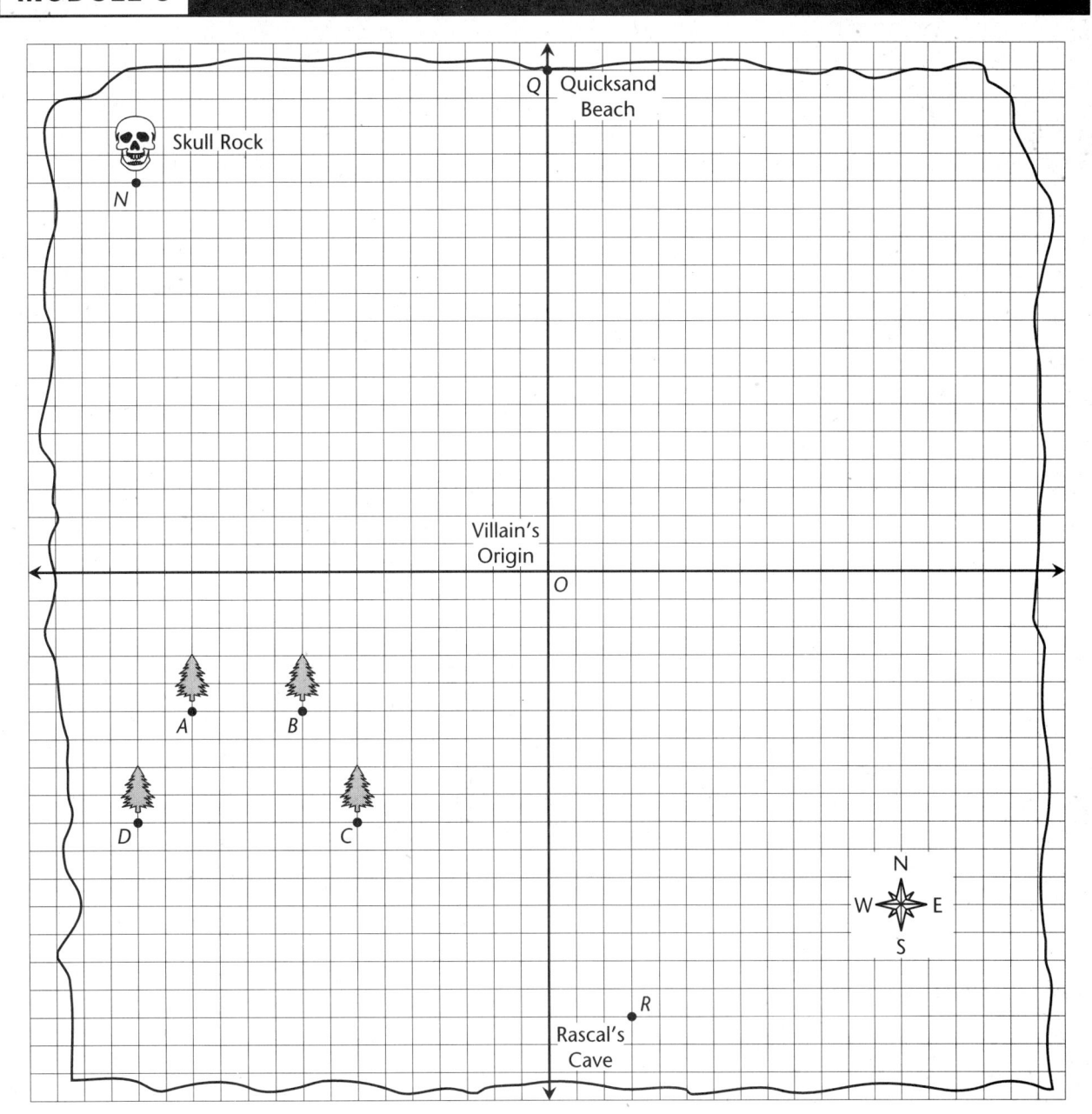

Answers

PRACTICE AND APPLICATIONS

Module 6, Section 1
1. a. 248 to 160, 248 : 160, $\frac{248}{160}$
b. 38 to 52, 38 : 52, $\frac{38}{52}$
c. 90 to 248, 90 : 248, $\frac{90}{248}$
d. 52 to 160, 52 : 160, $\frac{52}{160}$
e. 248 to 38, 248 : 38, $\frac{248}{38}$
f. 160 to 90, 160 : 90, $\frac{160}{90}$

2. a. ○○○○ □□□□□□
b. ☆☆ ◇◇◇◇◇◇◇
c. (cups and glasses)
d. (bananas and apples)
e. △△△△△ ▭

3. a. Yes. **b.** No. **c.** No. **d.** Yes. **e.** Yes. **f.** Yes.
g. Yes. **h.** No. **i.** No.
4. a. 8 to 5, 8 : 5, $\frac{8}{5}$ **b.** 5 to 8, 5 : 8, $\frac{5}{8}$

Module 6, Section 2
1. a. Yes. **b.** Yes. **c.** No. **d.** No. **e.** Yes. **f.** Yes.
g. No. **h.** Yes. **i.** Yes.
2. a. No. **b.** Yes. **c.** Yes. **d.** No.
3. a. 3 pages/min **b.** 750 km/day **c.** 23 mi/gal
d. $2\frac{2}{5}$ ft/step **e.** $6.25/book **f.** $6\frac{2}{3}$ ft/min
4. a. $2.25 for 15 lb **b.** $10.90 for 8 lb
c. $2.88 for 24 oz **d.** Neither is a better buy than the other.

5.
Number of miles	5	10	15	20	25
Time (minutes)	6	12	18	24	30

6. a. 540 ft, 5400 ft **b.** less; 5280 < 5400

Module 6, Section 3
1. a. 4 cm **b.** 36 cm **c.** 108 cm
2. a. 0.71 **b.** 0.44 **c.** 0.18 **d.** 0.53 **e.** 0.58 **f.** 0.19
3. a. $\frac{1}{6}$ **b.** $\frac{7}{10}$ **c.** $\frac{1}{4}$ **d.** $\frac{4}{5}$ **e.** $\frac{1}{8}$ **f.** $\frac{1}{5}$

4. a. about 0.63 **b.** Sample Response: $\frac{3}{5}$
c. Sample Response (based on the answer for part (b)):

Seated height (cm)	68	72	74	75
Standing height (cm)	113	120	124	125

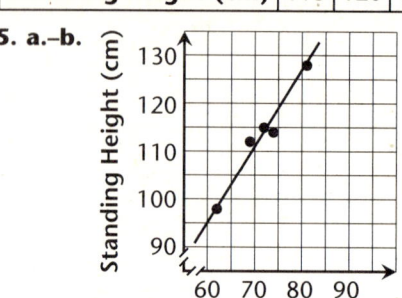

5. a.–b. (graph of Standing Height vs Seated Height)

c. Sample Response:

Seated height (cm)	68	76	79	75
Standing height (cm)	111	120	126	119

6. a. fitted line 2; The line is close to many of the points, and there are about the same number of points on either side of the line. **b.** Sample Response: 105 cm

Module 6, Section 4
1. a. Yes. **b.** Yes. **c.** No. **d.** No. **e.** Yes. **f.** No.
2. a. $\frac{12}{30}$ and $\frac{60}{150}$; $\frac{27}{72}$, $\frac{4.5}{12}$, and $\frac{18}{48}$
b. $\frac{5}{9}$ and $\frac{40}{72}$; $\frac{14}{8.5}$ and $\frac{56}{34}$
3. a. 45 **b.** 21 **c.** 45 **d.** 14 **e.** 28.8 **f.** 15 **g.** 25
h. 5 **i.** 3.6
4. a. $40.50 **b.** 22.5 ft **c.** not appropriate; Magazines may cost different amounts. **d.** 7 baseball caps **e.** not appropriate; Sample Response: It is not reasonable to assume that rescue missions needing helicopters occur at a steady rate hour to hour.

Module 6, Section 5
1. a. Corresponding sides: $\overline{AB}$ and $\overline{ED}$, $\overline{BC}$ and $\overline{DF}$, $\overline{AC}$ and $\overline{EF}$; Corresponding angles: $\angle A$ and $\angle E$, $\angle B$ and $\angle D$, $\angle C$ and $\angle F$. **b.** Corresponding sides: $\overline{AD}$ and $\overline{JM}$, $\overline{CD}$ and $\overline{LM}$, $\overline{AB}$ and $\overline{JK}$, $\overline{BC}$ and $\overline{KL}$; Corresponding angles: $\angle A$ and $\angle J$, $\angle B$ and $\angle K$, $\angle C$ and $\angle L$, $\angle D$ and $\angle M$.
2. a. not similar or congruent; The figures do not have the same shape. **b.** congruent
3. a. DE = 4, EF = 6 **b.** FG = HI = 12, FJ = IJ = 22.5
4. 7.5 ft
5. a. 32 ft **b.** 10 ft **c.** 28 in.
6. a. 1 in. : 15 ft **b.** 2.5 in. **c.** 7.5 ft **d.** 390 ft
7. a. 50° **b.** 145° **c.** 80°

8. a. [angle] **b.** [angle] **c.** [angle]
d. [angle] **e.** [angle] **f.** [angle]

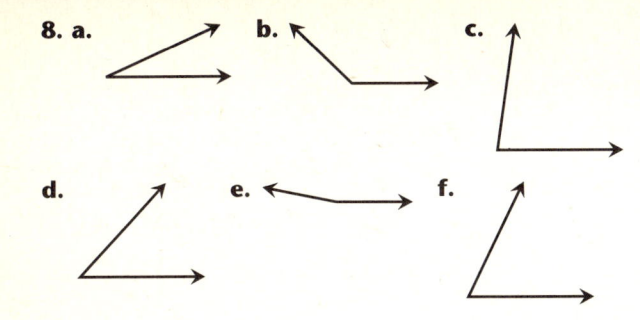

Module 6, Section 6
1. a. 13 **b.** 7 **c.** 14 **d.** 120 **e.** 84 **f.** 25 **g.** 21
h. 48 **i.** 36 **j.** 30 **k.** 54 **l.** 16 **m.** 3 **n.** 98 **o.** 210
2. a. $5 **b.** $10 **c.** $2.50 **d.** $12.50 **e.** $25
f. $12.50; Possible response: the second method
3. a. about 50% **b.** about 25% **c.** about 40%
d. about $33\frac{1}{3}$% **e.** about 75% **f.** about 50%
4. Sample Response: Use $\frac{3}{4}$ to obtain an estimate of 15 games; lower; because 76% is greater than $\frac{3}{4}$.
5. a. H1, H2, H3, H4, T1, T2, T3, T4 **b.** H2, H4, T2, T4
c. 50% **d.** about 20 times **e.** 25% **f.** about 15 times
6. a. [tree diagram: 1→1,2,3; 2→1,2,3; 3→1,2,3]
b. $\frac{1}{9}$ **c.** $\frac{3}{9}$ or $\frac{1}{3}$ **d.** $\frac{2}{9}$
7. a. $\frac{1}{10}$ **b.** $\frac{2}{10}$ or $\frac{1}{5}$ **c.** $\frac{4}{10}$ or $\frac{2}{5}$

Module 6, Sections 1–6
1. a. 3 : 5, $\frac{3}{5}$, 3 to 5 **b.** 6 : 2, $\frac{6}{2}$, 6 to 2
2. a. Yes. **b.** Yes. **c.** No.
3. 4 to 3, 4 : 3, $\frac{4}{3}$
4. a. 225 mi/day **b.** $24/art book **c.** 32 km/gal
5. a. $1.84 for 8 oranges **b.** $2.40 for 16 oz
6. 60, 240
7. a. 0.43 **b.** 0.22 **c.** 0.64 **d.** 0.84 **e.** 0.27 **f.** 0.42
8. a. $\frac{3}{4}$ **b.** $\frac{3}{10}$ **c.** $\frac{1}{5}$
9. a. 52.5 **b.** 24 **c.** 27
10. a. FG = 15, HG = 20 **b.** JK = LM = MN = OJ = 15
11. a. 45 ft **b.** 10.5 ft **c.** 33 yd
12. a. [angle] **b.** [angle] **c.** [angle]
13. a. 60 **b.** 22 **c.** 54

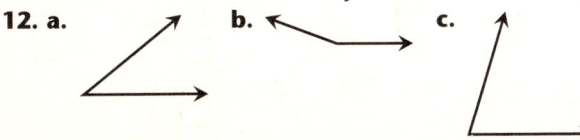

14. Accept reasonable estimates. Sample Responses are given. **a.** about 50% **b.** about 10% **c.** about 80%
15. a. $\frac{1}{2}$ **b.** $\frac{1}{16}$

STUDY GUIDE

Module 6, Section 1
1. a. 16 : 12 and 20 : 15 **b.** Yes; they are both equivalent to the fraction $\frac{4}{3}$.
2. a. 5 to 3; 5 : 3; $\frac{5}{3}$ **b.** 10 to 6; 10 : 6; $\frac{10}{6}$
c. Yes; they are both equivalent to the fraction $\frac{5}{3}$.
3. No.
4. Yes.
5. No.
6. Yes.
7. $\frac{1}{2}$ (or 1 : 2 or 1 to 2)
8. Hill B; Sample Response: The horizontal distances for the two climbs are the same; but the vertical distance for Hill B is twice as high as that of Hill A.
9. a. A(0, 1), B(2, 4), C(6, 10) **b.** 3; 2; $\frac{3}{2}$ (or $\frac{2}{3}$)
c. 6; 4; $\frac{6}{4}$ (or $\frac{4}{6}$) **d.** The ratios are equivalent.
e. The points lie on a line.
10. a. 70 ft **b.** about 58.1 ft; 60 ft; 30 ft, 60 ft, and 68 ft

c. Lengths of the Character Balloons in 1997 Macy's Thanksgiving Day Parade

10	0
9	
8	
7	8
6	0 0 1 2 4 7 8 8
5	5 8 9
4	
3	0 0 2 6

7 | 8 means 78 ft

Module 6, Section 2
1. Yes.
2. Yes.
3. No.
4. No.
5. Yes.
6. $\frac{39 \text{ km}}{1 \text{ h}}$ or 39 km/h
7. $\frac{\$4.05}{1 \text{ h}}$ or $4.05/h
8. $\frac{13 \text{ mi}}{1 \text{ gal}}$ or 13 mi/gal
9. a. 3 forms/h **b.** 48 h
10. a. about 35.7 ft/knot **b.** about 140 knots

11. a.

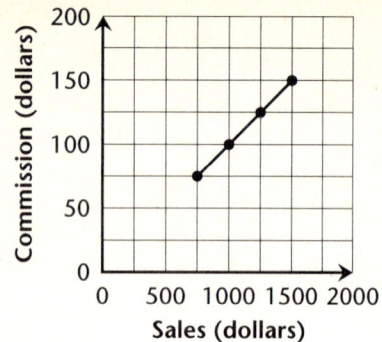

[Graph: Commission (dollars) vs Sales (dollars), with points plotted showing a linear relationship from about (750, 75) to (1500, 150)]

b. Sample Response: $90
c. Check students' work; Sample Response: $200
d. $1 of commission per $10 of sales; $90; $200; They are the same (or nearly the same).
12. 7 regions
13. Sample Response: about 1,400,000,000 people; about 3,500,000,000 people
14. Latin America and Europe
15. Oceania
16. Sample Response: about 2,500,000,000; about 6,000,000,000
17. Sample Response: about 7%; about 5%

Module 6, Section 3

1. 0.56
2. 0.64
3. 0.43
4. 0.46
5. a. $\frac{12}{9}$ or $\frac{4}{3}$, 1.33; $\frac{18}{9}$ or $\frac{2}{1}$, 2; $\frac{9}{9}$ or $\frac{1}{1}$, 1; $\frac{4.5}{9}$ or $\frac{1}{2}$, 0.5
b. Sample Response: The greater the ratio, the wider the rectangle. The smaller the ratio, the narrower the rectangle.
6. Sample Response: $\frac{1}{5}$
7. Sample Response: $\frac{1}{3}$
8. Sample Response: $\frac{4}{10}$ or $\frac{2}{5}$
9. $\frac{7}{10}$
10. about 17.5 in.
11. about 22.4 in.
12. Yes; Sample Response: The line is close to all the points, passing through two of them. Also, the same number of points fall on each side of the line.
13. 4 cm
14. 3 cm
15. Sample Response: about 15 cm
16. 65
17. rectangle or rhombus

Module 6, Section 4

1. $\frac{24}{36}$ and $\frac{30}{45}$; $\frac{8}{24}$ and $\frac{30}{90}$
2. $\frac{250}{1000}$, $\frac{7.2}{28.8}$, and $\frac{3.5}{14}$; $\frac{8}{2}$ and $\frac{67.6}{16.9}$

3. Sample Response: $\frac{1}{3} = \frac{10}{30}$
4. Sample Response: $\frac{3}{15} = \frac{8}{40}$
5. Sample Response: $\frac{7}{28} = \frac{6}{24}$
6. Yes.
7. Yes.
8. No.
9. 30
10. 28
11. 5
12. 12
13. a and b
14. c
15. about 10,064 fur seals
16. 4, 5, 6, or 7 regions; Sample Response: Make a list and draw a diagram.

4	5	6	7
0 lines intersect	2 lines intersect	3 lines intersect in 1 point	3 lines intersect in 3 points

17. 18 different meals
18. 45

Module 6, Section 5

1.

Part of △XYZ	Corresponding part of △MNO
∠X	∠M
∠Y	∠N
∠Z	∠O
$\overline{XY}$	$\overline{MN}$
$\overline{YZ}$	$\overline{NO}$
$\overline{ZX}$	$\overline{OM}$

2.

Part of quadrilateral ABCD	Corresponding part of quadrilateral RSTU
∠A	∠R
∠B	∠S
∠C	∠T
∠D	∠U
$\overline{AB}$	$\overline{RS}$
$\overline{BC}$	$\overline{ST}$
$\overline{CD}$	$\overline{TU}$
$\overline{DA}$	$\overline{UR}$

3. B and C; Sample Response: The corresponding sides are in proportion, with a ratio of 3 : 2.
4. WX = ZY = $\frac{10}{3}$ cm, WZ = 6 cm
5. 40 ft

6. a.

Method	Angle
Bus	108°
Car	72°
Train	130°
Walk	50°

b. Commuter Methods

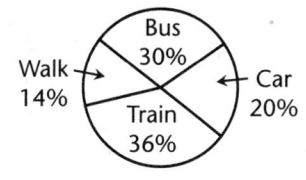

Walk 14%, Bus 30%, Car 20%, Train 36%

7. $\frac{2}{5}$ or 0.4
8. 108
9. 324
10. 81
11. 39

Module 6, Section 6
1. 179.5
2. 59
3. 600
4. 23
5. $9000
6. $\frac{8}{10} \times 25 = 20$ tests; higher, because $\frac{8}{10} = 80\%$ and 80% > 76%
7. Sample Response: about 50%
8. Sample Response: about 75%
9. Sample Response: about $33\frac{1}{3}\%$
10. Sample Response: about 20%
11. a.

Sweater	Skirt	Outcome
R	R	RR
R	W	RW
R	B	RB
W	R	WR
W	W	WW
W	B	WB

b. $\frac{2}{6}$ or $\frac{1}{3}$

12. a.

1st Spin, 2nd Spin, Outcome: AA, AB, AC, BA, BB, BC, CA, CB, CC

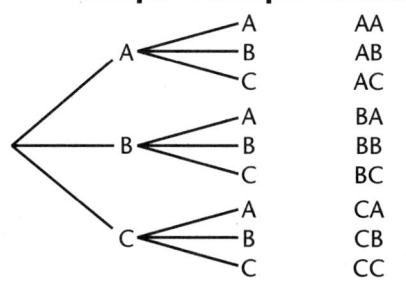

b. $\frac{1}{9}$; $\frac{5}{9}$

c. No; Sample Response: Paul's chance of winning is $\frac{1}{9}$ while Robyn's chance is $\frac{5}{9}$. Since both players do not have the same chance of winning, the game is not fair.
13. (9, 6)
14. $2^4 \cdot 3 \cdot 5$
15. 9 ft 2 in.

TECHNOLOGY

Module 6
1. about 98 cm
2. about 117 cm
3. $\frac{3}{4}$
4. about 86 cm

ASSESSMENT

Mid-Module 6 Quiz
1. $\frac{13}{16}$, 13 : 16, 13 to 16
2. $\frac{6}{13}$, 6 : 13, 6 to 13
3. $\frac{8}{3}$, 8 : 3, 8 to 3
4. Yes.
5. No.
6. No.
7. Yes.
8. $3\frac{3}{4}$ qt
9. Answers may vary. Check students' work.
10. $49\frac{3}{13}$ mi/h, or about 49.2 mi/h
11. $6.83 apiece
12. $181\frac{1}{4}$ lb/case
13. 64 oz for $5.99
14. a.

Number of guests	3	6	9	12	15	18	21
Dozens of cookies	2	4	6	8	10	12	14

b. 20 dozen
c. 27
15. 5 : 4, 10 : 1, 1 : 12

Sample Response: If the ratio is close to 1, you get a shape close to a rectangle. If the ratio is close to 0 or quite a bit greater than 1, then the trapezoid looks nearly triangular.
16. 0.32
17. 0.76
18. 0.89
19. 0.18

20.

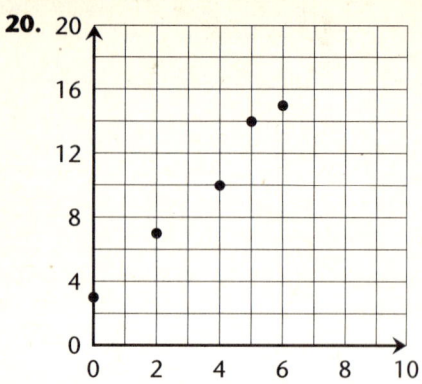

Accept reasonable estimates. Sample Responses: for x = 8, y is about 19; for x = 10, y is about 23.

Module 6 Test (Form A)
1. $\frac{12}{28}$, 12 : 28, 12 to 28
2. $\frac{9}{49}$, 9 : 49, 9 to 49
3. No.
4. Yes.
5. No.
6. a.

Length	1	2	3	4	5	6
Cost	$2.50	$5	$7.50	$10	$12.50	$15

b. $25   c. 13 yd

7. a.

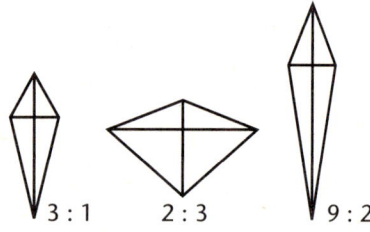

3 : 1   2 : 3   9 : 2

b. 3.0, 0.67, 4.5 c. Sample Response: If the ratio is much larger than 1, then the kite will be very "skinny."

8. Accept reasonable estimates. Sample Response:

Hours	$\frac{1}{2}$	$\frac{3}{4}$	1	$\frac{7}{8}$	$1\frac{1}{4}$
Grade	58	70	85	75	95

9. 45
10. 40
11. 64
12. Not appropriate; it is not realistic to think someone could run a marathon at the same rate of speed at which they run a mile.
13. 15 bottles
14. x = 21, y = 10
15. about 140°
16. 56
17. 240
18. 40
19. about 33%

20. a.

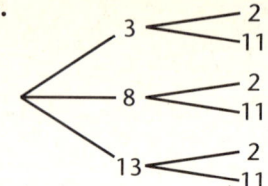

b. $\frac{2}{3}$ c. $33\frac{1}{3}$%

Module 6 Test (Form B)
1. $\frac{12}{30}$, 12 : 30, 12 to 30
2. $\frac{6}{30}$, 6 : 30, 6 to 30
3. Yes.
4. No.
5. Yes.
6. a.

Cheese (lb)	2	4	6	8	10
Cost	$10	$20	$30	$40	$50

b. $75   c. $3\frac{1}{2}$ lb

7. a.

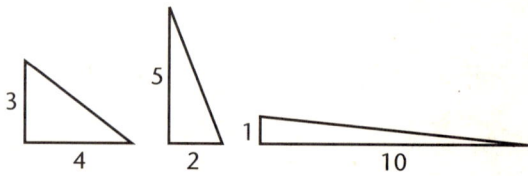

b. 1.33, 0.40, 10.0
c. Sample Response: The smaller the ratio, the taller and skinnier the triangle. If the ratio is much larger than 1, then the triangle will be short and wide.
8. Accept reasonable estimates. Sample Response:

Height (in.)	47	51	54	58	65
shoe size	3	4	$4\frac{1}{2}$	$5\frac{1}{2}$	7

9. 24
10. 8
11. 117
12. about 43 ft
13. Not appropriate; it is not reasonable to think that exercising $2\frac{1}{2}$ times as long will cause your heart rate to be multiplied by $2\frac{1}{2}$.
14. x = 12, y = 5
15. about 68°
16. 96
17. 85
18. 250
19. about 16 games

20. a.

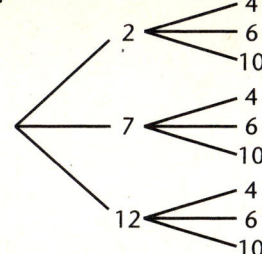

```
       ┌─ 4
    2 ─┼─ 6
    │  └─10
    │  ┌─ 4
    7 ─┼─ 6
    │  └─10
    │  ┌─ 4
   12 ─┼─ 6
       └─10
```

b. $\frac{5}{9}$ c. about 44% of the time

STANDARDIZED ASSESSMENT

Module 6
1. b
2. d
3. c
4. d
5. c
6. b
7. d
8. a
9. b
10. b
11. c
12. d

MODULE PERFORMANCE ASSESSMENT

Module 6

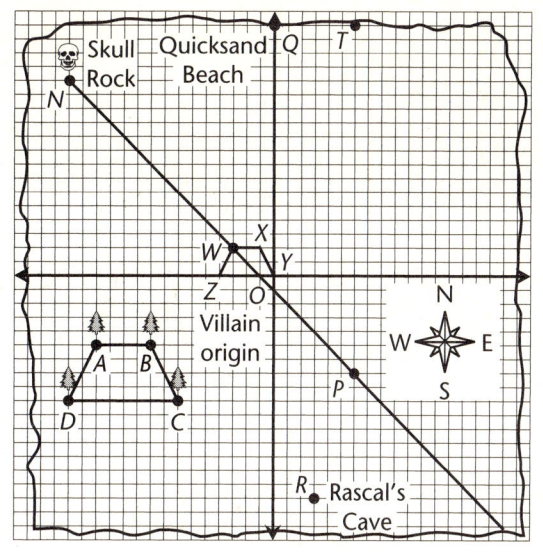

Step 4: east = 3; north = 9

Step 5: $\dfrac{\text{distance east from } R \text{ to } P}{\text{distance north from } R \text{ to } P} = \dfrac{3}{9}$;

$\dfrac{\text{treasure's distance east of } Q \text{ (unknown)}}{\text{treasure's distance north of } O} = \dfrac{\text{distance east from } R \text{ to } P}{\text{distance north from } R \text{ to } P}$

$\dfrac{\text{treasure's distance east of } Q}{18} = \dfrac{3}{9}$

treasure's distance east of Q = 6
The treasure is at T(6, 18).

Name _____ Date _____

MODULES 5 AND 6 TEST — CUMULATIVE

Write the fractions in order from least to greatest.

1. $\dfrac{2}{11}, \dfrac{7}{8}, \dfrac{3}{4}, \dfrac{2}{5}$

2. $\dfrac{9}{13}, \dfrac{1}{12}, \dfrac{3}{7}, \dfrac{3}{4}$

Replace each __?__ with the number that makes the statement true.

3. $6\dfrac{1}{4}$ yd = __?__ in.

4. 20 ft = __?__ yd

5. $3\dfrac{1}{4}$ mi = __?__ ft

Find each sum or difference. Write each answer in lowest terms.

6. $\dfrac{15}{27} + \dfrac{8}{18}$

7. $5\dfrac{2}{7} - 1\dfrac{1}{2}$

8. $\dfrac{7}{12} + 1\dfrac{3}{4}$

9. $17\dfrac{5}{6} - 12\dfrac{1}{3}$

10. Rachel has $8\dfrac{5}{16}$ yd of fabric. She plans to use $3\dfrac{3}{4}$ yd to make a dress. How much material will she have left?

Replace each __?__ with the number that makes the statement true.

11. $3\dfrac{1}{2}$ c = __?__ oz

12. 18 qt = __?__ gal

13. $5\dfrac{1}{4}$ gal = __?__ pt

14. Which of the following measures is/are *not* equivalent to 80 c?

   a. 40 pt   b. 10 qt   c. 560 oz   d. 5 gal

Find each product or quotient. Write each answer in lowest terms.

15. $\dfrac{3}{7} \cdot \dfrac{6}{14}$

16. $20 \div \dfrac{4}{5}$

17. $\dfrac{3}{16} \cdot \dfrac{4}{9}$

18. $2\dfrac{5}{8} \div \dfrac{3}{4}$

Write each ratio in three ways.

19. the ratio of the perimeter of the rectangle to the perimeter of the triangle

20. the ratio of the area of the rectangle to the area of the triangle

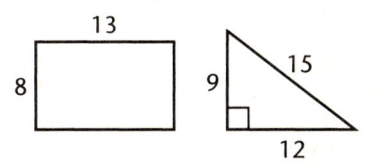

Tell whether or not the ratios are equivalent.

21. 4 : 9 and 9 : 25

22. $\dfrac{6}{20}$ and $\dfrac{24}{80}$

23. If it costs $108 to take a class of 24 students to the art museum, how much would it cost to take 60 students?

Name _____   Date _____

MODULES 5 AND 6 TEST — CUMULATIVE

Find a unit rate for each rate.

24. 192 mi in 3 h

25. $5.12 for 32 pencils

Find the missing term in each proportion.

26. $\dfrac{18}{42} = \dfrac{x}{70}$

27. $\dfrac{36}{60} = \dfrac{45}{y}$

28. $\dfrac{24}{96} = \dfrac{z}{200}$

If appropriate, use a proportion to solve Exercises 29 and 30. If it is not appropriate, explain why not.

29. A chef can make 12 sandwiches in 15 minutes. How many sandwiches can he make in $2\tfrac{1}{4}$ h?

30. During the first six days of April it rained $4\tfrac{3}{8}$ in. How much did it rain during the first 18 days of April?

31. The two rectangles are similar. Use a proportion to find the missing length.

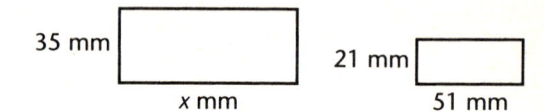

35 mm | x mm   21 mm | 51 mm

32. Use a protractor to measure ∠ABC.

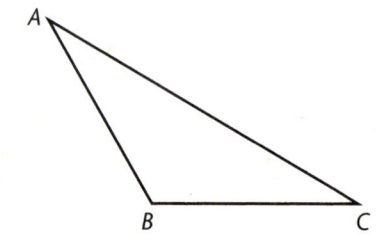

Find each value.

33. 60% of 330

34. 15% of 140

35. Anna and Brian are going to play Dueling Spinners. The one who spins the lower number wins.

   a. Make a tree diagram to find the possible outcomes.

   b. Find the probability that Anna beats Brian.

   c. What percent of the time do you expect Brian to win?

Anna: 3, 6, 10   Brian: 1, 4, 8, 9

CT-2 Math Thematics, Book 1

Answers

CUMULATIVE TEST

Modules 5 and 6
1. $\frac{2}{11}, \frac{2}{5}, \frac{3}{4}, \frac{7}{8}$
2. $\frac{1}{12}, \frac{3}{7}, \frac{9}{13}, \frac{3}{4}$
3. 225
4. $6\frac{2}{3}$
5. 17,160
6. 1
7. $3\frac{11}{14}$
8. $2\frac{1}{3}$
9. $5\frac{1}{2}$
10. $4\frac{9}{16}$
11. 28
12. $4\frac{1}{2}$
13. 42
14. b and c
15. $\frac{9}{49}$
16. 25
17. $\frac{1}{12}$
18. $3\frac{1}{2}$
19. $\frac{7}{6}$, 7 : 6, 7 to 6
20. $\frac{52}{27}$, 52 : 27, 52 to 27
21. No.
22. Yes.
23. $270
24. 64 mi/h
25. $.16/pencil
26. 30
27. 75
28. 50
29. 108 sandwiches
30. Not appropriate; it is not reasonable to think that rain will continue at the same rate.
31. 85 mm
32. about 120°
33. 198
34. 21

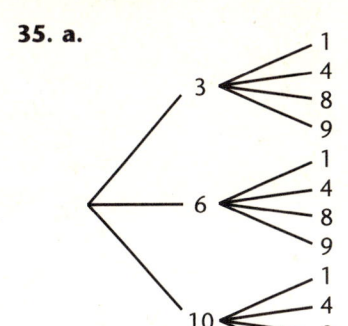

35. a. [tree diagram: 3 → 1, 4, 8, 9; 6 → 1, 4, 8, 9; 10 → 1, 4, 8, 9]

b. $\frac{5}{12}$
c. about 58%